EVERGLADES
WILDFLOWERS

EVERGLADES
WILDFLOWERS

A Field Guide to Wildflowers of the Historic Everglades,
including Big Cypress, Corkscrew, and Fakahatchee Swamps

Second Edition

ROGER L. HAMMER

FALCONGUIDES

GUILFORD, CONNECTICUT
HELENA, MONTANA
AN IMPRINT OF ROWMAN & LITTLEFIELD

FALCONGUIDES®

An imprint of Rowman & Littlefield
Falcon, FalconGuides, and Outfit Your Mind are registered trademarks of Rowman & Littlefield.

Distributed by NATIONAL BOOK NETWORK

Copyright © 2014 by Rowman & Littlefield

All photos by Roger L. Hammer unless otherwise noted.
Illustrations by DD Dowden

British Library Cataloguing-in-Publication Information available

Library of Congress Cataloging-in-Publication Data available

ISBN 978-0-7627-8753-1 (paperback)

∞™ The paper used in this publication meets the minimum requirements of American National Standard for Information Sciences—Permanence of Paper for Printed Library Materials, ANSI/NISO Z39.48-1992.

TO MY WIFE, MICHELLE, FOR HER LOVE, SUPPORT, AND WILLINGNESS TO WADE AROUND IN SWAMPS WITH ME. WE MAY NEVER HAVE MET IF NOT FOR A WILD ORCHID.

"The everglades . . . Preserves a unique american landscape. Not all who learn to know the country find it attractive, but few are unmoved by it. Many who came to know it well, have found that the charm of the everglades country grows with acquaintance and sharpens the memory. This feeling is difficult to phrase, especially for one who feels it keenly. For me it is compounded of many experiences, by no means all pleasant, and small insights gained after long struggle—so personal that it can scarcely be communicated. If you are susceptible to the everglades, you may then begin to know that this long misused and often hostile wilderness holds a fascination you will never be able to shake off."

—William B. Robertson Jr., *In Everglades Natural History,* December 1953

CONTENTS

ACKNOWLEDGMENTS

 I am deeply humbled as I begin to think of all the people who so graciously shared their time, friendship, and knowledge with me over the years. There are so many that I could not begin to acknowledge them all in such a limited space. So, to everyone who has ever spent time with me in the field, passed on a bit of cherished knowledge, or simply talked with me about wildflowers, my deepest and most sincere gratitude is yours. And I could not have wished for a better field companion than my new partner in life, Michelle. Her love, companionship, and steadfast support made spending days away from home, and the many hours spent slogging through swamps in waist-deep water with belligerent water moccasins, more endurable.

To the many members of the Florida Native Plant Society, Tropical Audubon Society, and the North American Butterfly Association—thank you for your genuine friendship and shared interests. Equal appreciation goes to the staff and volunteers at Everglades National Park, Biscayne National Park, Big Cypress National Preserve, Corkscrew Swamp Sanctuary, the CREW Marsh, and the marvelous state and county parks that dot the region. Their dedication to the environment helps preserve the real Florida for this and future generations. I must also thank Carlyle Luer for his monumental 1972 book on the native orchids of Florida that started me on my quest to discover the botanical riches in my home state. Spending time with him in the field searching for orchids is a cherished memory.

I owe immeasurable gratitude to my grandparents, Clarence and Olive Postle, my parents, Bob and Martha Stickland, and my brother, Russell, for influencing my life through my formative years growing up in Central Florida back when there was an abundance of wild Florida waiting to be explored. And we all should thank the pioneer botanists who described the natural splendor of Florida before much of it was lost to development. For me their writings about Old Florida bring about feelings of both envy and gratitude.

I have been blessed to count among my friends George N. Avery (1922–1983), Donovan S. Correll (1908–1983), and William "Dr. Bill" Robertson, Jr. (1924–2000). They were all an inspiration to anyone who had the good fortune to know them. And, of course, to Marjory Stoneman Douglas (1890–1998), whose elegant prose brought deserved attention to her beloved River of Grass where her ashes were spread. Sipping straight whiskey with her in her Coconut Grove cottage was one of life's special moments. Also to the memory of my dear friend, next-door neighbor, and fellow rum connoisseur, John C. Ogden (1938–2012), whose footprints will forever mingle with those of wood storks and spoonbills in the Everglades. John's vision of adapative management for Everglades restoration is underway and is destined to help bring about the changes needed to return the Everglades to their former grandeur.

For their companionship and valued friendship I am indebted to Keith Bradley, Brenda Brooks, Russ Clusman, Saul Friess, Deb Hanson, Karen Johnson, Carol Lippincott, Paul Marcellini, Chuck McCartney, Gil Nelson, Mike Owen, Robert Riefer, Jimi Sadle, and Glen Stacell. They are among many who have either shared time with me in the field over the years or let me know when rare plants were in flower. Mike Owen was especially helpful by cheerfully accompanying me on long slogs into remote areas of the Fakahatchee Swamp in search of flowering orchids.

This guide is the result of the knowledge and works of countless people but endless thanks are owed to Maryanne Biggar, Keith Bradley, Doug Goldman, Bruce F. Hansen, Chuck McCartney, and Richard P. Wunderlin for generously contributing their taxonomic expertise and tolerating my many botanical questions. They are all treasured friends and their knowledge made this a much better book than it might otherwise have been. I am also indebted to my friend Dan Austin whose book on Florida ethnobotany explained many of the Latin name derivations offered in this guide. And thanks also to the Belgian Trappist monks who brew Chimay ale, which was used for celebratory purposes to toast photographing rare and difficult-to-find wildflowers.

And lastly, a standing ovation is due to the entire staff of Globe Pequot Press for their combined efforts in putting this book together. My gratitude to everyone, heartfelt as it is, seems entirely inadequate.

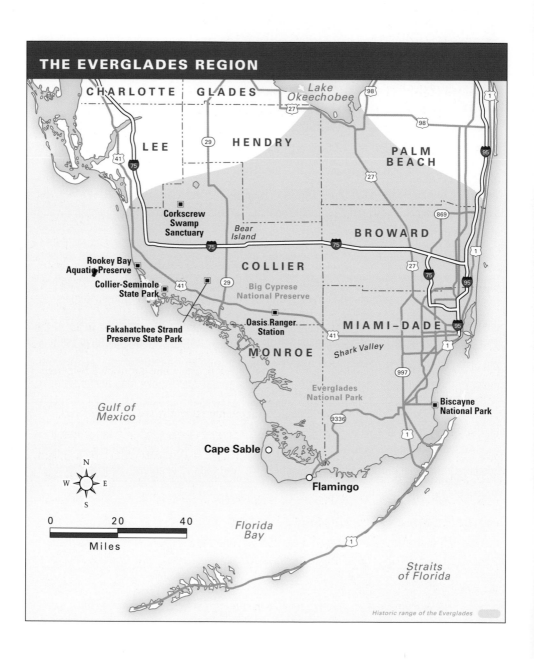

THE EVERGLADES REGION

CHARLOTTE | GLADES | *Lake Okeechobee* 98

LEE | HENDRY 29

PALM BEACH

Corkscrew Swamp Sanctuary

Bear Island

BROWARD

Rookey Bay Aquatic Preserve

COLLIER

Collier-Seminole State Park

Big Cypress National Preserve

Fakahatchee Strand Preserve State Park

Oasis Ranger Station

MIAMI-DADE

MONROE

Shark Valley

Everglades National Park

Biscayne National Park

Gulf of Mexico

Cape Sable ○

Flamingo

N
W E
S

0   20   40
Miles

Florida Bay

Straits of Florida

INTRODUCTION

The Historic Everglades

The Everglades once covered some 13,000 square miles from Lake Okeechobee south to the Gulf of Mexico, Florida Bay, and Biscayne Bay, literally encompassing all of southern mainland Florida with differing yet intrinsically connected ecosystems. The most famous of the Florida wetlands, the pre-drainage Everglades were complex and included the vast Big Cypress Swamp in southwest Florida and the broad mangrove estuaries along the coastlines.

The popular term, "River of Grass," oversimplifies the Everglades. They were, and still are, an interrelated ecosystem with distinct subregions, including broad prairies that typically were flooded only during the summer rainy season and deeper interior sloughs that remained flooded in all but the driest years. Grasses and sedges dominated the true Everglades and were interspersed with many small tree islands. Stretching southward along the inland edge of Biscayne Bay and then angling west into the heart of the Everglades was a wide, elevated ridge of limestone called the Miami Rock Ridge, which diverted much of the freshwater flow south and southwest like a wide, shallow, vegetated river. The Miami Rock Ridge was covered with seemingly endless pine forests occasionally interrupted by dense tropical hardwood forests called "hammocks."

When land finally gave way to the sea the vegetation abruptly changed to coastal strand and tidal marsh behind a muddy shoreline rimmed by entangled thickets of mangroves, sometimes reaching 20 miles inland. Creeks, bays, and islands dotted the southern coast and great expanses of seagrass meadows stretched across shallow, mud-bottomed bays between mainland Florida and the rocky Florida Keys. Together these interconnected habitats formed one vast ecosystem—the Everglades.

To define the ecological boundaries of the present-day Everglades would be difficult because of the diversion of the natural water flow from Lake Okeechobee and also because the eastern boundary of Everglades National Park to Biscayne Bay has been lost to development and agriculture. But even though human activities over the past century have substantially altered the natural water regime of this great watershed, the Everglades remain a fascinating and valuable ecosystem. The true Everglades are still today dependent on adjacent ecosystems, most particularly the Big Cypress Swamp, through which water still flows to nourish the river of grass and the shallow bays that are its final destination.

Elevations on the Miami Rock Ridge average 3 to 12 feet above sea level, declining imperceptibly toward the sea. Shallow, linear depressions that cut through the Miami Rock Ridge south of present-day Miami historically allowed surface water to flow through these openings. Some of it nourished Biscayne Bay, but most of the flow was channeled into Florida Bay to the south and the Gulf of Mexico to the west. Although overland water flow still occurs across the Big Cypress Swamp and through much of Everglades National Park, the freshwater flow that once nourished Biscayne Bay and eastern Florida Bay has been cut off by a series of canals and levees. These were built to help accommodate agricultural interests and a burgeoning human population in Miami-Dade County. The Comprehensive Everglades Restoration Plan is destined to restore the water flow in this region to the benefit of the plants and animals that call it home.

Habitats

The Everglades are a mosaic of different plant communities. Wildflower enthusiasts should pay the closest attention to open, sunny habitats, such as pineland and prairies, particularly if these habitats burned recently. Fire plays an important ecological role and many wildflowers bloom profusely following fire.

Pinelands

Pineland habitat in southern Florida may have an understory dominated by saw palmetto (*Serenoa repens*), grasses, or a rich array of understory shrubs and herbs mixed with hardwood trees that are kept shrubby by fire. Pineland habitat on the Miami Rock Ridge in Miami-Dade County is characterized by limestone outcroppings. This is an imperiled plant community called pine rockland. The principal upland area in Everglades National Park is Long Pine Key, which is nearly 20,000 acres of pine rockland interspersed with more than 120 tropical hardwood hammocks. Like much of the flora of southern Florida, most pine rockland plants have tropical affinities and occur no farther north than the southernmost

Pine rockland

Florida counties. Others are endemic and occur nowhere else on Earth. In contrast to the dry, rocky pinelands of the Miami Rock Ridge, the pine flatwoods of the Big Cypress Swamp and Corkscrew Swamp regions differ by having moist, sandy soils and a more temperate inventory of plants. In most southern Florida pinelands there is a single overstory tree, the slash pine (*Pinus elliottii*).

Tropical Hammocks

Hammock may be taken from the word *hamac*, meaning "sleeping place" in the language of the Taino, an extinct, aboriginal Arawakan people of the Bahamas and Greater Antilles. Hammocks are dense forests of broad-leaved hardwood trees surrounded by a contrasting plant community—usually pineland, freshwater marsh, or even mangroves. They are shady, humid forests dominated by trees of tropical origin. They occur on slightly elevated locations and are usually spared from fire because of the moist, partially decayed leaf litter and humid atmosphere that create a microclimate within the understory. They are often associated with deep solution holes carved out of the limestone that hold water during the wet season.

Tropical hammock

Cypress Swamps and Mixed Hardwood Swamps

Cypress swamps and mixed hardwood swamps are the dominant features of the Everglades region north of Everglades National Park. Although flooded throughout much of the year, southern Florida's swamps are typically dry in winter and spring. As water in the aquifer rises during the rainy season it soon

Mixed hardwood swamp

Cypress swamp

saturates the soil and overland flow begins.

Some cypress swamps have different configurations. Cypress domes are rounded, dome-shaped forests of cypress (*Taxodium* spp.) that form around deeper water than the surrounding area. The taller trees are in the center.

Slough

Cypress strands are similar except they are linear in configuration and resemble a forested, shallow river. Mixed hardwood swamps are characterized by bald cypress (*Taxodium distichum*), pond cypress (*Taxodium ascendens*), and a host of mostly temperate zone hardwood trees. In the interior of these swamps are deeper sloughs (pronounced *slews*) that remain flooded well into the dry season. Sloughs are often characterized by pond-apple (*Annona glabra*) and pop ash (*Fraxinus caroliniana*) trees that prefer to grow in deeper water. These trees are often draped with epiphytic ferns, bromeliads, orchids, and mosses.

Flatwoods and Prairies

The term *flatwoods* is generally used for prairies, savannas, and meadows but flatwoods may also have trees (typically pines) scattered here and there. These are called *pine flatwoods*. Prairies may have different substrates that affect the dominating vegeta-

Everglades prairie

tion. Marl substrate generally favors muhly grass (*Muhlenbergia capillaris*) while peaty soils favor sawgrass (*Cladium jamaicense*), which is actually a sedge that covers vast expanses of the Everglades region and what Marjory Stoneman Douglas termed a "River of Grass." These two prairie types are often called Everglades prairies or simply "glades" by locals. Prairies that are dominated by cordgrass (*Spartina*) are referred to

Wet prairie

as wet prairies even though they are no wetter than other prairie types. Prairies are great habitats to explore for wildflowers, especially within the first year after a burn.

Saltmarsh

Saltmarsh habitat is generally found on marl soils of coastal areas that are inundated periodically by salt or brackish water and develop where mangroves are not dense enough to create an abundance of shade. Because saltmarsh plants must be able to tolerate salty soil, the species diversity is lower than in most other plant communities. The dominant plants in saltmarshes are saltwort (*Batis maritima*), glasswort (*Sarcocornia ambigua*), and sea blite (*Suaeda linearis*).

Saltmarsh

Mangrove Forests

Mangroves occur along Florida's muddy and rocky shorelines. They dominate the fringes of Florida Bay, Biscayne Bay, and the Gulf of Mexico in southern Florida and are an important habitat for birds and countless

Mangroves

marine organisms. These forests are comprised of the red mangrove (*Rhizophora mangle*), black mangrove (*Avicennia germinans*), white mangrove (*Laguncularia racemosa*), and buttonwood (*Conocarpus erectus*).

Beach Dunes

Its long, sandy beaches make much of Florida's shoreline famous. Dune plants are hardy because they must be tolerant of dry, sandy soils, salt spray, and periodic inundation by seawater during tidal action and storm surges. Natural beaches in the Everglades region occur at Cape Sable and Highland Beach in Everglades National Park and are accessible only by canoes,

Beach dune

kayaks, sailboats, or powerboats. Key Biscayne, which is accessible by a causeway, is a sand barrier island between Biscayne Bay and the Straits of Florida. Dune plants help stabilize the sand and some of the more interesting species are burrowing four-o'clock (*Okenia hypogaea*), sea oats (*Uniola paniculata*), inkberry (*Scaevola plumieri*), railroad vine (*Ipomoea pes-caprae*), and bay bean (*Canavalia rosea*).

About the Second Edition

Welcome to the second edition of *Everglades Wildflowers.* This expanded and improved guide differs from the 2002 edition in several ways. The most significant change is that woody species have mostly been omitted and more species are now two per page in order to make room for a greater diversity of herbaceous wildflowers, which are what most people envision when they hear the word *wildflower.*

There have been a number of taxonomic revisions in recent years. Some species names have changed and others have even been moved to different genera by taxonomists. Members of the genus *Aster* in the Americas, for instance, are now placed in the genus *Symphyotrichum,* which almost seems like changing the name of apple pie. In a few cases some plants have been assigned to different families, such as the entire milkweed family (Asclepiadaceae) being relegated to the dogbane family (Apocynaceae) and the turnera family (Turneraceae) being placed in the passionflower family (Passifloraceae). As a consequence, some species will be in a different order than they were in the first edition of this guide. Because of new interpretations some of the botanical name derivations have been revised, too.

Due to the increasing popularity of butterfly and hummingbird gardening a special effort has been made to include more information regarding which species are larval host plants for butterflies (and moths) as well as which species produce blossoms that are attractive to butterflies and hummingbirds for nectar or pollen. The author and the publisher hope you enjoy this new and more comprehensive wildflower guide to the Everglades region.

How to Use This Guide

The plants in this guide are placed in six color groups based on the most prominent color of the flower or inflorescence. Many flowers can be multicolored, the color may change as the flower matures, or there may be different color forms within a species, so the reader is advised to check more than one color group. The bracts on some plants are more colorful than the flowers, so those species may be in a different color section than the actual color of the flowers. Within each color group, the plants are arranged alphabetically, first by the botanical name of the family, then by genus, and last by the species. Some plants are further divided into subspecies or varieties. Photographs do not always depict the actual flower size so the description of the flower should help the reader gain a sense of scale. The common names used in this guide are those in common usage in Florida but these names are not universal and often change from region to region within the plant's natural range.

Scientific names are universally recognized and those used in this guide mostly conform to those in the *Guide to the Vascular Plants of Florida* (third edition, 2011), or the online *Atlas of Florida Vascular Plants* (www.florida.plantatlas.usf.edu). In some cases the nomenclature follows the *Flora of North America* (floranorthamerica.org).

In this system of binomial classification, each plant has a two-word name, comprised first of the genus and then the species. An example of a genus within the aster family is *Rudbeckia,* which includes the coneflowers. The name that follows the genus is the species. There are many species in the genus *Rudbeckia* but one is called *Rudbeckia hirta,* which tells you it is a black-eyed Susan. The names are usually derived from either Greek or Latin words that describe a feature of the plant, its region of origin, or are Latinized versions of a person it was named to honor. Swedish naturalist Carl Linnaeus (1707–1778) created the binomial nomenclature system in use today and he even Latinized his own name to Carolus Linnaeus.

The **Description** section in this guide gives the reader information regarding leaf type, size, and shape; the arrangement of the leaves on the stem; flower size, color, and shape; and in some cases, the characteristics of the fruits.

The **Bloom Season** is next, and this is a general time of year that a particular species can be expected to bloom. Keep in mind that the flowering season of a plant can vary from one place to another. Some species flower continuously or sporadically throughout the entire year and are indicated as "All year" in the Bloom Season section.

The **Habitat/Range** section describes the typical habitat and geographical range of the plant. Some plants found in the Everglades may also grow in suitable habitats farther north in the United States but many of them have natural ranges that extend into the tropics. In many cases the term "Neotropics" is used to describe the range of plants that are distributed through the American tropics, including the Bahamas and West Indies. Some plants in this guide are endemic to Florida, being found nowhere else in the world.

Plants in this guide are native to Florida unless specifically stated otherwise. Nonnative plants included in this guide are those that are naturalized in Florida and can be commonly found growing wild in natural habitats. In the **Comments** section will be information on the derivation of the botanical name in English for each species. This is offered to give the reader a better understanding of botanical names. Other information in this section may include medicinal or poisonous properties, uses by wildlife, comparisons to related species, and horticultural attributes.

Stewardship and Outdoor Ethics

Please remember that the beauty of flowers is not solely for our pleasure. What we see and admire has a very serious biological function for the plant. The flower's purpose is to become pollinated and produce seeds to help ensure survival of its species. Flowers often reward pollinators by offering pollen or nectar. Many species in this guide are federal or state-listed endangered or threatened species and most of them occur within national, state, or regional parks and preserves where they are protected. It makes common sense to leave native wildflowers where you find them, not only for the benefit of the plant and its pollinators, but also for future wildflower enthusiasts like yourself.

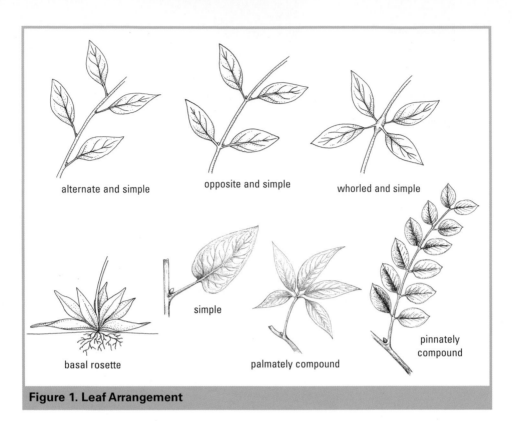

alternate and simple

opposite and simple

whorled and simple

basal rosette

simple

palmately compound

pinnately compound

Figure 1. Leaf Arrangement

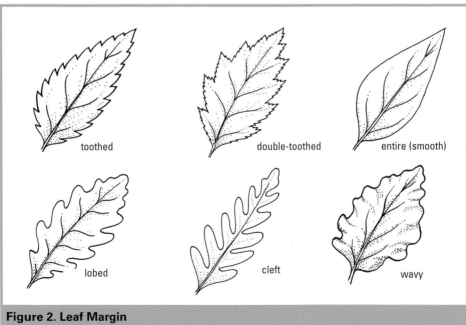

toothed

double-toothed

entire (smooth)

lobed

cleft

wavy

Figure 2. Leaf Margin

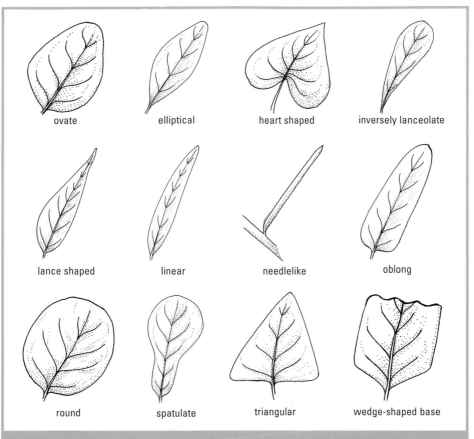

ovate   elliptical   heart shaped   inversely lanceolate

lance shaped   linear   needlelike   oblong

round   spatulate   triangular   wedge-shaped base

Figure 3. Leaf Shapes

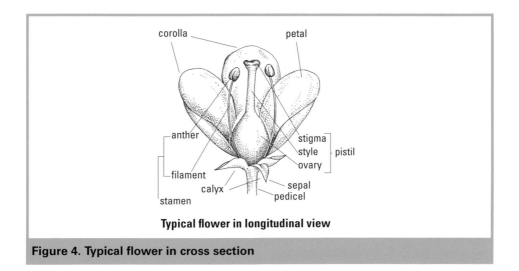

corolla   petal

anther

filament

stamen

calyx   sepal   pedicel

stigma   style   ovary   pistil

Typical flower in longitudinal view

Figure 4. Typical flower in cross section

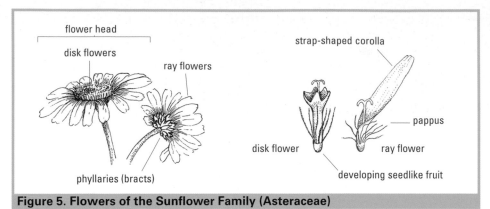

Figure 5. Flowers of the Sunflower Family (Asteraceae)

Figure 6. Flower of the Pea Family (Fabaceae)

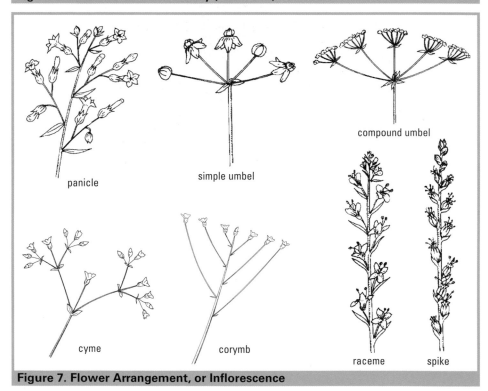

Figure 7. Flower Arrangement, or Inflorescence

BLUE AND PURPLE FLOWERS

Commelina erecta

This section includes flowers ranging from pale blue to deep indigo and from lavender to violet. Since lavender flowers grade into pink, you should check the Pink section if you do not find the flower you are looking for here.

PINELAND TWINFLOWER
Dyschoriste angusta (A. Gray) Small
Acanthus Family (Acanthaceae)

Description: Pineland twinflower has 4"–8" stems and nearly sessile linear to narrowly lanceolate opposite leaves. The leaves average ⅜" long and are covered with small hairs. The funnel-shaped flowers have 5 lobes with darker purple dots on the lower lobe. The flowers are in the upper leaf axils and measure ⁵⁄₁₆"–⅜" long and about ¼" wide.

Bloom Season: All year

Habitat/Range: Pinelands and prairies of central and southern Florida to the Bahamas.

Comments: *Dyschoriste* is a Greek word meaning "difficult to separate," referring to the valves of the capsule. The name *angusta* means "narrow," in reference to the leaf shape. Some members of this genus are used in the Caribbean to cure "pains in the waistline" and to "relieve women's tiredness." It is the only member of the genus in Everglades National Park and is a larval host plant of the common buckeye butterfly.

OBLONGLEAF TWINFLOWER
Dyschoriste oblongifolia (Michx.) Kuntze
Acanthus Family (Acanthaceae)

Description: This species is 2"–10" tall with opposite, sessile leaves. The leaves are typically oblong, ⅜"–1⅛" long, and coarsely hairy. The axillary, 5-lobed flowers are blue or purplish, measuring ⅝"–¾" long and ⅜"–½" wide.

Bloom Season: March–September

Habitat/Range: Flatwoods and sandhills along the coastal plain from South Carolina south in Florida to the Corkscrew Swamp region in Collier County.

Comments: The name *oblongifolia* means "oblong leaves." The flowers of oblongleaf twinflower are larger than those of the previous species. This is one of many wildflowers with a southern range that barely reaches the Everglades region. It is common in the CREW Marsh near Corkscrew Swamp where it grows in company with the pineland twinflower. Butterfly gardeners sometimes cultivate this species as a larval host plant of the common buckeye butterfly.

PINELAND WATERWILLOW

Justicia angusta (Chapm.) Small
(Also *Justicia ovata* [Walter] Lindau var. *angusta*
[Chapm.] R. W. Long)
Acanthus Family (Acanthaceae)

Description: Pineland waterwillow is emergent
in shallow water and has small, opposite, linear
leaves that are either sessile or with short
petioles. The flowers are usually solitary on long
stems and each flower is pale purple to violet,
⅜"–½" wide, with a 2-lobed upper lip and a
3-lobed lower lip. The upper lip is strongly curled.

Bloom Season: All year

Habitat/Range: Freshwater wetlands of Florida
and Georgia.

Comments: *Justicia* commemorates James Justice
(1698–1763), a Scottish gardener who wrote
about practical gardening in a cold temperate
climate. The name *angusta* alludes to the narrow
leaf shape. Of the 5 native members of this genus
in Florida this is the only species found in the
Everglades region. It is a larval host plant of the
'Seminole' Texas crescent in northern Florida.

GREEN SHRIMP-PLANT

Ruellia blechum L.
(Also *Blechum pyramidatum* [Lam.] Urb.)
Acanthus Family (Acanthaceae)

Description: The hairy, ovate leaves are opposite
along square stems and range from 1"–3" long
and ½"–1½" wide with entire margins. Flowers are
on upright spikes to 1½"–3" tall with overlapping
green bracts. The violet (or white) flowers are
about ⁵⁄₁₆" wide.

Bloom Season: All year

Habitat/Range: Pinelands, hammock margins, and
disturbed sites of Florida. Native to the Neotropics.

Comments: *Ruellia* honors French herbalist Jean
de la Ruelle (1474–1537). The name *blechum* is a
Greek name originally applied to a genus. Although
this plant is a common naturalized weed in Florida
it is often tolerated in home landscapes because
it is a larval host plant of the beautiful and rare
malachite butterfly. The young larvae hide in the
floral bracts. Many members of this family have
flowers that are subtended by colorful bracts and
some are popular garden subjects.

THICKLEAF WILD PETUNIA
Ruellia succulenta Small
Acanthus Family (Acanthaceae)

Description: The leaves of this low-growing species can be green or reddish purple. It averages 4"–8" tall with opposite, elliptic to lanceolate leaves that are mostly 1"–3" long and covered with short hairs. The 5-lobed, trumpet-shaped flowers are 1"–1½" wide and vary from light purple to pink.

Bloom Season: All year

Habitat/Range: Endemic to rocky pinelands and flatwoods of southern Florida.

Comments: The name *succulenta* refers to the somewhat succulent leaves. This is a larval host plant of the common buckeye butterfly and the malachite butterfly in southern Florida. It is locally common and is sometimes cultivated by butterfly gardeners in the southernmost Florida counties. The naturalized Mexican bluebell *(Ruellia simplex)* reaches 4' tall and hairyflower wild petunia *(Ruellia ciliatiflora)* is a pernicious lawn weed in Florida. Both have similar flowers.

FRAGRANT ERYNGO
Eryngium aromaticum Baldwin
Carrot Family (Apiaceae)

Description: The thick, ovate leaves average 1"–2½" long and are irregularly toothed. The main stem is erect but the lower branches typically spread horizontally along the ground. The whorled stem leaves are deeply divided into 3 pointed lobes and the pale blue flowers are in globose, ½" bristly heads.

Bloom Season: September–January

Habitat/Range: Sandy habitats of Florida, Georgia, and Alabama.

Comments: *Eryngium* means "to belch," alluding to medicinal uses to help avoid flatulence. The name *aromaticum* refers to the aromatic leaves that smell strongly of fresh carrots when crushed. Rattlesnake master is a common name used for many members of this genus and relates to the ineffective use by Native Americans as an antidote for rattlesnake bite. Some species attract an exceptional variety of butterflies when in flower and are larval host plants of the black swallowtail butterfly.

DOLL'S DAISY
Boltonia diffusa Elliott
Aster Family (Asteraceae)

Description: This stoloniferous species typically reaches 1'–2' in height but may be taller. Stems are slender with linear to narrowly lanceolate leaves that measure 1"–4" long and about ⅛"–¼" wide. Flower heads average ⅜" wide with numerous, narrow, violet, ray flowers. The involucre is cone shaped.

Bloom Season: July–December

Habitat/Range: Floodplains from North Carolina and Illinois south to Texas and Florida.

Comments: *Boltonia* commemorates English mycologist and botanist James Bolton (1735–1799) whose first published work was on the natural history of British songbirds. The name *diffusa* refers to the diffusely branched inflorescence. The cone-shaped involucre helps distinguish this species from similar-looking species in the genus *Symphyotrichum* (Asteraceae) that share its habitat and flowering season. It is locally common throughout the Everglades region.

FLORIDA PAINTBRUSH
Carphephorus corymbosus (Nutt.) Torr. & A. Gray
Aster Family (Asteraceae)

Description: From a basal rosette of leaves arises a single, erect, leafy stem to 3' tall or more, topped by tightly bunched ⅜" heads of pink disk flowers. The stem leaves are much smaller than the basal leaves. Fruits are 10-angled, cone-shaped achenes. The flower heads of this species are larger than any of the wetland *Carphephorus* species in Florida.

Bloom Season: June–November

Habitat/Range: Upland sandy habitats of Florida, Georgia, and South Carolina.

Comments: *Carphephorus* means "chaff-bearing," in reference to the bract (chaff) at the base of the flowers. The name *corymbosus* refers to the flat-topped floral arrangement, a corymb. This striking species is also called coastalplain chaffhead and attracts many species of butterflies when in flower. Green lynx spiders are pollinator predators and are often found on the flower heads waiting for a hapless insect to visit.

17

PINELAND PURPLE

Carphephorus odoratissimus (G. F. Gmel.) var. *sub-tropicanus* (DeLaney et al) Wunderlin & B. F. Hansen
Aster Family (Asteraceae)

Description: This relative of the Florida paint-brush is a simple-stemmed perennial from 1"–3' tall when in flower. The basal leaves are typically oblong lanceolate and range from 2"–12" long and ⅜"–2" wide. Each flower head is about ¼" in diameter.

Bloom Season: June–November

Habitat/Range: Endemic to sandy flatwoods from central Florida south to Collier County.

Comments: The name *odoratissimus* means "very fragrant," in reference to the vanilla-scented leaves of the typical variety called vanillaleaf *(Carphephorus odoratissimus* var. *odoratissimus)*, which has a more northern distribution in Florida. Pineland purple has no leaf fragrance. The name *subtropicanus* refers to its subtropical range in Florida. Butterflies visit the flowers and it is a larval host plant of the little metalmark butterfly.

HAIRY CHAFFHEAD

Carphephorus paniculatus (J. F. Gmel.) H. Hebert
Aster Family (Asteraceae)

Description: The reddish purple stems of this species are densely hairy and average 20"–30" tall. The basal leaves are narrowly elliptic and vary from 1"–10" long with much smaller stem (cauline) leaves. Flowers are congested in a columnar array with each flower measuring about 3⁄16" wide.

Bloom Season: August–January

Habitat/Range: Wet flatwoods and bogs from North Carolina to Alabama south in Florida to Palm Beach and Collier Counties.

Comments: The name *paniculatus* relates to the tightly bunched panicles of flowers. Butterflies visit the flowers but in less profusion than they do with other species, perhaps because there is no floral scent. It is also called deertongue due to the large basal leaves shaped like the tongue of a deer. This species is locally common in Corkscrew Swamp, the CREW Marsh, and the Bear Island region of the Big Cypress Swamp in Collier County.

CAPE SABLE THOROUGHWORT
Chromolaena frustrata (B. L. Rob.) R. M. King & H. Rob
Aster Family (Asteraceae)

Description: The stems have short, soft, scattered hairs with 3-nerved, elliptic-lanceolate leaves from ½"–1" long with shallowly toothed margins. Flower heads are in clusters of 2–6 with pale blue to lavender corollas.

Bloom Season: All year

Habitat/Range: Endemic to coastal hammocks and rock barrens of Monroe County, Florida (Florida Keys and mainland), and near West Lake in Everglades National Park (Miami-Dade County).

Comments: *Chromolaena* alludes to the colored involucral bracts on some species. The name *frustrata* relates to botanist Benjamin Lincoln Robinson (1864–1935) becoming frustrated by this Florida endemic being confused with a related Jamaican species. It does not occur on Cape Sable but the entire area from Flamingo to the southwest tip of Florida was once called "Cape Sable." It is a state-listed endangered species.

BLUE MISTFLOWER
Conoclinium coelestinum (L.) DC.
Aster Family (Asteraceae)

Description: The stems of this quaint and colorful rhizomatous species are usually erect to about 12" tall with triangular to ovate leaves ranging from 1"–2½" long and half as wide. The floral heads are blue to blue-violet, each measuring about ⅜" wide.

Bloom Season: May–December

Habitat/Range: Coastal and inland habitats, including floodplains, pine savannas, pine-oak woodlands, and roadsides of the eastern United States.

Comments: *Conoclinium* means "cone bed," alluding to the conical receptacles. The name *coelestinum* refers to the sky-blue flowers. Blue mistflower attracts a dazzling assortment of butterflies but is only occasionally cultivated by butterfly gardeners. It is the only member of the genus in Florida. Bluemink *(Ageratum houstonianum)* has similar flowers but is not rhizomatous and is naturalized along roadsides of central and southern Florida.

ELEPHANT FOOT

Elephantopus elatus Bertol.
Aster Family (Asteraceae)

Description: The unmistakable basal leaves of elephant foot reach up to 10" long and 3" wide. The leaves are elliptic in shape and scalloped or toothed along the margins. The flowering stem is covered with spreading hairs and can reach 24"–48" tall. It is topped with small, violet flowers and 3 triangular, leaflike bracts.

Bloom Season: April–November

Habitat/Range: Sandhills and flatwoods from South Carolina to Arkansas south in Florida to the Big Cypress Swamp.

Comments: *Elephantopus* means "elephant foot," and is believed to be an aboriginal name of a species in India. The name *elatus* means "tall," in reference to the flowering stem. Three other species occur in Florida but none of them range into the Everglades region. Many insects visit the flowers, including a variety of butterflies and moths. Some species are used medicinally to treat asthma and other respiratory ailments.

WOODLAND LETTUCE

Lactuca floridana (L.) Gaertn.
Aster Family (Asteraceae)

Description: Most leaves of this species are deeply and irregularly lobed but may become ovate or elliptic up the flowering stem. Plants reach 3'–5' tall at flowering with an open branching habit near the top of the plant. Flower heads are ⅜"–½" wide.

Bloom Season: February–October

Habitat/Range: Wet flatwoods, open forests, and disturbed sites from Canada across the eastern half of the United States south through Florida.

Comments: *Lactuca* alludes to the milky latex. The name *floridana* means "of Florida" and refers to where this species was first collected in 1753. It is also called Florida lettuce. The leaves of this species are edible when cooked as greens but are bitter eaten raw. A close relative *(Lactuca sativa)* is the leaf and head lettuce of gardens and marketplaces. The milky sap of *Lactuca* species was once believed to be narcotic and was even called "lettuce opium."

SCALELEAF ASTER
Symphyotrichum adnatum [Nutt.] G. L. Nesom
Aster Family (Asteraceae)

Description: The upper leaves of this common species are appressed tightly to the brittle, wire-like stems, somewhat resembling scales. Flowering stems reach 2' tall and the 1½"–2" basal leaves are alternate and rough to the touch. Mature plants are much branched. Each flower is about ¾" in diameter with light blue to lilac ray flowers and yellow disk flowers.

Bloom Season: All year

Habitat/Range: Sandhills and flatwoods of the southeastern United States and the Bahamas.

Comments: *Symphyotrichum* is Greek for "junction" and "hair," perhaps alluding to the bristles on the European cultivar used to describe the genus. The genus *Symphyotrichum* replaces *Aster* in the New World. The name *adnatum* is Latin for "joined to" and refers to the clasping upper leaves. Small butterflies, especially crescents, blues, and hairstreaks, visit the disk flowers for nectar.

CLIMBING ASTER
Symphyotrichum carolinianum (Walter) Wunderlin & B. F. Hansen
(Also *Aster carolinianus* Walter)

Aster Family (Asteraceae)

Description: The lower leaves of this vinelike shrub constrict below the middle and have a clasping base. The smaller upper leaves clasp nearly around the stems. Leaves are elliptic to lanceolate and range from ¾"–2⅜" long. Flowers are along the upper portion of the stems and reach 1"–1½" wide. The ray flowers vary from pale pink to rosy purple.

Bloom Season: October–May

Habitat/Range: Freshwater wetlands throughout the southeastern United States.

Comments: The name *carolinianum* means "of the Carolinas." Climbing aster is sometimes cultivated for its attractive flowers that are visited by bees and butterflies. Vigorous plants can climb 15' or more into trees and over shrubs. It is common in the Everglades region and blooms well into spring in years with mild winters. It is also called Carolina aster.

EASTERN SILVERY ASTER

Symphyotrichum concolor (L.) G. L. Nesom
Aster Family (Asteraceae)

Description: The common name derived from the silvery hairs that cover both sides of the leaves. The decorative leaves are elliptic-lanceolate, usually canted up the stem, and measure up to 2" long and ½" wide. The basal leaves wither before flowering. Flowering stems average 1'–2' tall and are topped by stalked heads of flowers with 8–16 blue rays.

Bloom Season: All year

Habitat/Range: Sandhills and flatwoods from New England south along the coastal plain to Texas and Florida.

Comments: The name *concolor* means "one-colored," in reference to the ray flowers. Eastern silvery aster is sporadic in the Everglades region but is most common in open prairies that have recently burned and in sandy pineland habitat east of Everglades National Park. It also occurs on Big Pine Key in the Florida Keys. It is distinctive and not easily confused with other species in the region.

ELLIOTT'S ASTER

Symphyotrichum elliottii (Torr. & A. Gray) G. L. Nesom
Aster Family (Asteraceae)

Description: Elliott's aster has long rhizomes that create large colonies. The stems are mostly smooth, sometimes purplish pink, and can reach 5' tall. The toothed, elliptic leaves measure 2"–9" long and ⅜"–2" wide. The flower heads measure about 1" wide with rays that range from lavender to pale pink or white.

Bloom Season: August–December

Habitat/Range: Wet flatwoods, marshes, bogs, and roadsides across the southeastern United States.

Comments: The name *elliottii* honors American legislator, banker, and botanist Stephen Elliott (1771–1830) of South Carolina. Small butterflies visit the disk flowers. Native-plant enthusiasts sometimes cultivate this species but it requires permanently wet soil and may spread well out of bounds if given the proper conditions. It puts on an eyecatching display along roadside ditches in the Everglades region in late fall.

FLORIDA BELLFLOWER
Campanula floridana S. Watson ex A. Gray
Bellflower Family (Campanulaceae)

Description: The leaves of this species are linear lanceolate, ½"–1½" long and ⅟₁₆"–¼" wide, with entire or obscurely toothed margins. The flowers are ½"–⅝" wide with 5 narrow, widely spreading lobes subtended by green sepals.

Bloom Season: All year

Habitat/Range: Endemic to pond margins and freshwater marshes of peninsular Florida into the central Panhandle.

Comments: *Campanula* means "a bell" and references the flower shape of some members of the genus. The name *floridana* means "of Florida." Of the 3 Florida native *Campanula* species this is one of 2 endemics and the only one that reaches the Everglades region. The flowers are difficult to see because they are often hidden among competing vegetation. It ranges south in Florida to the CREW Marsh and Corkscrew Swamp but does not occur in the Big Cypress National Preserve or Everglades National Park.

BAY LOBELIA
Lobelia feayana A. Gray
Bellflower Family (Campanulaceae)

Description: The basal leaves of this trailing species are ¼"–⅝" long and broadly ovate or kidney shaped. The upper leaves are elliptic, sometimes with scalloped margins. The flowers are about ⁵⁄₁₆" wide and range from pale blue to pinkish violet.

Bloom Season: All year

Habitat/Range: Endemic to moist habitats from the eastern Florida Panhandle south into the Big Cypress Swamp.

Comments: *Lobelia* commemorates Flemish herbalist Matthias de l'Obel (1538–1616). The name *feayana* honors physician and botanist William T. Féay (1803–1879). When an insect disturbs lobelia flowers the pollen is discharged through pores at the tip of the anthers. Native Americans used lobelias to treat syphilis but studies in Europe found it to be ineffective. Carolus Linnaeus (1707–1778) even named one species *Lobelia syphilitica*. The small flowers of bay lobelia can turn roadsides into a blue carpet.

GLADES LOBELIA
Lobelia glandulosa Walter
Bellflower Family (Campanulaceae)

Description: The blue flowers of glades lobelia stand out among the grasses of open prairies. The 2'–3' stems bear linear or lanceolate, alternate leaves that typically have small, gland-tipped teeth along the margins. The ½" flowers have 2 lips, the upper one strongly curled with 2 lobes, and the bottom one divided into 3 lobes. The lower lip and the throat are hairy.

Bloom Season: All year

Habitat/Range: Freshwater wetlands throughout Florida north to Mississippi and Virginia.

Comments: The name *glandulosa* refers to the gland-tipped teeth on the leaves. Many lobelias contain poisonous, narcotic sap that causes convulsions and even death to humans if ingested in quantity. Lobelias contain the tropane alkaloid *lobeline* and have been used to expel mucus, induce vomiting, and to treat venereal diseases. Hummingbirds visit the flowers of this species for nectar.

WHITEMOUTH DAYFLOWER
Commelina erecta L.
(Also *Commelina elegans* Kunth)
Spiderwort Family (Commelinaceae)

Description: The sheathed, linear leaves measure 1"–6" long, ³⁄₁₆"–½" wide, and alternately clasp the stem. Each flower is about 1" wide with 2 large blue (rarely white) petals and a much smaller white petal.

Bloom Season: All year

Habitat/Range: Dry, open woodlands from Texas and North Carolina through Florida and the West Indies.

Comments: *Commelina* honors Dutch botanists Jan (1629–1692) and his nephew Caspar (1667–1732) Commelin. A story holds that a third relative never accomplished much in the field of botany, depicted in the flowers by the 2 prominent petals and a third insignificant petal. The name *erecta* refers to the erect growth habit. The name dayflower relates to the ephemeral flowers that open once and congeal by late morning. Common dayflower *(Commelina diffusa)* is a naturalized vine of disturbed sites with much smaller flowers.

OCEANBLUE MORNING GLORY
Ipomoea indica (Burm.) Merr.
Morning-Glory Family (Convolvulaceae)

Description: Oceanblue morning glory produces 2"–4" heart-shaped or 3-lobed, hairy, alternate leaves. The funnel-shaped, 2"–3" flowers vary from blue, pinkish violet, or purple. The flowers have stripes (nectar guides) radiating outward from the floral tube.

Bloom Season: All year

Habitat/Range: A wide range of habitats of Florida and the New World tropics.

Comments: *Ipomoea* is Greek for "wormlike," alluding to the twining habit. The name *indica* denotes "of India," revealing the wide natural range of the species. The roots are used as a purgative and the seeds of some members of this family are hallucinogenic. Skipper butterflies crawl down the floral tube seeking nectar and Sphinx moths visit the flowers after dusk. The similar Tievine *(Ipomoea cordatotriloba)* has 3-lobed cordate leaves and dark centered flowers that range from purple to pink.

RAILROAD VINE
Ipomoea pes-caprae (L.) R. Br. subsp. *brasiliensis* (L.) Ooststr.
Morning-Glory Family (Convolvulaceae)

Description: This trailing vine has rounded or oblong, 2"–4" leaves that are notched at the tip. The stems can extend 20' or more in length and help entrap drifting sand. The funnel-shaped flowers are typically solitary, each measuring 2"–3" wide with rose-purple stripes radiating outward from the throat and serve as nectar guides for insects.

Bloom Season: All year

Habitat/Range: Beach dunes and rocky shorelines of tropical and subtropical regions worldwide.

Comments: The name *pes-caprae* means "goat's foot," referring to the leaf shape. The name *brasiliensis* means "of Brazil," where this subspecies was first collected. Ocean currents disperse the seeds of this global traveler. In ancient Hawaii the flowers were used as a soothing sheath after circumcision and the stems were used to smite the ocean to bring rough waves for enemies at sea.

SALTMARSH MORNING GLORY

Ipomoea sagittata Poir.
Morning-Glory Family (Convolvulaceae)

Description: The leaves of this twining vine are very narrowly arrow-shaped and range from 1½"–4" long and ⅜"–¾" wide. Showy, funnel-shaped flowers appear from the leaf axils and measure 2½"–3" wide, ranging from rose purple to lavender with a darker throat.

Bloom Season: Sporadically all year but principally in the summer and fall rainy season

Habitat/Range: Brackish and freshwater marshes of the southeastern United States, Mexico, Guatemala, Bahamas, Cuba, and Jamaica.

Comments: The name *sagittata* refers to the strongly sagittate (arrow shaped) leaves that cannot be confused with any other native morning glory. Flower production of this species is highly dependent upon rainfall, with many more flowers appearing during wet years. The common name refers to saltmarsh habitat but it is equally common in freshwater marshes, including cypress swamps.

ROCKLAND MORNING GLORY

Ipomoea tenuissima Choisy
Morning-Glory Family (Convolvulaceae)

Description: The slender stems of this trailing vine are covered with hairs, as are the ¾"–2" long and ¼"–⅜" wide arrow-shaped leaves. Flowers are funnel shaped, typically solitary, and measure about ¾" wide. Flower color ranges from purple to light pinkish purple with a darker center.

Bloom Season: All year

Habitat/Range: Pine rocklands of Florida (Miami-Dade County) and the West Indies.

Comments: The name *tenuissima* means "slender" or "thin," in reference to the narrow stems. This species seldom twines but may climb up low vegetation. It is a state-listed endangered species because its pine rockland habitat in southern Miami-Dade County is critically imperiled. It benefits from fire and will disappear if its habitat has not burned within about 5 years. Resource managers purposely set fires (prescribed burns) to benefit fire-dependent plants.

LITTLEBELL
Ipomoea triloba L.
Morning-Glory Family (Convolvulaceae)

Description: Littlebell is a fast-growing, rather petite vine that twines over low vegetation. The heart-shaped leaves typically have 3 lobes and range from 1"–2" long with a nearly equal width. Flowers are somewhat hexagonal with pointed lobes and range from ⅜"–½" wide.

Bloom Season: All year

Habitat/Range: Pinelands, fencerows, and disturbed sites of Florida. Native to the Neotropics.

Comments: The name *triloba* refers to the 3 lobes on the leaves. This is an invasive species in Florida but it does not displace or smother out native vegetation like other invasive vines. The hexagonal shape of the flowers is diagnostic. White-flowered forms are rare. The common name relates to the flowers resembling little bells. The most well-known morning glory is the sweet potato *(Ipomoea batatas)*, cultivated for its edible root tubers. It is called *boniato* in Spanish-speaking countries.

SKYBLUE CLUSTERVINE
Jacquemontia pentanthos (Jacq.) G. Don
Morning-Glory Family (Convolvulaceae)

Description: This slender, twining vine bears alternate, heart-shaped leaves that range from ¾"–2½" long and ⅜"–2½" wide. Very showy, sky blue, broadly funnel-shaped flowers are about ¾" wide and appear in open clusters from the leaf axils.

Bloom Season: All year

Habitat/Range: Hammock margins and edges of swamps from southern Florida to the Greater Antilles, Mexico, and Central America.

Comments: *Jacquemontia* honors French botanist Victor Jacquemont (1801–1832) who undertook a scientific survey of India in 1828 but succumbed to a tropical disease. The name *pentanthos* means "with five stamens." This state-listed endangered species puts on a spectacular display of eye-catching blossoms that cover the plant. For native-plant enthusiasts this attractive species is a worthy garden subject suitable for a small arbor, fence, or trellis.

SPURRED BUTTERFLY PEA
Centrosema virginianum (L.) Benth.
Pea Family (Fabaceae)

Description: This is a rather petite, perennial vine with trailing or twining stems. The compound leaves are alternate and divided into 3 narrowly lanceolate leaflets, each about 1"–1⅜" long. The flowers are solitary or in pairs, ¾"–1¼" long, and range in color from purplish lavender to nearly white. The keel is uppermost and there is a blunt spur at the base of the upper petal.

Bloom Season: All year

Habitat/Range: Pinelands, hammock margins, and coastal strand of the southeastern United States, Bermuda, and the Neotropics.

Comments: *Centrosema* is Greek for "spur" and "standard," in reference to the spurred upper petal (standard). The name *virginianum* means "of Virginia," where this species was first collected in the 1830s. The common name alludes to the butterfly-shaped flowers but the long-tailed skipper uses the plant as larval food. Gardeners sometimes cultivate it.

BEGGAR TICKS
Desmodium incanum DC.
Pea Family (Fabaceae)

Description: The alternate, compound leaves of this weedy species are divided into 3 elliptic leaflets that are ¾"–4" long, usually lighter colored around the midvein, and densely hairy on the lower surface. The lowers are ¼" long, each with a standard petal, 2 lateral wing petals, and 2 lower keel petals. The pods are in 3–9 segments, each about ¼" long and ⅛" wide.

Bloom Season: All year

Habitat/Range: Sandhills, pinelands, and disturbed sites of warm regions worldwide.

Comments: *Desmodium* is Greek for "a chain" or "bond," in reference to the joined segments of the pods. The name *incanum* means "ash-colored," alluding to the color of the leaf hairs. Although it is a larval host plant of the long-tailed skipper, dorantes longtail, silver-spotted skipper, and hoary edge butterflies in Florida, it is regarded as a pest because the pods stick tightly to hair and clothing and must be pulled or scraped off.

SWEETHEARTS
Desmodium triflorum (L.) DC.
Pea Family (Fabaceae)

Description: This prostrate, mat-forming weed has leaves divided into 3 rounded leaflets that measure ¼"–⁵⁄₁₆" long and up to ⅛"–¼" wide. Pinkish purple flowers are in axillary clusters and range from ⅛"–³⁄₁₆" long. The pods are segmented and measure ½" long and ⅛" wide. Like many other members of the genus, the seeds cling to hair and clothing.

Bloom Season: All year

Habitat/Range: Pinelands, lawns, and disturbed sites throughout much of Florida. Native to Asia.

Comments: The name *triflorum* means "three flowers." It is assumed that the original specimen used to describe the species had groups of 3 flowers. This and other members of the genus are used in the Caribbean to make a soothing bath. This weedy species is sometimes grown purposely as a groundcover. It is common along roadsides of Long Pine Key and other open lawn areas in Everglades National Park where it grows low enough to escape mowing.

WILD BUSHBEAN
Macroptilium lathyroides (L.) Urb.
(Also *Phaseolus lathyroides* L.)
Pea Family (Fabaceae)

Description: This weedy species has prostrate or ascending stems to 3' long. The compound leaves are divided into 3 linear, oblong leaflets from 1"–2½" long and ⅜"–1" wide. The reddish purple flowers are produced on long stems that exceed the leaves. The lower leaf surface is smooth or with sparse stiff hairs.

Bloom Season: All year

Habitat/Range: Pinelands and disturbed sites throughout most of Florida. Native to the Neotropics.

Comments: *Macroptilium* means "long winged," referring to the long wing petals that protrude at odd angles. The name *lathyroides* refers to the resemblance of this species to the genus *Lathyrus* (Fabaceae). A similar nonnative species *(Macroptilium atropurpureum)* shares its habitat in Florida but it has velvety pubescence on the lower surface of the leaves. Wild bushbean is regarded as a peasant crop in Latin America.

FOURLEAF VETCH
Vicia acutifolia Elliott
Pea Family (Fabaceae)

Description: Fourleaf vetch bears evenly pinnate, compound leaves with a terminal leaflet modified into a tendril. The narrowly linear leaflets number 2–6 (usually 4) and range from ½"–1¼" long and up to ⅛" wide. The ¼" flowers are pale blue or white with purple markings.

Bloom Season: All year

Habitat/Range: Freshwater to brackish wetlands and moist disturbed sites of the southeastern United States and the Bahamas.

Comments: *Vicia* is an ancient Latin name that means *victorious* but without explanation regarding how it relates to this genus. The name *acutifolia* refers to the pointed leaflets. The seeds are edible as famine food when cooked but the consumption of raw seeds can lead to tremors, jaundice, hepatitis, and liver damage typical of cyanide poisoning. The flowers open late in the afternoon. It is also called sand vetch and is a larval host plant of the clouded sulphur butterfly.

SEASIDE GENTIAN
Eustoma exaltatum (L.) Salisb. ex G. Don
Gentian Family (Gentianaceae)

Description: Seaside gentian is an annual with fleshy, gray green, opposite leaves that clasp the stem. The plant reaches about 1'–3' tall with elliptic leaves that measure ¾"–2½" long and half as wide. The tuliplike, ¾", 5-lobed flowers are either white or rose-purple, but always with a dark purple center.

Bloom Season: All year

Habitat/Range: Coastal areas of central and southern Florida through the West Indies and Mexico to South America.

Comments: *Eustoma* is Greek for "true" and "mouth," in reference to the showy, cupped flowers. The name *exaltatum* means "lofty," alluding to the upright growth habit. The two color forms of this species often grow together, but one or the other may dominate some populations. There are only 3 species distributed from southern North America to northern South America. A leaf tea has been used as a wash for the eyes and to reduce fever.

SPINY FALSE FIDDLELEAF
Hydrolea capsularis (L.) Druce
(Also *Hydrolea spinosa* L.)
False Fiddleleaf Family (Hydroleaceae)

Description: This herbaceous shrub reaches about 4' tall. Very sticky hairs cover the stems and leaves and there are sharp, ½" spines in the leaf axils. Leaves measure 1"–2" long and ⅜"–½" wide. The attractive flowers are ¾" wide.

Bloom Season: All year

Habitat/Range: Disturbed soils of Miami-Dade County, Florida. Native to Texas and the Neotropics.

Comments: *Hydrolea* translates to "water-loving." The name *capsularis* means "having capsules." This species appeared in the Hole-in-the-Donut region of Everglades National Park in 1986 where it still persists in disturbed marl soils. The Hole-in-the-Donut is abandoned agricultural land being restored to natural habitat by removing nonnative invasive plants and scraping the soil below grade to allow flooding in the rainy season. It has been a resounding success and is still ongoing.

SKYFLOWER
Hydrolea corymbosa J. Macbr. ex Elliott
False Fiddleleaf Family (Hydroleaceae)

Description: Skyflower may reach 2' tall with spirally arranged leaves on smooth stems. The leaves are elliptic to lanceolate, mostly 1"–2" long and half as wide. Azure blue flowers, each about ¾"–1" wide, are produced in flat-topped clusters.

Bloom Season: May–November

Habitat/Range: Freshwater wetlands and roadside ditches of the southeastern United States.

Comments: The name *corymbosa* refers to the corymb of flowers. A corymb is a flat-topped cluster of flowers that progressively open from the outside inward. Members of this genus are autogamous, meaning their own pollen fertilizes the flowers. There is hardly a richer blue on any other wildflower but skyflower is not widely cultivated because it requires shallow water or permanently wet soil to be successfully grown. The leaves of some species have cleansing and healing effects when applied as a poultice.

BLUEFLAG
Iris savannarum Small
(Also *Iris hexagona* Walter var. *savannarum* [Small] R. C. Foster)
Iris Family (Iridaceae)

Description: The flat, linear, swordlike leaves of this species reach 4' long and 1" wide, spreading in one plane like a fan. The showy flowers reach 4"–5" across. The capsules are not ridged (6-sided) like they are on other species.

Bloom Season: March–June

Habitat/Range: Endemic to freshwater wetlands of Florida.

Comments: *Iris* relates to the mythological Greek goddess who appeared as a rainbow and sent messages to the gods. The name *savannarum* alludes to growing in savannas (prairies). Some botanists lump this species in with *Iris hexagona* while others consider *Iris hexagona* to be a critically rare species known only from 2 Florida counties (Dixie and Taylor) with a single, small, disjunct population in South Carolina. They cite capsule shape, leaf color, bloom season, winter dormancy, and floral differences to separate *Iris savannarum* from *Iris hexagona*. It is both confusing and controversial. Regardless, this is a striking plant when in flower and it is common in the Corkscrew Swamp region and along strand forests in the Big Cypress Swamp, yet it is entirely absent from Everglades National Park. It is also called Dixie iris.

NARROWLEAF BLUE-EYED GRASS
Sisyrinchium angustifolium Mill.
(Also *Sisyrinchium atlanticum* E. P. Bicknell)
Iris Family (Iridaceae)

Description: The leaves of this common species are in a fanlike arrangement, growing in tufts from rhizomes and resembling a grass when not in flower. The leaves are narrowly linear and average 8"–14" long and 1/16"–1/8" wide. The starlike flowers are about 1/2" wide.

Bloom Season: Principally January–August

Habitat/Range: Wet soils from Newfoundland south to Texas and Florida.

Comments: *Sisyrinchium* is a name used by Greek philosopher Theophrastus (372–287 BC) for a related plant. The name *angustifolium* means "narrow leaved." This is the most common of the 4 native members of the genus in Florida and is frequent along roadsides that traverse its natural habitat. Native-plant enthusiasts sometimes cultivate it. The Neotropical *Sisyrinchium vaginatum* has been used for birth control in South America.

EASTERN FALSE DRAGONHEAD
Physostegia purpurea (Walter) S. F. Blake
Mint Family (Lamiaceae)

Description: The leaf margins may be scalloped or with pointed teeth. The upper leaves are greatly reduced in size compared to the basal leaves. Flowering plants range from 1'–3' tall and are topped with paired flowers spaced opposite each other along the stem. The flowers are 1 3/8"–2" long with deeply lobed lips. The throat is lined with rose purple dots.

Bloom Season: June–November

Habitat/Range: Freshwater marshes and swamps of Florida, Georgia, and the Carolinas.

Comments: *Physostegia* is Greek for "bladder" and "covering," alluding to the inflated calyx covering the fruits. The name *purpurea* refers to the purple flowers, even though they range from rose purple to light pink. Another common name is obedient plant because the flowers can be repositioned and will then obediently stay where they are put. The flowers are irresistible to butterflies.

WILD PENNYROYAL

Piloblephis rigida (W. Bartram ex Benth.) Raf.
Mint Family (Lamiaceae)

Description: The hairy, ascending stems of this brittle species form mounds from 6"–24" tall. The needlelike leaves measure ⅜" long and ¹⁄₁₆" wide and are highly aromatic when crushed. Small, lavender flowers are in compact, conelike spikes at the branch tips. The upper lip is 3-lobed, and the lower lip is 2-lobed.

Bloom Season: All year

Habitat/Range: Sandy habitats from Florida to the Bahamas.

Comments: *Piloblephis* means "hairy eyelid" and relates to the hairlike pubescence on the sepals. The name *rigida* means "stiff," alluding to the leaves. The minty leaves are used to flavor soups and stews, and also medicinally to cure fever and other ailments. It makes a refreshing tea by steeping the leaves in sweetened water. It ranges south into southern Miami-Dade County and is common in the CREW Marsh (Collier County). It is absent from Everglades National Park.

LYRELEAF SAGE

Salvia lyrata L.
Mint Family (Lamiaceae)

Description: The wavy, spatulate or oval basal leaves range from 2"–6" long and are divided partway to the midrib, with a broad, rounded tip. The hairy flower spike is 4"–24" tall and bears purple flowers mottled with white. Each flower is about ⅜" long and ³⁄₁₆" wide.

Bloom Season: February–November

Habitat/Range: Hammocks and pinelands from Missouri and Connecticut south to Texas and Florida.

Comments: *Salvia* is Latin for "safe" or "well," alluding to the medicinal values bestowed upon some species. The name *lyrata* means "lyre shaped," in reference to the leaves. Many members of this genus are favorites of gardeners and have a long history of herbal and medicinal uses dating back to Pliny (AD 23–79) and Dioscorides (AD 40–80). In 16th-century America extracts of this plant were used as an ineffective cure for cancer. In the Everglades region it occurs in Corkscrew Swamp and the CREW Marsh.

WEST INDIAN SAGE
Salvia occidentalis Sw.
Mint Family (Lamiaceae)

Description: The branching stems of this species typically scramble across nearby vegetation. The toothed, strongly aromatic, 1"–1½" leaves are ovate. The flowers have included stamens and are on long terminal spikes, each flower measuring about ⅛". Fruits are glandular pubescent and cling to hair and clothing.

Bloom Season: All year

Habitat/Range: Disturbed sites of central and southern Florida, Bahamas, and the Neotropics.

Comments: The name *occidentalis* refers to its range in the Western Hemisphere. This is a relatively common weedy species in urban areas throughout its Florida range and is frequent in the Hole-in-the-Donut region of Everglades National Park and other disturbed sites. A related species *(Salvia divinorum)* from Mexican cloud forests has psychoactive principles and causes divinitory visions and hallucinations. It is used in Mexico for spiritual healing.

HAVANA SKULLCAP
Scutellaria havanensis Jacq.
Mint Family (Lamiaceae)

Description: This quaint little plant has slender stems covered with minute hairs. The opposite, softly hairy leaves are ovate, ⅜"–⅝" long, with entire or slightly toothed margins. The delicate ⅝" long and ½" wide, blue flowers emerge from the upper leaf axils. Each flower has a 3-lobed lower lip with 2 parallel white stripes.

Bloom Season: All year

Habitat/Range: Rocky pinelands from southern Florida to the Bahamas and Greater Antilles.

Comments: *Scutellaria* is Latin for "small dish," an allusion to the prominent pouch on the calyx. The name *havanensis* means "of Havana," the capital city of Cuba where it was first discovered in 1760. The name "skullcap" is based on the resemblance of the flowers of some species to a type of military helmet worn by American colonists. Cubans use this plant to treat infections, swelling of the feet, and psoriasis. The seeds are used to treat sarcoptic mange.

FORKED BLUECURLS
Trichostema dichotomum L.
Mint Family (Lamiaceae)

Description: Forked bluecurls reaches 2' tall and has square stems covered by minute, glandular hairs. The oblong to ovate leaves are opposite, about 2" long and ¾" wide, with entire margins. Flowers are in 3- to 7-flowered axillary clusters with curled stamens.

Bloom Season: Principally June–November

Habitat/Range: Sandy soils of beaches and dry woodlands through the eastern United States to the Bahamas.

Comments: *Trichostema* is Greek for "hair" and "stamen," in reference to the slender stalks of the anthers. The name *dichotomum* means "forked," alluding to the forked inflorescence. The flowers are scarcely noticeable without close inspection of the plant. Some members of this genus are allelopathic, capable of chemically inhibiting the growth of other plants growing nearby to limit competition. Narrowleaf bluecurls *(Trichostema setaceum)* occurs in central and northern Florida.

SMALL BUTTERWORT
Pinguicula pumila Michx.
Bladderwort Family (Lentibulariaceae)

Description: This is a very petite plant with a small basal rosette of leaves that are viscid to the touch. The leaves are elliptic to ovate and measure ⅜"–1" long. Flower spikes may reach 8" tall. Each spike is topped by a single flower that measures about ⅜" wide, varying from blue, violet, or pink to white and marked with purple or yellow.

Bloom Season: All year

Habitat/Range: Damp soils of the southeastern United States to Texas and the Bahamas.

Comments: *Pinguicula* alludes to the greasy texture of the leaf surface. The name *pumila* means "little," referring to its small stature. Butterworts are carnivorous and trap small insects on the leaves where they are digested by glandular enzyme secretions. The leaves were used to curdle milk, hence the name "butterwort." It typically prefers damp soils but can be found growing on limestone outcroppings in Everglades National Park.

PURPLE BLADDERWORT

Utricularia purpurea Walter
Bladderwort Family (Lentibulariaceae)

Description: Like other members of the genus, this aquatic, carnivorous species has filament-like leaves that branch into threadlike segments. There is usually a bladderlike trap at the end of the segments. Flower spikes can reach 6" tall, each topped by 1–4 light purple or violet, ⅜" flowers.

Bloom Season: All year

Habitat/Range: Fresh or brackish wetlands of the southeastern United States to the West Indies.

Comments: *Utricularia* is Latin for "small bag," referring to the traps on the leaves. When a tiny aquatic organism triggers a trap it is sucked inside and the trap closes. Once captured, enzymes absorb nutrients from the prey. The name *purpurea* refers to the purple flowers. This species may be floating or stranded in mud and is the most common of the 4 species in Florida with purple or violet flowers. There are 10 other Florida species that bear yellow flowers.

WINGED LOOSESTRIFE

Lythrum alatum Pursh var. *lanceolatum* (Elliott) Torr. & A. Gray ex Rothr.
Loosestrife Family (Lythraceae)

Description: The leaves are opposite on the lower stem, alternate above, and average ¾"–2" long and ¼"–⅜" wide with axillary flowers that range from white to pinkish-lavender and measure about ½" wide. Plants are typically about 2'–3' tall but may reach twice that height.

Bloom Season: March–September

Habitat/Range: Freshwater *wetlands from Virginia to Texas south through Florida.*

Comments: *Lythrum* means "blood" and alludes to the red flowers of *Lythrum salicaria* and to its use to stop bleeding. The name *alatum* refers to the strongly winged central stem. The name *lanceolatum* relates to the lanceolate leaves. Many species of bees and butterflies are attracted to the flowers yet it is seldom cultivated. "Loosestrife" is derived from a word meaning "ending strife." Wand loosestrife *(Lythrum lineare)* is similar but with linear leaves.

FIRE FLAG

Thalia geniculata L.
Arrowroot Family (Marantaceae)

Description: Fireflag grows to 6'–9' tall and is easily identified by its broad, lanceolate leaf blade held at an angle atop the petiole. The leaves reach 3' long and 1' wide. The odd-shaped flowers have 3 purple petals, 3 small sepals, and hang in pairs on zigzagging stems.

Bloom Season: May–January

Habitat/Range: Freshwater wetlands of Florida and the West Indies.

Comments: *Thalia* honors German physician and botanist Johannes Thal (1542–1583). The name *geniculata* means "with knees," referring to the jointed stems. When alligators move through thickets of this plant the leaves wave back and forth, giving rise to another common name, alligator flag. The larvae of the Brazilian skipper butterfly and the stinging caterpillars of the io moth and saddleback moth eat the leaves. It is very common in the Everglades region, often forming dense thickets. The roots are survival food.

BURROWING FOUR-O'CLOCK

Okenia hypogaea Schltdl. & Cham.
Four-O'Clock Family (Nyctaginaceae)

Description: The leaves of this annual are opposite, densely pubescent, and range from 1"–1½" long and ¾"–1" wide. The 5-lobed, rose-purple, ¾" flowers are solitary in the leaf axils. The flowers bend down after fertilization, pushing the developing fruits underground to ripen. This prevents them from being washed away by tides.

Bloom Season: March–November

Habitat/Range: Beach dunes from eastern-central to southwest Florida and Mexico.

Comments: *Okenia* honors German naturalist Lorenz Oken (1779–1851) who is best known for dividing animals into 5 distinct classes. The name *hypogaea* means "underground," in reference to the fruits that develop beneath the sand. Another common name is beach peanut. This plant is one of the most attractive dune plants in Florida but habitat destruction due to beachfront development has placed it on the endangered species list.

TROPICAL ROYAL-BLUE WATERLILY
Nymphaea elegans Hook.
Waterlily Family (Nymphaeaceae)

Description: The leaves of this species are rounded and deeply notched at the base, ranging from 4"–8" in diameter (green above, purple below). The petals of the fragrant, solitary flowers are usually lightly tinged with violet. The flowers are held 4"–8" above the water surface and range from 2½"–4" wide.

Bloom Season: April–November

Habitat/Range: Freshwater habitats of the eastern United States to Canada and the Bahamas.

Comments: *Nymphaea* is Greek for "water nymph." The Greek word "nymph" means "young girl" and in this case refers to the mythological water nymphs associated with rivers, ponds, lakes, or the sea, and who hardly ever wore clothing. The name *elegans* means "elegant." It is also called elegant waterlily. In the Everglades region it can be found in the canal along Turner River Road in the Big Cypress Swamp and around Corkscrew Swamp in Collier County.

PANTROPICAL WIDELIP ORCHID
Liparis nervosa (Thunb.) Lindl.
(Also *Liparis elata* Lindl.)
Orchid Family (Orchidaceae)

Description: This attractive terrestrial or semi-epiphytic orchid produces large leaves that sheathe the pseudobulb. The leaves can reach 10" long and 5" wide and are pleated longitudinally. The erect flower spike produces up to 30 flowers. Each flower is ⅜"–½" wide with greenish purple sepals and petals and a purple lip.

Bloom Season: July–October

Habitat/Range: Hardwood forests and swamps of central and southern Florida through the Neotropics.

Comments: *Liparis* translates to "greasy" or "glossy," alluding to either the oily-feeling leaves or their glossy luster. The name *nervosa* means "prominently nerved," in reference to the leaf veins. In the Everglades region this endangered orchid is very local and can be found growing on rotting stumps and floating logs in the Faka-hatchee Swamp in Collier County, often in the company of mosses.

CLAMSHELL ORCHID
Prosthechea cochleata (La Llave & Lex.) W. E. Higgins
(Also *Encyclia cochleata* [L.] Dressler)
Orchid Family (Orchidaceae)

Description: The clamshell orchid has 1–3 linear-lanceolate leaves arising from a green, compressed pseudobulb. The leaves average 4"–12" long and ½"–1" wide. The purple lip of the flower is held uppermost and shaped like the valve of a clamshell. The sepals and petals are yellow, narrow, and twisted below the lip.

Bloom Season: October–May

Habitat/Range: Hardwood forests and swamps of southern Florida, the West Indies, and Mexico to South America.

Comments: *Prosthechea* refers to the appendage on the back of the column. The name *cochleata* means "shell shaped," alluding to the lip where it gets its common name. This orchid was first discovered in Florida in 1877 by botanist Abram P. Garber (1838–1881). It was once abundant in southern Florida's hardwood hammocks and swamps but is now a state-listed endangered species.

MAYPOP
Passiflora incarnata L.
Passionflower Family (Passifloraceae)

Description: Maypop is a high-climbing, aggressive vine with 3-lobed leaves from 3"–4" wide. The showy, fragrant flowers are 2½"–3¼" wide with pink to pale purple sepals and petals. The ovoid, yellowish-green fruits are 2"–2½" wide.

Bloom Season: April–October

Habitat/Range: A variety of habitats throughout the eastern United States.

Comments: *Passiflora* is Latin for "passion flower" and relates to the crucifixion of Christ because the floral parts were believed by 17th-century Spanish Jesuits to represent 10 apostles (minus Peter and Judas), the crown-of-thorns, and 3 nails. The name *incarnata* means "flesh colored," alluding to the fruits. It is a larval host plant of heliconian butterflies as well as the plebeian sphinx moth. The Cherokee called it *ocoee* and is the name source of the Ocoee River in Tennessee and the town of Ocoee in Florida. It is also called apricot vine.

BLUE WATER HYSSOP
Bacopa caroliniana (Walter) B. L. Rob.
Plantain Family (Plantaginaceae)

Description: The mat-forming succulent stems and leaves of this species smell like lemon when crushed. The stems are typically about 6" tall, with opposite, sessile, softly hairy leaves that alternate in direction on the stem. The leaves are ovate to about ⅝" long and ¼"–½" wide. The ⅜", 5-lobed, bright blue flowers are solitary in the upper leaf axils.

Bloom Season: May–November

Habitat/Range: Freshwater wetlands from Florida to Virginia and Texas.

Comments: *Bacopa* is an aboriginal name among indigenous people of French Guiana. The name *caroliniana* means "of the Carolinas." Another common name, lemon bacopa, refers to the pungent, lemonlike odor emitted from crushed leaves. The name "hyssop" relates to the garden herb anise *(Hyssopus officinalis)*. This and other members of the figwort family (Scrophulariaceae) were recently moved to the Plantaginaceae.

BLUE TOADFLAX
Linaria canadensis (L.) Chaz.
Plantain Family (Plantaginaceae)

Description: This biennial reaches 8"–24" tall with narrowly linear, alternate leaves measuring ⅜"–1" long. Smaller but wider leaves on the prostrate stems are opposite or whorled. Flowers are violet and white with 3 rounded posterior lobes. Flowers measure about 5/16" long and nearly as wide.

Bloom Season: February–May

Habitat/Range: Fields and roadsides from Florida to California north to British Columbia and Nova Scotia.

Comments: *Linaria* alludes to the leaves of *Linaria vulgaris*, which resemble a species of *Linum* (Linaceae). The name *canadensis* means "of Canada." The Iroquois used leaves of a related species as an anti-love medicine and also to treat bewitching. Flowers were given to babies to keep them from crying and the leaves were brewed as a sedating tea. It does not occur in Everglades National Park. It is a larval host plant of the common buckeye butterfly.

SAVANNAH FALSE PIMPERNEL
Lindernia grandiflora Nutt.
Plantain Family (Plantaginaceae)

Description: This species has prostrate or ascending stems with opposite, clasping, ovate leaves measuring up to ⅜" long and ½" wide. The slender flower stems are axillary and topped by a single flower. The flowers are about ¼" wide with a purple-spotted lip.

Bloom Season: All year

Habitat/Range: Freshwater wetlands from Georgia south in Florida to Everglades National Park.

Comments: *Lindernia* honors German botanist Franz Balthazar von Lindern (1682–1755). The name *grandiflora* means "large flowers" compared to those of other species in the genus. It is also called angel's tears or blue moneywort and is found throughout the Everglades region. It is common along the shady trails that traverse mesic flatwoods within the 60,000-acre CREW Marsh in Collier County. The naturalized exotic *Lindernia crustacea* differs by having a purple line across the lower lip.

WATER HYACINTH
Eichhornia crassipes (Mart.) Solms.
Pickerelweed Family (Pontederiaceae)

Description: This unmistakable floating, aquatic perennial has spongy, inflated petioles topped by a nearly round leaf blade. The showy flowers are produced on erect succulent stems. The roots are black.

Bloom Season: Sporadically all year

Habitat/Range: Freshwater habitats throughout Florida. Native to Brazil.

Comments: *Eichhornia* honors Prussian statesman Johann Albrecht Friedr Eichhorn (1779–1856). The name *crassipes* refers to the inflated petioles that provide buoyancy. This federal noxious weed grows at explosive rates and is capable of reproducing vegetatively from 2 to 1,200 plants in just 4 months. Dense rafts of plants prevent sunlight from penetrating the water and impede recreational activities such as boating, swimming, and fishing. It was introduced at the World Industrial & Cotton Centennial Exposition held in Louisiana in 1884.

PICKERELWEED
Pontederia cordata L.
Pickerelweed Family (Pontederiaceae)

Description: Pickerelweed is an aquatic species with fleshy, heart-shaped or lanceolate leaves. Plants usually emerge from standing water, reaching 3' tall, with leaf blades measuring 4"–8" long and 1"–4" wide. The erect flower spike is densely covered with blue (rarely white), 2-lipped flowers with yellow markings. The flowers are about ³⁄₁₆"–¼" wide.

Bloom Season: All year

Habitat/Range: Freshwater wetlands from Virginia to Missouri and Texas south through Florida and the Neotropics.

Comments: *Pontederia* honors Italian botanist and professor Guilo Pontedera (1688–1757). The name *cordata* means "heart shaped," in reference to the leaf blade. The common name refers to the pickerel, a fish that often uses this plant for cover, especially when young. The flowers attract bees and a multitude of butterflies. It is exceptionally common along roadside ditches and canals.

PINE HYACINTH
Clematis baldwinii Torr. & A. Gray
Buttercup Family (Ranunculaceae)

Description: Pine hyacinth reaches 8"–24" tall with linear or broadly lanceolate leaves that average 1"–4" long and often deeply divided into 5 segments. The nodding flowers are 1"–2" long with curled, frilly sepals that are purple or white and elevated well above the foliage.

Bloom Season: February–November

Habitat/Range: Endemic to flatwoods and pinelands from Flagler County south through mainland Florida.

Comments: *Clematis* was a name used by Greek naturalist Dioscorides (A.D. 40–80) for a climbing plant with long, flexible branches. The name *baldwinii* honors Pennsylvania physician and botanist William Baldwin (1779–1819). The name *hyacinth* relates to Hyacinthus, a boy in Greek mythology who is said to have died accidentally from a discus thrown by Apollo, who then made a flower from the boy's blood. Seeds may take a year or more to germinate but the result is worth the wait.

BLUEHEARTS
Buchnera americana L.
(Also *Buchnera floridana* Gand.)
Figwort Family (Scrophulariaceae)

Description: The frail stems of bluehearts average 8"–12" tall with narrow, opposite leaves that reduce in size up the stem. The lower leaves range from 1"–2" long and ¼"–⅜" wide. Violet or white 5-lobed flowers top the slender flowering stem. The flowers are about ⅜" wide with 1 to several open at a time.

Bloom Season: All year

Habitat/Range: Pinelands, marshes, and roadsides of the eastern United States to the Bahamas, Greater Antilles, and Central America.

Comments: *Buchnera* honors German botanist Johann Gottfried Büchner (1695–1749) who wrote books in Latin. The name *americana* means "of America." White-flowered forms are frequent in the Corkscrew Swamp and CREW Marsh regions. This species can become parasitic under certain conditions to gain sustenance from another plant for survival. It is a larval host plant of the common buckeye butterfly.

BLUE PORTERWEED
Stachytarpheta jamaicensis (L.) Vahl
Verbena Family (Verbenaceae)

Description: Blue porterweed has low-spreading branches and is typically only about 10" tall. The leaves range from 1"–4" long and ¾"–1¾" wide with coarse teeth along the margins. The green, quill-like spikes produce 1 to several flowers at a time, each about ⅜" wide.

Bloom Season: All year

Habitat/Range: Pinelands, forest margins, and disturbed sites from Alabama through Florida to Bermuda and the Neotropics.

Comments: *Stachytarpheta* alludes to the thick flower spike. The name *jamaicensis* means "of Jamaica." The name porterweed relates to a porterlike brew concocted from the leaves and used medicinally to treat everything from coughs to syphilis. It is a superb butterfly attractor and a larval host plant of the tropical buckeye butterfly. The taller (to 6'), nonnative *Stachytarpheta cayennensis* is often sold by nursery growers as is this Florida native.

WOOD VIOLET
Viola palmata L.
Violet Family (Violaceae)

Description: The variable leaves are typically palmately lobed with blades averaging 1"–2" long. Flowers are solitary atop stems that reach 1½"–3" tall. Individual flowers are about ¾"–1" tall and range from dark to light blue or purple.

Bloom Season: March–July

Habitat/Range: Sandhills and flatwoods from Ontario and Maine south across the eastern United States to Texas and Florida.

Comments: *Viola* is the classical name for the violet. The name *palmata* refers to the palmate leaves. Because this species is so variable it has a lengthy list of synonyms. It is also called early blue violet and is the state flower of Rhode Island. It ranges through northern and central Florida south into the Corkscrew Swamp region of Collier County where it typically grows in association with other members of the genus. There are 9 native violets in Florida and 1 naturalized exotic species from Europe *(Viola tricolor).*

COMMON BLUE VIOLET
Viola sororia Willd.
(Also *Viola floridana* Brainerd)
Violet Family (Violaceae)

Description: The nearly orbicular leaves form a basal rosette and measure 1"–3" across. The leaves are toothed with long petioles. The flowers are about ¾" wide and consist of 5 rounded petals ranging from pale to rich blue. It is not stoloniferous like many other species.

Bloom Season: March–July

Habitat/Range: Mesic forests of the eastern and midwestern United States north into Canada.

Comments: The name *sororia* means "sisterly," alluding to its resemblance to other species. The flowers are fragrant but they contain chemicals that can briefly turn off the ability of humans to detect the scent consecutively. Hover flies (pictured) seek nectar from the flowers. There are no *Viola* species within Everglades National Park but this and other species are locally common in the Big Cypress Swamp and Corkscrew Swamp regions, including the CREW Marsh.

PINK FLOWERS

Sabatia stellaris

This section includes flowers ranging from pale pink to deep magenta. Many species with pink flowers also have white flower variations. You may need to check the Blue and Purple, Red, or White sections of this book if the flower you are searching for is not found here.

PINELAND PINKLET
Stenandrium dulce (Cav.) Nees
(Also *Stenandrium dulce* [Cav.] Nees var. *floridanum* A. Gray)
Acanthus Family (Acanthaceae)

Description: Pineland pinklet has smooth, dark green leaves in a rosette that lies flat on the ground. The leaves are somewhat ovate and measure ¾"–1¼" long. The scape typically stands 3"–4" tall. The flowers are on a short spike with leafy bracts. The flowers are sweetly fragrant and reach about ⅜"–½" wide.

Bloom Season: All year

Habitat/Range: Wet pinelands and prairies of central and southern Florida and from Texas through Mexico to Chile.

Comments: *Stenandrium* is Greek for "tight anthers." The name *dulce* means "sweet," referring to the sweet-scented flowers. Another common name is rattlesnake flower, in reference to its use by Seminoles as a perceived remedy for rattlesnake bite. The Miccosukee believe that bags of leaves placed near sleeping babies keep them from dreaming about scary animals.

SEA PURSLANE
Sesuvium portulacastrum (L.) L.
Carpetweed Family (Aizoaceae)

Description: The succulent stems of this trailing species are reddish with opposite, fleshy leaves that reach 2" long and ½" wide. The leaves are green or tinged with red. The ⅜" starlike flowers are solitary in the leaf axils, with pink petal-like sepals and numerous stamens.

Bloom Season: All year

Habitat/Range: Tropical and subtropical coastal shorelines worldwide.

Comments: *Sesuvium* relates to the Sesuvii, a Gallic tribe from present-day France mentioned by Julius Caesar (100–44 BC). The name *portulacastrum* refers to its resemblance to members of the genus *Portulaca*, the purslanes. Sea purslane has been used effectively to treat scurvy (vitamin C deficiency) and is sold in Asian markets. In the Caribbean the pulverized leaves are used to soothe puncture wounds caused by venomous fish. It is common along both coastlines of Florida and is an important dune stabilizer.

ROSE MILKWEED

Asclepias incarnata L.
Dogbane Family (Apocynaceae)

Description: Rose milkweed is an erect, usually multi-stemmed species that averages 2'–4' tall. The opposite, narrowly lanceolate leaves may reach 6" long and 1½" wide. Small, pink to mauve flowers each have 5 reflexed petals and an elevated crown. Seeds are attached to tufts of white fiber and are dispersed by wind.

Bloom Season: June–August

Habitat/Range: Freshwater wetlands of the eastern United States.

Comments: *Asclepias* was named for Aesculapius, the legendary Greek god of medicine. The name *incarnata* means "flesh colored," in reference to the pink flower color. This species ranges south through the Big Cypress Swamp into Everglades National Park. Like other members of the genus it is a larval host plant of the monarch and queen butterflies. The flowers emit a pleasant fragrance reminiscent of cinnamon. It is very localized in the Everglades region but more common northward.

LONGLEAF MILKWEED

Asclepias longifolia Michx.
Dogbane Family (Apocynaceae)

Description: The long, narrow leaves of this species reach 6" long and ⅛"–⅜" wide. The leaves have small hairs on the veins of the lower surface with scattered hairs on the upper surface. All parts exude milky sap if broken. The corolla lobes are pinkish purple with white bases and are strongly reflexed.

Bloom Season: February–September

Habitat/Range: Wet soils of pinelands and prairies from Delaware to Louisiana and Florida.

Comments: The name *longifolia* means "long leaved." This species is infrequent and sporadic in wet prairies throughout the Everglades region. It is a larval host plant for monarch and queen butterflies that are specialized to feed on *Asclepias* despite chemical defenses in the leaves. Birds that attempt to eat their larvae find them distasteful and even toxic. There are 21 native members of this genus in Florida and 2 are endemic to the state.

MADAGASCAR PERIWINKLE
Catharanthus roseus (L.) G. Don
Dogbane Family (Apocynaceae)

Description: This species is well known in cultivation. It reaches 2' tall with opposite, elliptic, hairy leaves with a white midvein. Leaves range from 2"–3" long and ½"–1" wide. Showy 5-lobed flowers are in terminal clusters, each flower measuring 1½"–2" wide. Flowers are uniformly rosy pink with a darker center or white with a dark pink center.

Bloom Season: All year

Habitat/Range: Dry habitats, including beach dunes, throughout central and southern Florida. Native to Madagascar.

Comments: *Catharanthus* means "pure flower" and the name *roseus* means "rose colored." This plant is commonly cultivated and widely naturalized in Florida. Alkaloids in the leaves are effective in treating childhood leukemia and Hodgkin's disease. Other alkaloids are being tested for the treatment of diabetes, influenza, and polio. The plant is poisonous to people and livestock if eaten.

PURPLE THISTLE
Cirsium horridulum Michx.
Aster Family (Asteraceae)

Description: The spiny, lobed, or deeply incised leaves of this biennial form a rosette. The basal leaves reach 12" long and 2" wide, becoming shorter up the flowering stem. The stem leaves are clasping and not as deeply cut. The flower heads range from 2"–3" in diameter and vary from rosy purple to lavender or white.

Bloom Season: All year

Habitat/Range: Pinelands, prairies, and roadsides of the eastern United States, Mexico, and the Bahamas.

Comments: *Cirsium* means "swollen vein," alluding to members of the genus used medicinally to treat varicose veins. The name *horridulum* means "prickly" or "bristly." The flowers attract a variety of insects, including butterflies. In Greek mythology thistles appeared on Earth to grieve the loss of Daphnis, a shepherd said to be the inventor of pastoral poetry. It is a larval host plant of the little metalmark and painted lady butterflies in Florida.

NUTTALL'S THISTLE
Cirsium nuttallii DC.
Aster Family (Asteraceae)

Description: This very spiny biennial reaches 10' tall, often branching near the top, with strongly ribbed stems. Leaves are sessile, 4"–10" long and 1"–4" wide, with sharp spines on the tips of the lobes. Heads of pink to lavender disk flowers are ⅝"–1" wide and shaped like a shaving brush.

Bloom Season: April–August

Habitat/Range: Wet pine savannas, flatwoods, and roadsides from North Carolina to Louisiana south through mainland Florida.

Comments: The name *nuttallii* honors English botanist Thomas Nuttall (1786–1839) who traveled in Florida in 1830. Six other Florida native plants also honor Nuttall. A host of insects visit the flowers, including a wide variety of butterflies. This plant is often found in pastures where it escapes grazing by livestock due to the abundance of sharp spines. Green lynx spiders often hide on the flowers to grab an easy meal when an insect stops to visit.

BLAZING STAR
Liatris spicata (L.) Willd.
Aster Family (Asteraceae)

Description: Numerous narrowly linear, 3–5-nerved leaves appear grasslike near the bottom of the stem and average 5"–7" long and ³⁄₁₆"–³⁄₈" wide, becoming smaller up the flowering stem. Flowers are in groups of 4–10, deep rose pink (rarely white), and opening from the top of the spike downward.

Bloom Season: June–December

Habitat/Range: Moist prairies and pinelands from Florida to Louisiana north to Canada.

Comments: *Liatris* may have come from the Gaelic *liatrus*, or "spoon-shaped," and refer to the shape of the tuberous roots on some species. The name *spicata* means "a spike," alluding to the spike of flowers. This common species blooms in abundance following fire and attracts a profusion of butterflies. It is grown as a commercial cut flower under the name Floristan violet. There are 4 other species in the Everglades region and all have similar flowers so check the leaf characteristics.

ROSE RUSH
Lygodesmia aphylla (Nutt.) DC.
Aster Family (Asteraceae)

Description: The erect, rushlike, 12"–32" tall stems of rose rush sometimes fork near the top with leaves that are either represented by narrow scales or by a few elongated, linear blades near the base. Basal leaves are often absent during flowering. Flowers are light rose lavender to about 1³⁄₈" wide with petals that are squared off and toothed at the tip.

Bloom Season: March–August

Habitat/Range: Sandy flatwoods and scrub from Georgia south in Florida to Broward and Collier Counties.

Comments: *Lygodesmia* is from the Greek *lygos*, "a pliant twig," and *desme*, "a bundle," referring to the clustered rushlike stems. The name *aphylla* means "without leaves," in reference to the bare stems and few leaves produced by the plant. The flowers attract butterflies but the buds do not open until midmorning and close by late afternoon. The sap of some species turns blue when chewed like gum.

ROSY CAMPHORWEED
Pluchea baccharis (Mill.) Pruski
(Also *Pluchea rosea* R. K. Godfrey)
Aster Family (Asteraceae)

Description: Copious soft hairs give this plant a fuzzy appearance. It typically grows less than 12" tall with alternate, sessile leaves. The lower leaves are square at the base, ¾"–2¾" long and ¼"–1¼" wide. The leaves smell like camphor when crushed. Rose pink disk flowers are in compact heads.

Bloom Season: All year

Habitat/Range: Freshwater wetlands of the southeastern United States, West Indies, and Mexico.

Comments: *Pluchea* honors French abbot and naturalist Noël-Antoine Pluche (1688–1761). The name *baccharis* may come from the Greek *bakcharis,* used by Dioscorides (AD 40–80). Pioneer settlers in the southeastern United States placed the aromatic leaves of this and related species in their bedding to deter fleas, hence another colloquial name, marsh fleabane. The flowers attract hairstreaks and other small butterflies.

SALTMARSH FLEABANE
Pluchea odorata (L.) Cass.
Aster Family (Asteraceae)

Description: This attractive plant grows to 4' tall. The aromatic leaves are ovate to lanceolate, ranging from 2"–5" long and 1½"–2½" wide, more or less clustered toward the branch tips, with fine, glandular hairs on the lower surface. The scented, pink flower heads are numerous in dense, flat-topped clusters.

Bloom Season: All year

Habitat/Range: Coastal and inland marshes of the southeastern United States and the Neotropics.

Comments: The name *odorata* means "fragrant," in reference to the aromatic leaves and flowers. In the Caribbean the leaves are used in a tea to relieve colds, night sweats, menstrual difficulties, and stomach disorders. This species deserves attention from butterfly gardeners because the flowers are highly attractive to an assortment of butterflies. Despite its common name, this plant can also be found growing in freshwater habitats.

FLORIDA IRONWEED
Vernonia blodgettii Small
Aster Family (Asteraceae)

Description: The smooth stems bear alternate, sessile, linear or narrowly lanceolate leaves that range from 2"–4" long and up to ½" wide. The rayless flower heads are few to numerous in open clusters. The disk flowers are bright pinkish lavender.

Bloom Season: All year

Habitat/Range: Pinelands and prairie margins of Florida and the northern Bahamas.

Comments: *Vernonia* honors 17th-century English botanist William Vernon who collected plants in North America. The name *blodgettii* commemorates botanist John Loomis Blodgett (1809–1853), who is regarded as the most important figure in southern Florida's early botanical history. Another prominent Florida botanist, John Kunkel Small (1869–1938), named this species in honor of Blodgett's contributions to the field of botany. It was once thought to be endemic to Florida until it was discovered on Andros Island in the Bahamas.

POTBELLY AIRPLANT

Tillandsia paucifolia Baker
(Also *Tillandsia circinnata* Schltdl., misapplied)
Pineapple Family (Bromeliaceae)

Description: This squat, urn-shaped, epiphytic bromeliad produces just a few thick, contorted, or curled leaves. Small, scurfy scales cover the leaves, giving the plant a silvery gray appearance. Plants average 2"–4" tall and are either solitary or in small clusters. The erect or curved flower spike is 1½"–3" tall and covered with overlapping pink bracts. Tubular lavender flowers emerge from behind the bracts.

Bloom Season: March–July

Habitat/Range: Cypress and mangrove forests from Florida, the West Indies, and Mexico to Colombia.

Comments: *Tillandsia* honors Swedish physician and botanist Elias Erici Tillands (1640–1693), who cataloged the plants of Abo, Finland. The name *paucifolia* means "few leaves." This species is capable of tolerating dry, harsh conditions where there are few available nutrients.

FUZZYWUZZY AIRPLANT

Tillandsia pruinosa Sw.
Pineapple Family (Bromeliaceae)

Description: This quaint, epiphytic bromeliad stands 2"–5" tall and resembles a small octopus. The narrow, twisting leaves emerge from a swollen, bulbous base and are covered with dense, silvery hairs. Tubular purple flowers, to about ⅛" wide, emerge singly from behind pink, fuzzy bracts.

Bloom Season: Principally November–March

Habitat/Range: Forested swamps from southwestern Florida to the West Indies and Brazil.

Comments: The name *pruinosa* means "hoarfrost" or "frosty," alluding to the silvery hairs that cover the plant. In Florida this endangered species is restricted to hardwood swamps of Collier County and is easily the rarest member of the genus in Florida. It grows singly or in small clusters, typically low on trees in dappled sunlight. It is also called hoary airplant or hairy airplant and has been described as resembling a small, hairy octopus.

FLORIDA SCRUB ROSELING
Callisia ornata (Small) G. C. Tucker
Spiderwort Family (Commelinaceae)

Description: The narrowly linear leaves are ascending and average 4"–6" long and ⅛" wide or less. The 3-petaled flowers are about ¾" wide and range in color from pale pink to rich rose pink (rarely white).

Bloom Season: March–September

Habitat/Range: Endemic to scrub and sandhills from the Florida Panhandle to Broward and Collier Counties.

Comments: *Callisia* means "beauty" and refers to the leaves of *Callisia repens*. The name *ornata* relates to the ornate flowers of this species. The southern range of this species in Florida includes the CREW Marsh where it grows in small colonies in open, sandy locations. This is the only endemic member of the genus in Florida. It was originally placed in the genus *Cuthbertia* by botanist John Kunkel Small (1869–1938) to honor amateur botanist Alfred Cuthbert (1857–1932) who collected plants in Florida and Georgia.

DWARF SUNDEW
Drosera brevifolia Pursh.
Sundew Family (Droseraceae)

Description: The spoon-shaped leaves form a ⅜"–½" rosette and the leaf blades are covered with numerous gland-tipped tentacles (glandular trichomes) that exude a glistening, sticky secretion. Small, 5-petaled pink (rarely white) flowers are held atop thin, erect stems.

Bloom Season: Typically April–June

Habitat/Range: Wet, acidic soils of flatwoods and bogs from North Carolina to Texas south in Florida to the Big Cypress Swamp.

Comments: *Drosera* means "dewy," alluding to the secretions that resemble dew and glisten in the sun (sundew). The name *brevifolia* refers to the short leaves. This plant entraps small insects that are then dissolved by the secretions. It sometimes grows in the company of the larger pink sundew *(Drosera capillaris)* north of the Everglades region. The leaf secretions have been used to treat warts and corns and were once believed to be a powerful aphrodisiac.

BAY BEAN
Canavalia rosea (Sw.) DC.
Pea Family (Fabaceae)

Description: This spreading vine has leathery leaves that are divided into 3 large leaflets. Each leaflet is almost circular in outline and measures 2½"–4" long and 2"–3" wide. Flowers are in axillary racemes with 2–3 rosy, ¾" flowers produced at each node. The pods are 5"–6" long and 1"–1½" wide.

Bloom Season: All year

Habitat/Range: Beach dunes of tropical and warm temperate regions worldwide.

Comments: *Canavalia* is derived from *kavavali,* a name meaning "forest climber" in India. The name *rosea* refers to the rose-colored flowers. The seeds contain chemicals that are toxic to ingest but the leaves are eaten in Asia. Ocean currents transport the buoyant seeds around all parts of the world. It helps stabilize dunes by trapping sand with its long stems and is a larval host plant of the day-flying faithful beauty moth. Two other species *(Canavalia brasiliensis* and *C. ensiformis)* are naturalized in Florida.

SANDHILL PRAIRIECLOVER
Dalea carnea (Michx.) Poir
Pea Family (Fabaceae)

Description: This species reaches 18"–24" tall and typically forms mounds of stems that are covered with dainty, 1" flower clusters in summer. The alternate, compound leaves are finely dissected and appear featherlike.

Bloom Season: July–October

Habitat/Range: Sandy habitats of peninsular Florida and Georgia.

Comments: *Dalea* commemorates English physician and botanist Samuel Dale (1659–1739). The name *carnea* means "flesh pink" in reference to the flowers. Sandhill prairieclover is a larval host plant of the southern dogface butterfly north of the Everglades region. Small butterflies and day-flying moths occasionally visit the flowers but bees are the most frequent visitors, especially bumblebees. It is present in the CREW Marsh (Collier County) and in sandy pinelands east of Everglades National Park (Miami-Dade County).

FLORIDA HAMMOCK MILKPEA
Galactia striata (Jacq.) Urb.
Pea Family (Fabaceae)

Description: The leaves of this twining legume are divided into 3 ovate-elliptic leaflets, each measuring about 1½"–2½" long and ¾"–1" wide. The ⅜" flowers differ from other species by the thin, white stripes on the standard.

Bloom Season: All year

Habitat/Range: Coastal hammocks of southern Florida (including the Florida Keys) and the Neotropics.

Comments: *Galactia* means "milk-yielding," a name first used in 1756 to describe a species with milky sap. The name *striata* refers to the striations on the standard. This is the larval host plant of the zestos skipper butterfly that has recently disappeared from Florida. It was last reported in Key West but has not been seen since January 2004. Aerial spraying for mosquito control and the spread of imported fire ants that attack butterfly eggs and larvae may have contributed to its demise. Florida hammock milkpea also occurs in the Bahamas and Greater Antilles.

EASTERN MILKPEA
Galactia volubilis (L.) Britton
Pea Family (Fabaceae)

Description: Eastern milkpea is a slender, twining (sometimes prostrate) vine with leaves divided into 3 oblong leaflets from ⅜"–1¾" long and half as wide (the terminal leaflet is longest). Flowers measure about ½"–⅝" long.

Bloom Season: All year

Habitat/Range: Sandhills, scrub, and dry forests of the Eastern United States and West Indies.

Comments: The name *volubilis* relates to its twining habit. Downy milkpea *(Galactia regularis)* is similar but differs principally by having a much-exerted inflorescence. Some botanists separate *Galactia pinetorum* and *Galactia smallii* as Florida endemic species, citing differences in leaflet shape and pubescence, while others relegate them as synonyms of this widespread species. This is a larval host plant of the cassius blue, ceraunus blue, gray hairstreak, silver spotted skipper, and zarucco duskywing butterflies.

FLORIDA SENSITIVE BRIER
Mimosa quadrivalvis L. var. *angustata* (Torr. & A. Gray) Barneby
Pea Family (Fabaceae)

Description: The thorny stems are ribbed and may trail 6' or more, scrambling across low vegetation. The bipinnately compound leaves have numerous fine leaflets and are almost fernlike in appearance. The balls of flowers are about ½" wide.

Bloom Season: May–November

Habitat/Range: Scrub and sandhills of peninsular Florida and Georgia.

Comments: *Mimosa* means "mimic," and refers to the leaflets on some species that close when touched. The name *quadrivalvis* means "4 valves," in reference to the 4 valves of the pods. The name *angustata* means "narrowed." The small, recurved thorns can make walking through patches of this vining species a painful experience. The thorns are not there solely to torment people but rather to hook onto nearby vegetation for the purpose of climbing in lieu of twining or using tendrils. They also deter herbivores.

POWDERPUFF
Mimosa strigillosa Torr. & A. Gray
Pea Family (Fabaceae)

Description: This thornless, hairy, mat-forming species spreads by rhizomes and bears alternate, bipinnate leaves that are divided into as many as 21 pairs of small, linear leaflets. The leaflets are sensitive and close when touched. The flower heads are oblong in outline (taller than wide) and consist mostly of pink stamens.

Bloom Season: March–September

Habitat/Range: Sandy habitats and roadsides of Florida and Texas south into Mexico.

Comments: The name *strigillosa* refers to the minute, straight, appressed (strigose) hairs. This plant is becoming a popular ground cover because it spreads rapidly by rhizomes that criss-cross to form a dense, ground-hugging mat. It is sometimes used in road medians and parking lot islands because it can tolerate foot traffic and drought. The flowers attract bees and the leaves serve as larval food for the little yellow butterfly.

CORAL HOARYPEA

Tephrosia angustissima Shuttlew. ex Chapm. var. *corallicola* (Small) Isely
Pea Family (Fabaceae)

Description: This legume has hairy stems that spread outward from a taproot with hairy compound leaves that average 2"–2½" long. The narrow leaflets range from ⅜"–½" long and ⅛"–¼" wide. The flowers are about ⅜" wide.

Bloom Season: March–October

Habitat/Range: Pine rocklands of southern Florida (historically Collier and Miami-Dade Counties) and Cuba.

Comments: *Tephrosia* means "ash colored" and refers to the grayish tint of the leaves created by the hairs. The name *angustissima* refers to the narrow leaflets and the name *corallicola* alludes to it growing on coral rock (actually oolitic limestone). John Kunkel Small (1869–1938) first discovered it near Coconut Grove in 1904. George Newton Avery (1922–1983) found a population in Miami-Dade County in 1978 and this remains the only extant population in Florida. It is critically imperiled.

COASTAL ROSEGENTIAN

Sabatia calycina (Lam.) A. Heller
Gentian Family (Gentianaceae)

Description: The upper stem leaves are slightly larger than those lower on the stem and are mostly elliptic, averaging ½"–¾" long and ⅛"–¼" wide. There can be 5–7 corolla lobes ranging from pink to white and with wide calyx lobes visible behind the corolla lobes. The centers of the flowers may be green or yellow, sometimes surrounded by an irregular reddish circle. The flowers average ⅝"–¾" wide.

Bloom Season: April–October

Habitat/Range: Floodplain forests and flatwoods of the southeastern United States.

Comments: *Sabatia* honors 18th-century Italian botanist Liberato Sabbati who was the keeper of the botanical garden in Rome. The name *calycina* refers to the conspicuous calyx lobes, which help tell it apart from other species in the Everglades region. This species is locally common in and around the swamps of southwestern Florida but absent from Everglades National Park.

BARTRAM'S ROSEGENTIAN
Sabatia decandra (Walter) R. M. Harper
(Also *Sabatia bartramii* Wilbur)
Gentian Family (Gentianaceae)

Description: The rosette of lower leaves are spatulate or narrowly oblong, 1½"–3½" long and ⅜"–⅝" wide. The upper stem leaves are equal to or narrower than the stem. The 2"–2¾" very showy flowers have 10–14 corolla lobes that range from rich rosy magenta to pale pink (rarely white).

Bloom Season: May–September

Habitat/Range: Freshwater wetlands of the southeastern United States south in Florida to the Big Cypress National Preserve and adjacent wetland ecosystems to the west.

Comments: The name *decandra* refers to the 10 stamens. There is hardly a more spectacular flower adorning the sunny prairies surrounding the swamps of southwestern Florida during the wet season yet it does not occur within Everglades National Park. It is most commonly seen in the dreadful heat of summer when mosquitoes are as thick as the humidity and rains have flooded its habitat. It is similar to *Sabatia dodecandra* of northern Florida but it has upper stem leaves that are much wider than the stem. The common name honors John Bartram (1699–1777) and his renowned naturalist son William Bartram (1739–1823). Ahaya the Cowkeeper, who was the chief of the Alachua Seminole tribe of northern Florida, referred to William as *puc-puggee* (the flower hunter).

LARGEFLOWER ROSEGENTIAN
Sabatia grandiflora (A. Gray) Small
Gentian Family (Gentianaceae)

Description: The uppermost leaves of this annual are thick, wrinkled, and not as wide as the stem, which helps differentiate it from the following species. The lower leaves measure ¾"–1½" long to ¼" wide. The flowers may reach 1¾" wide and vary in color from deep rose to pale pink (rarely white).

Bloom Season: All year

Habitat/Range: Wet flatwoods and marshes of Alabama, Georgia, Florida, and Cuba.

Comments: The name *grandiflora* refers to its large flowers compared to some members of the genus. It is occasional from the Panhandle to the Florida Keys and was first collected in Florida along the Indian River in Brevard County in 1874. The Seminole used this and the following species to treat "sun sickness" and to make a bitter tonic as a substitute for quinine. It was also taken as an aid to indigestion. Other species were used to treat yellow fever and to promote appetite and digestion.

ROSE OF PLYMOUTH
Sabatia stellaris Pursh.
Gentian Family (Gentianaceae)

Description: The prominently veined uppermost leaves of this species are thin, smooth, and equal to or wider than the stem. The lower leaves are ½"–1¼" long and ³⁄₁₆" wide. The 1"–1½" flowers have 5 (rarely 6) lobes that vary from deep rose to pale pink, white, or 2-toned pink and white. A red, jagged line encircles the base of the corolla lobes.

Bloom Season: All year, peaking in springtime

Habitat/Range: Brackish and freshwater wetlands from New England to Louisiana south through Florida, Bahamas, Cuba, and Mexico.

Comments: The name *stellaris* refers to the starlike flowers. This is the most frequently encountered of the 12 members of the genus that occur in Florida. It is also called marsh pink and sea pink within its natural range. The name rose of Plymouth derived from 17th-century Pilgrims of Plymouth, Massachusetts, who wrongly believed the name *Sabatia* referred to the Sabbath.

CAROLINA CRANESBILL
Geranium carolinianum L.
Geranium Family (Geraniaceae)

Description: The finely pubescent, palmate leaves average 1"–2" wide and are deeply dissected with secondary lobes. The flowers are pink to nearly white and measure about ⁵⁄₁₆" wide. The fruits are about ¼" wide and are divided into 5 segments with a narrow ½" long, erect beak.

Bloom Season: January–June

Habitat/Range: Moist, shady trails and disturbed sites throughout much of North America.

Comments: *Geranium* means "a crane," alluding to the long beak on the fruits that was thought by Linnaeus to resemble a crane's bill. The name *carolinianum* refers to the Carolinas. The plant has been used medicinally to treat such ills as dysentery, skin rash, diarrhea, wounds, and cancer. Small bees and hover flies visit the blossoms for nectar. It is a frequent weed in residential areas throughout Florida, especially in shady moist areas. Ground doves and mourning doves feed on the seeds.

FLORIDA BETONY
Stachys floridana Shuttlew. ex Beth.
Mint Family (Lamiaceae)

Description: This square-stemmed herb spreads by rhizomes and tubers, often forming dense roadside colonies. The hairy, somewhat heart-shaped, opposite leaves range from 1"–2" long and ⅜"–¾" wide. The ⅜" flowers are in whorls along an erect spike.

Bloom Season: March–November

Habitat/Range: Flatwoods and roadsides from Virginia to Texas south through mainland Florida.

Comments: *Stachys* means "ear of grain" and alludes to the spiked inflorescence. The name *floridana* relates to Florida, where it was first collected near Tallahassee in 1843. It is also called woundwort for its uses to treat wounds and also rattlesnake weed in reference to the segmented tubers that resemble a rattlesnake's rattle. Another common name is Florida hedgenettle. The tubers are edible raw or cooked and resemble radishes in flavor. It is aggressive in cultivation and can quickly spread out of bounds.

WOOD SAGE

Teucrium canadense L.
Mint Family (Lamiaceae)

Description: This cold-tolerant wildflower produces erect, 1'–3' square stems. The opposite leaves are hairy and range from narrowly lanceolate to elliptic, 2"–4½" long, ⅜"–2" wide, with scalloped margins. Pale pink to lavender, wide-lipped, ⅜"–¾" flowers are held on upright stems. The plant spreads by rhizomes and can form extensive colonies.

Bloom Season: April–November

Habitat/Range: Freshwater wetlands of the eastern United States into Canada.

Comments: *Teucrium* honors Teucer, the mythological king of Troy who is said to have been the son of the Scamander River and the nymph Idaea. The name *canadense* means "of Canada." It is also called American germander. Some species in this genus are used as a catnip substitute and to brew a medicinal tea to treat facial muscle twitching caused by St. Vitus' dance, a motor nerve disorder once thought to be cured only by a pilgrimage to the shrine of Saint Vitus.

STIFFHAIR WAXWEED

Cuphea strigulosa Kunth
Loosestrife Family (Lythraceae)

Description: The slightly hairy red stems of this species are 12"–24" tall and lined with small, opposite, nearly sessile leaves that measure ½"–1" long and half as wide. The 6-petaled, axillary flowers measure ⅜" wide and are subtended by a striped, urnlike calyx.

Bloom Season: All year

Habitat/Range: Disturbed wetlands of Broward and Miami-Dade Counties. Native to the Neotropics.

Comments: *Cuphea* means "hump," alluding to the swollen base of the calyx. The name *strigulosa* refers to the small, straight, appressed (strigulose) hairs. This species is spreading rapidly in Everglades National Park, especially along firebreak roads of Long Pine Key and in the Hole-in-the-Donut region where it was first discovered in 1995 by Everglades National Park research collaborators Rick (1942–) and Jean (1942–) Seavey. German botanist Carl Sigismund Kunth (1788–1850) described it in 1824.

SWAMP ROSEMALLOW
Hibiscus grandiflorus Micx.
Mallow Family (Malvaceae)

Description: Swamp rosemallow is shrubby from 6'–10' tall with softly hairy leaves and long petioles. The leaves are mostly 3-lobed with irregular teeth along the margins and measure 4"–7" long and up to 6" wide. The attractive, 4"–5" flowers appear in the leaf axils and may be white or pink, always with a red center.

Bloom Season: May–September

Habitat/Range: Freshwater wetlands from southeastern Georgia to Louisiana south through mainland Florida.

Comments: *Hibiscus* is an ancient Greek name for "mallow." The name *grandiflorus* refers to the large flowers. Water garden enthusiasts sometimes cultivate this species for its captivating flowers. The stems die back in winter, then resprout in spring. Orioles and hummingbirds sip nectar from the flowers and bees are frequently seen gathering the pollen. Lindenleaf rosemallow *(Hibiscus furcellatus)* is similar but has smaller, rosy pink flowers with a darker center and mostly occurs north of the Everglades region in dry to moist sites. Florida native *Hibiscus* species are related to the well-known *Hibiscus rosa-sinensis,* cultivated worldwide with many named cultivars but now unknown in the wild in its native China.

SALT MARSH MALLOW
Kosteletzkya pentacarpos (L.) Ledeb.
(Also *Kosteletzkya virginica* [L.] Presl.)
Mallow Family (Malvaceae)

Description: This shrubby plant has hairs covering the leaves and the 2'–5' stems. The 1"–3" leaves may be triangular or lobed with irregular teeth along the margins. The flowers are 1¼"–2" wide.

Bloom Season: All year

Habitat/Range: Brackish and freshwater wetlands from New York to Texas south through Florida to the Greater Antilles, Bermuda, and Europe.

Comments: *Kosteletzkya* honors Czechoslovakian botanist Vincenz Franz Kosteletzky (1801–1887). The name *pentacarpos* refers to the 5 carpels that make up the ovule-bearing part of the flower. This species has recently gained attention as a source of biodiesel fuel. The roots can be dried, ground into a paste, and then roasted to make marshmallows. The leaves can be eaten raw, cooked as a pot herb, or used to thicken soups. The cooking water can be whipped to make meringue.

BRETONICA PELUDA
Melochia spicata (L.) Fryxell
Hibiscus Family (Malvaceae)

Description: The Spanish common name means "hairy bretonica" and refers to the densely pubescent, ovate-oblong leaves that range from ¾"–1½" long. The pink to violet, ½" flowers are bell shaped and appear from the upper leaf axils.

Bloom Season: All year

Habitat/Range: Sandhills and flatwoods of Florida, Georgia, and the Neotropics.

Comments: *Melochia* is an Arabic name relating to mallows. The name *spicata* refers to flowers arranged in a spike. This genus was previously included in the cacao family (Sterculiaceae) but recent taxonomic revisions determined that the Sterculiaceae is obsolete as a valid classification. This species is locally common in sandy habitats of the northern Big Cypress and Corkscrew Swamp regions but is absent from Everglades National Park. It is closely allied to cacao *(Theobroma cacao)*, used to make cocoa powder and chocolate.

CAESAR WEED
Urena lobata L.
Mallow Family (Malvaceae)

Description: This semi-woody species reaches 3'–9' tall with palmate, 7-veined, alternate leaves averaging 1½"–4" long and 1"–4" wide. Leaf shape varies from broadly ovate to suborbicular with shallow lobes and serrate margins, the upper surface rough to the touch. The axillary flowers average ½" wide. The ¼" fruits cling to hair and clothing.

Bloom Season: All year

Habitat/Range: A cosmopolitan weed of swamps, upland forests, pinelands, and disturbed sites. Native to eastern India.

Comments: *Urena* is a name from the Malabar region of India. The name *lobata* refers to the lobed leaves. This plant has been used as a substitute for jute, a glossy fiber usually derived from members of the genus *Corchorus* and used chiefly for burlap and twine. It invades natural habitats in Florida and is listed by the Florida Exotic Pest Plant Council. If the fruits get entangled in hair they must be cut out with scissors.

PALE MEADOWBEAUTY
Rhexia mariana L.
Melastome Family (Melastomataceae)

Description: This species may reach 30" tall and has narrow, linear, toothed leaves that range from ½"–3" long and ⅛"–¼" wide. The stems are unequally 4-sided. The petals measure ¾"–1" long and about ½" wide. The petals fall off easily when touched.

Bloom Season: February–November

Habitat/Range: Wet flatwoods from New York to Texas and Missouri south in Florida to the Big Cypress and Corkscrew Swamp regions.

Comments: *Rhexia* is a name used by Roman scholar Pliny (AD 23–79) for a plant useful in treating ruptures. The name *mariana* refers to the state of Maryland where this species was first collected in 1700 and described in 1753 by Carolus Linnaeus (1707–1778). It is also called Maryland meadowbeauty. It closely resembles West Indian meadowbeauty *(Rhexia cubensis)* that shares its habitat in the northwestern Everglades region. No members of this genus occur within Everglades National Park.

SOUTHERN BEEBLOSSOM
Gaura angustifolia Michx.
Evening Primrose Family (Onagraceae)

Description: Southern beeblossom is a tall, wispy plant with leaves that are 1½"–5" long, narrowly oblong or lanceolate, with toothed margins. Tubular flowers, each about 1" wide, open white at sunset and then fade to pink the next day. Each flower has 4 petals, 4 sepals, and 8 stamens.

Bloom Season: February–November

Habitat/Range: Dry pinelands, coastal dunes, and roadsides of the southeastern United States and the Bahamas.

Comments: *Gaura* is from the Greek *gauros*, meaning "proud" or "superb," which relates to the attractive flowers of this genus. The name *angustifolia* refers to the narrow leaves. It has been used in herbal folk medicine in the southeastern United States to treat pain and inflammation. Bees visit the flowers and the leaves are larval food for the beautiful clouded crimson moth and a hummingbird-like hawkmoth called the proud sphinx or gaura sphinx.

FLOR DE PASMO
Bletia patula Hook.
Orchid Family (Orchidaceae)

Description: Pleated, narrowly elliptic leaves measuring 10"–24" long and ½"–1½" wide arise from ovoid psuedobulbs. The flowers are pink to rosy purple (rarely white) and are about 1½" long and wide.

Bloom Season: March–June

Habitat/Range: Pinelands and marl soils of Florida (Miami-Dade County) through the Neotropics.

Comments: *Bletia* honors Luis Blet, an 18th-century apothecary who joined expeditions to the New World to collect medicinal plants. The name *patula* relates to the spreading sepals and petals. Two small populations of albino forms of this species were collected in a Miami-Dade County pineland in 1947 and it was not seen again in Florida until a small patch of plants was discovered in Everglades National Park shortly after Hurricane Wilma in 2005. The common name is Spanish for "flower of astonishment" or "amazing flower." It is a critically imperiled endangered species in Florida.

PINE-PINK
Bletia purpurea (Lam.) DC.
Orchid Family (Orchidaceae)

Description: The palmlike leaves of this orchid are attached to hard, ovoid pseudobulbs. The leaves are linear-lanceolate, pleated longitudinally, and range from 6"–18" long and 1"–2" wide. The flower spike (to 5') arises from the base of the pseudobulb and is branched near the top. Flowers are ½"–¾" wide and are typically bright rose pink.

Bloom Season: January–June

Habitat/Range: Rocky soils of pinelands or on stumps and floating logs in swamps of southern Florida and the Neotropics.

Comments: The name *purpurea* means "purple" but the flowers are more pink than purple. Some Florida populations of this orchid become self-pollinated in bud (cleistogamous) and never fully open. It is locally common in rocky, marl soils throughout the Everglades region, especially on Long Pine Key in Everglades National Park and through the western Big Cypress Swamp to Corkscrew Swamp and the CREW Marsh.

BEARDED GRASSPINK
Calopogon barbatus (Walter) Ames
Orchid Family (Orchidaceae)

Description: The 3"–10" linear leaves are appressed to the inflorescence with up to 12 flowers crowded at the top of the stem. The bright magenta to pale pink (rarely white) ¾" flowers typically open simultaneously to create an attractive display. The odorless flowers are non-resupinate (the lip is uppermost).

Bloom Season: February–May

Habitat/Range: Wet flatwoods and bogs from North Carolina to Louisiana south in Florida to Palm Beach and Collier Counties.

Comments: *Calopogon* means "beautiful beard," alluding to the bristles on the lip. The name *barbatus* means "bearded." Members of this genus offer no pollinator reward but bees mistake the bristles on the lip for a tuft of stamens and the weight of the bee causes the lip to bend downward, pressing the hapless insect onto the sticky pollinia. The attached pollinia will then be transferred to the next flower the bee visits.

MANYFLOWERED GRASSPINK
Calopogon multiflorus Lindl.
Orchid Family (Orchidaceae)

Description: Characterisitics of this species are its strong floral perfume and purple flower stem (rachis) that turns green after flowering. The narrowly linear leaves range to 6" long but may double in length at flowering. The attractive flowers are about ¾" and may number up to 15, mostly open at the same time.

Bloom Season: Principally April–May

Habitat/Range: Wet flatwoods and damp meadows from North and South Carolina across southern Georgia to eastern Louisiana south through most of mainland Florida.

Comments: The name *multiflorus* refers to the many flowers that typically open at the same time. In the Everglades region this orchid is found in the Bear Island Unit of the Big Cypress National Preserve where it was not known to occur until the mid-1990s. It is highly dependent on fire to trigger flowering and may skip flowering for years until its habitat burns again.

PALE GRASSPINK
Calopogon pallidus Chapm.
Orchid Family (Orchidaceae)

Description: There are 1–2 narrowly linear ribbed leaves that measure 4"–8" long and up to ³⁄₁₆" wide that are about half as tall as the flowering stem. The 2 lateral sepals are distinctively upturned and often wavy. The faintly fragrant, widely spaced, pale pink (rarely magenta or white) flowers measure ¾"–⅝" wide and open sequentially up the stem over a long period.

Bloom Season: March–June (rarely later)

Habitat/Range: Bogs, wet flatwoods, and meadows from Virginia to eastern Louisiana south in Florida to Broward and Collier Counties.

Comments: The name *pallidus* relates to the typically pallid (pale) flowers. This species often grows in association with other members of the genus but the upturned lateral sepals make the pale grasspink easy to identify. Natural hybrids of this and other species are known from Florida. There are only 5 species in this genus and 4 of them occur in Florida.

SIMPSON'S GRASSPINK

Calopogon tuberosus (L.) BSP var. *simpsonii*
Magrath
Orchid Family (Orchidaceae)

Description: From 1–5 erect, linear, lanceolate leaves arise from an underground corm with leaves ranging from 12"–16" long and ⅜"–½" wide. The flowers consist of 3 sepals and 3 petals, with the upper petal modified into a bristled lip, typical of the genus. The flowers average 1¼" wide and vary in color from magenta to pure white.

Bloom Season: March–July

Habitat/Range: Sunny marshes and wet flatwoods of southern Florida, Cuba, and the Bahamas.

Comments: The name *tuberosus* refers to the underground tuberous corms. The name *simpsonii* honors revered naturalist Charles Torrey Simpson (1846–1932) who settled in Miami in 1902. This is the only *Calopogon* in Everglades National Park and is by far the most common species in the Everglades region. It is more robust than the typical variety that ranges across the eastern United States to southeastern Canada.

DELICATE VIOLET ORCHID

Ionopsis utricularioides (Sw.) Lindl.
Orchid Family (Orchidaceae)

Description: This epiphytic species has 1–5 thick, prominently ribbed leaves that average 2"–4" long and ⅜"–⅝" wide. The flowers are produced in an airy panicle and individual flowers are pink to nearly white with pinkish purple venation. Small sepals and petals are above the much larger, broadly spreading 2-lobed lip. The lip is typically about ⅜" wide.

Bloom Season: December–June

Habitat/Range: Hardwood swamps of southern mainland Florida, West Indies, and the Neotropics.

Comments: *Ionopsis* means the flowers resemble those of a violet (Violaceae). The name *utricularioides* refers to the similarity of the flowers to those of *Utricularia*, the bladderworts. This critically imperiled state-listed endangered species tends to grow on small branches and twigs of the host tree and is sometimes found hanging in midair connected by only a few thin roots.

TINY ORCHID
Lepanthopsis melanantha (Rchb.f.) Ames
Orchid Family (Orchidaceae)

Description: This minuscule orchid forms small clusters that stand only 1½"–2¾" tall with thin stems topped by a single leaf blade that measures up to 1⅛" long and ½" wide. The purplish pink flowers are in a single rank and barely measure ⅛" long.

Bloom Season: Sporadically all year

Habitat/Range: Epiphytic in the Fakahatchee Swamp (Collier County) to the Greater Antilles.

Comments: *Lepanthopsis* refers to similarities to the orchid genus *Lepenthes*. The name *melanantha* translates to "black flower" and alludes to the flowers turning black when dried. This critically imperiled orchid is so rare in Florida that very few people have ever seen it in the wild. It inhabits remote, nearly inaccessible sloughs deep in the Fakahatchee Swamp, typically growing just above the swamp water on mossy tree trunks. Finding it is truly a memory not soon forgotten.

MONK ORCHID
Oeceoclades maculata (Lindl.) Lindl.
(Also *Eulophidium maculatum* [Lindl.] Pfitzer)
Orchid Family (Orchidaceae)

Description: This terrestrial orchid has leathery, lanceolate leaves attached to a pseudobulb. The mottled 2-tone green leaves range from 4"–8" long and ¾"–2" wide. The erect flower spike is topped by 6–12 flowers, each measuring about ½" wide.

Bloom Season: September–October

Habitat/Range: Shady leaf litter of forests, groves, and urban areas of central and southern Florida. Native to Africa.

Comments: *Oeceoclades* means "private branch," in reference to its separation from the genus *Angraecum*. The name *maculata* relates to the mottled leaves. It was first discovered in Florida in Matheson Hammock (Miami-Dade County) in 1974. It has since spread rapidly across the lower half of the state where it colonizes forests and shady mulched areas in urban landscapes. It is self-pollinated by rain (rain-assisted autogamy).

COOT BAY DANCING LADY ORCHID

Trichocentrum carthagenense (Jacq.) M. W. Chase
& N. H. Williams
Orchid Family (Orchidaceae)

Description: The rigid, keeled leaves average about 12"–15" long and 3"–4" wide with purple flecks. The flowers are on branched, arching spikes, each measuring about ½" wide.

Bloom Season: April–May

Habitat/Range: Mangrove forests of southwestern Florida (Monroe County) and the Neotropics.

Comments: *Trichocentrum* relates to the nectarless spur of the flowers. The name *carthagenense* refers to Cartagena, Colombia, where it was first collected in 1760. Botanist John Kunkel Small (1869–1938) collected this orchid once in Florida near Coot Bay (now Everglades National Park) in April 1916 and the specimen is in the New York Botanical Garden herbarium. It doubtfully still occurs in Florida but the vast mangrove country of the Everglades is mostly unexplored. Vegetatively it resembles the mule-ear orchid *(Trichocentrum undulatum)* that occurs in the same region.

FLAXLEAF FALSE FOXGLOVE

Agalinis linifolia (Nutt.) Britton
Broomrape Family (Orobanchaceae)

Description: The sparsely branched stems of this species reach 3' tall with very narrow, linear leaves from ¾"–2" long. The ⅝"–1" hairy flowers are somewhat bell shaped and the throat is adorned with dark pink spots.

Bloom Season: June–November

Habitat/Range: Freshwater wetlands from Delaware to Louisiana south through mainland Florida.

Comments: The genus *Agalinis* and the species name *linifolia* both refer to the resemblance of the leaves to flax in the genus *Linum* (Linaceae). Some species can derive sustenance from other plants by becoming parasitic. Members of this genus are larval host plants of the common buckeye butterfly in Florida. This is a common wetland species in the Everglades region and the only species in the United States that is perennial. Three other species range south into the Everglades region and have very similar flowers.

GULF HAIRAWN MUHLY GRASS

Muhlenbergia capillaris (Lam.) Trin. var. *filipes*
(M. A. Curtis) Chapm. ex Beal
Grass Family (Poaceae)

Description: This common Everglades grass has narrow, rolled leaf blades to 3' long and ¹⁄₁₆" wide. The airy panicles are finely branched with mauve or pinkish flowers. The panicles range from 6"–24" tall and 4"–10" wide.

Bloom Season: September–November

Habitat/Range: Prairies, flatwoods, and dunes from Massachusetts to Texas south through Florida, the West Indies, and Mexico.

Comments: *Muhlenbergia* honors Gotthilf Henry Ernest Muhlenberg (1753–1815), a Pennsylvanian Lutheran minister who later studied botany. The name *capillaris* means "hairlike" and the name *filipes* means "with threadlike stalks." It is sometimes used in mass plantings along roadsides and in urban landscapes and is eyecatching when in flower, especially in autumn when it transforms the vast Everglades prairies into a sea of pink.

DRUMHEADS

Polygala cruciata L.
Milkwort Family (Polygalaceae)

Description: Drumheads has whorled, linear, or linear-elliptic leaves with the lower leaves smaller than those above. The leaves average ³⁄₈"–1½" long. The raceme is dense, mostly oblong in outline, with a compact arrangement of flowers that open progressively from the bottom upward. Two of the sepals are formed into petal-like wings and are colored like the petals. These are white when fresh but become pinkish violet.

Bloom Season: March–September

Habitat/Range: Flatwoods and wet meadows from Maine to Minnesota and Texas, south in Florida to Broward and Collier Counties.

Comments: *Polygala* means "much milk," in the fanciful belief that milkworts could increase milk flow in cattle. The word *gala*, or "milk," also makes up the word "galaxy," as in the Milky Way. The name *cruciata* means "forming a cross," alluding to the flower shape. It is locally common in the Corkscrew Swamp region.

PROCESSION FLOWER
Polygala incarnata L.
Milkwort Family (Polygalaceae)

Description: The leaves of this species are linear, often with their bases appressed to the stem, and measure ¼"–½" long. The tubular flowers are about ³⁄₁₆" long. The flowers are twice as long as the wings and have 3 petals that unite into a tube, flaring into 6 lobes. White-flowered plants are occasional throughout its range.

Bloom Season: All year

Habitat/Range: Sandy soil in open, sunny habitats from New York to Ontario and Wisconsin south to Florida and Mexico.

Comments: The name *incarnata* means "flesh colored," in reference to the pink flower color. The word "wort" in milkwort is an old Anglo-Saxon name that simply means "plant." Milkworts once received unmerited fame as a remedy for snakebite but many species are still used medicinally for respiratory ailments. The seeds are dispersed by ants, which harvest them to consume the nutritious arils.

SHOWY MILKWORT
Polygala violacea Aubl.
(Also *Polygala grandiflora* Walter)
Milkwort Family (Polygalaceae)

Description: The stems of this species are 8"–16" tall with narrow, lanceolate, alternate leaves that exude milky sap when broken. The leaves average ½"–1½" long and ¼"–³⁄₈" wide. Flowers are on terminal spikes and the small corolla is nestled between 2 winglike, pinkish violet (rarely white) sepals that measure ³⁄₁₆"–⁵⁄₁₆" long. The upper petals are yellow tipped.

Bloom Season: All year

Habitat/Range: Pinelands and prairies of the southeastern United States to the Bahamas.

Comments: The name *violacea* refers to the pinkish violet sepals. The flowers of this common species are orchidlike in appearance. Although small, the flowers are much larger than other members of the genus, as noted by the botanical synonym *Polygala grandiflora*. It can easily be overlooked due to its diminutive stature. Small native bees serve as effective pollinators.

KISS-ME-QUICK
Portulaca pilosa L.
Purslane Family (Portulacaceae)

Description: The prostrate, succulent stems have long, shaggy, white hairs in the leaf axils. The leaves are sessile (or nearly so) with narrow, succulent blades to about ½" long and less than ⅛" wide. Flowers are clustered at the branch tips and are surrounded by hairs. Each flower is about ⅜" wide.

Bloom Season: All year

Habitat/Range: Sandy habitats from Florida and Georgia to Texas and the Neotropics.

Comments: *Portulaca* is an ancient Latin name first applied to field purslane *(Portulaca oleracea)*. The name *pilosa* means "with long soft hairs." The leaves are used as an herbal tea and are high in omega-3 fatty acids. Kiss-me-quick is a name given to various things that are attractive, including kiss-me-quick bonnets worn by fashionable women in the 1800s with ribbons that were tied under the chin on one side with "kissing strings" and a short lock of hair curled in front of each ear.

COKER'S GOLDEN CREEPER
Ernodea cokeri Britton ex Coker
Madder Family (Rubiaceae)

Description: The finely hairy stems have narrowly linear, sessile, clustered leaves that measure ½"–1½" long and ³⁄₁₆" wide or less. Each leaf has a single longitudinal nerve. Tubular, 4-lobed flowers open white but then turn pink or reddish. The oval, ¼" fruits are orangish yellow.

Bloom Season: All year

Habitat/Range: Pine rocklands of southern Florida (southern Miami-Dade County and Big Pine Key in Monroe County) and the Bahamas.

Comments: *Ernodea* is Greek for "offshoot," alluding to the many leafy branches produced along the stem. The name *cokeri* honors North Carolina botanist William Chambers Coker (1872–1953). This species was thought to be endemic to the Bahamas until 1996 when specimens collected in Florida as early as 1904 were correctly identified. It is a critically imperiled state-listed endangered species with only a few Florida populations.

BEACH CREEPER
Ernodea littoralis Sw.
Madder Family (Rubiaceae)

Description: The glossy, opposite leaves of this mounding plant are lanceolate and range from ¾"–1½" long and ¼"–½" wide with 3–5 longitudinal nerves. The tubular, pink or white (rarely yellow) flowers have 4 strongly curled lobes and measure ½"–⅝" long. The oval, ¼" fruits are golden yellow.

Bloom Season: Sporadically all year

Habitat/Range: Dunes of central and southern Florida to the Neotropics.

Comments: The name *littoralis* refers to its coastal habitat, the littoral zone. It is also called golden creeper and coughbush. Landscapers use this species as a drought- and salt-tolerant ground cover and in border plantings where it will thrive in the most inhospitable dry, sandy soils. It forms mounds of leafy stems and is very ornamental when in flower or fruit. The leaves of this and the previous species can be confused with members of the related genus *Spermacoce* that share their habitat.

LARGEFLOWER MEXICAN CLOVER
Richardia grandiflora (Cham. & Schltdl.) Schult. & Schult. f.
Madder Family (Rubiaceae)

Description: The prostrate hairy stems have opposite, hairy, lanceolate leaves from ⅜"–¾" long. The trumpet-shaped flowers are 6-lobed, light pink with a white throat, and measure about ⅜" wide. The flowers close at night and are produced in terminal and axillary clusters.

Bloom Season: All year

Habitat/Range: Pinelands, lawns, and disturbed sites of central and southern Florida. Native to South America.

Comments: Linnaeus named the genus *Richardia* using the first name of British physician and botanist Richard Richardson (1663–1741). The name *grandiflora* means "large flowers," referring to the size of the flowers of this species compared to others in the genus. The flowers of this attractive lawn and roadside weed attract bees and an array of butterflies. There are 4 members of this genus in Florida but none are native to the state.

HERB-OF-GRACE
Bacopa monnieri (L.) Pennell
Figwort Family (Scrophulariaceae)

Description: The opposite, spatulate leaves of this succulent, mat-forming species range from ³⁄₁₆"–½" long. The 5-lobed, pale pink flowers are produced from the leaf axils and are about ¼" wide.

Bloom Season: All year

Habitat/Range: Freshwater and brackish wetlands through the southeastern United States and tropical regions worldwide.

Comments: *Bacopa* is an aboriginal name among indigenous people of French Guiana. The name *monnieri* honors Louis Guillaume le Monnier (1717–1799), a French scientist who studied electricity but received such ridicule he became a botanist. Although this is a larval host plant of the white peacock butterfly, gardeners seldom cultivate it. It is sold in capsule form and promoted as a nutritional supplement to promote brain health, memory, and emotional comfort. It is called *brahmi* in a form of alternative medicine in India.

BEACH VERBENA
Glandularia maritima Small
(Also *Verbena maritima* [Small] Small)
Verbena Family (Verbenaceae)

Description: The opposite leaves of beach verbena may be variously lobed, toothed, or deeply incised, and average about 1½" long and 1" wide. The stems spread near the ground with ascending tips. Hairy, pink or rosy purple, 5-lobed flowers are clustered on slender, terminal spikes and measure ³⁄₈"–½" wide. Each lobe is indented at the tip.

Bloom Season: All year

Habitat/Range: Endemic to dunes and sandy pinelands of central and southern mainland Florida, mostly along the east coast, but also inland.

Comments: *Glandularia* relates to the glandular appearance around the stigmas. The name *maritima* is a reference to "maritime," or "growing by the sea." This is a state-listed endangered species due to its limited habitat and range. It is cultivated by butterfly gardeners in Florida and performs well in dry sunny areas. It is also called coastal mock vervain.

RED AND ORANGE FLOWERS

Asclepias tuberosa

This section includes flowers ranging from pale orange to deep red and burgundy. Many species of flowers will turn orange, red, or burgundy as they age. If these flowers were once white or yellow when they were young, you may need to check those sections if the flower you are looking for is not found here.

SIXANGLE FOLDWING

Dicliptera sexangularis (L.) Juss.
(Also *Dicliptera assurgens* [L.] Juss. var. *vahliana*
[Nees] M. Gómez)
Acanthus Family (Acanthaceae)

Description: The 6-angled stems of this bushy herb can reach 4' tall. The opposite leaves are ovate and range from 1½"–2" long and ¾"–1¼" wide but may be much larger. Red, hairy, tubular flowers are curved, flattened vertically, and range from ¾"–1" long.

Bloom Season: All year

Habitat/Range: Coastal strand and along the edges of salt marshes, hammocks, and mangroves from central Florida southward to the Neotropics.

Comments: *Dicliptera* is Greek for "folding" and "wing," referring to the 2 winglike divisions of the seed capsule. The name *sexangularis* means "six angled," alluding to the stems. Butterflies and hummingbirds visit the flowers but this species is extraordinarily weedy in cultivation, spreading quickly from seed with abandon. It is the larval host plant of the Cuban crescent butterfly.

SCARLET MILKWEED

Asclepias curassavica L.
Dogbane Family (Apocynaceae)

Description: Scarlet milkweed is a perennial with opposite, lanceolate leaves that exude milky sap when broken. The leaves range from 2"–6" long and ¾"–1½" wide. The ⅜" flowers are in flat-topped clusters and are usually 2-toned orange and yellow but some plants have solid yellow flowers.

Bloom Season: All year

Habitat/Range: Roadsides, canal banks, and other disturbed sites of central and southern Florida. Native to the Neotropics.

Comments: *Asclepias* was named for Aesculapius, the legendary Greek god of medicine. The name *curassavica* refers to Curaçao, an island country in the Lesser Antilles where the lectotype was collected in 1954. It is widely cultivated in Florida by butterfly enthusiasts as a nectar source and larval host plant for monarch, queen, and soldier butterflies but it is also a larval host plant of the milkweed tussock moth in parts of Florida.

PRAIRIE MILKWEED
Asclepias lanceolata Walter
Dogbane Family (Apocynaceae)

Description: The linear or narrowly lanceolate leaves of this attractive native wetland species are 4"–8" long and ⅛"–½" wide. Flowers are in terminal clusters and measure about ¼" wide. The corolla lobes are reflexed and arch downward beneath the 5-lobed calyx. The flowers are generally 2-toned red and reddish orange. Like other members of the genus the seeds are wind dispersed.

Bloom Season: All year

Habitat/Range: Wet prairies from New Jersey to Texas through mainland Florida.

Comments: The name *lanceolata* refers to the lance-shaped leaves. The flowers are showy and typically stand well above competing vegetation in wet prairies throughout the Everglades region. Although the leaves are larval food for monarch and queen butterflies it requires permanently wet soil to be successfully cultivated. Other common names are purple silkweed and fewflowered milkweed.

BUTTERFLY MILKWEED
Asclepias tuberosa L.
Dogbane Family (Apocynaceae)

Description: The coarsely hairy leaves of this semi-woody species range from 2"–4" long and ½"–1" wide. The leaves do not exude milky sap when broken. Flat-topped flower clusters terminate each stem. Individual flowers measure ¼"–⅜" and are uniformly light orange to dark reddish orange.

Bloom Season: All year

Habitat/Range: Dry, sandy soils throughout much of the United States.

Comments: The name *tuberosa* refers to the tuberous roots. This well-known milkweed is cultivated for its attractive blossoms, drought tolerance, and butterfly-attracting attributes. Native Americans brewed a tea from the leaves to induce vomiting during rituals but the plant is poisonous if eaten in quantity. A tea from the root has been used medicinally as an expectorant to treat whooping cough and pneumonia. Its use to treat pleurisy gave rise to the name pleurisy root in parts of its native range.

TASSELFLOWER
Emilia fosbergii Nicolson
Aster Family (Asteraceae)

Description: This weedy species has clasping leaves with the blade reduced to a winged petiole bearing entire, toothed, or slightly lobed margins. The stems are hairy. Cylindric, somewhat urn-shaped involucres subtend the red (rarely pink or violet) shaving-brush-like flower heads.

Bloom Season: All year

Habitat/Range: Pinelands and disturbed sites through most of Florida. Native to the Old World.

Comments: *Emilia* is believed to be a personal name (Emilie) given without comment by Alexandre Henri Gabriel de Cassini (1781–1832), who named the genus. The name *fosbergii* honors Smithsonian Institution botanist Francis Raymond Fosberg (1908–1993). This is a common weed of roadsides and other disturbed areas. It is often tolerated as a weed in gardens because the flowers attract small butterflies. Lilac tasselflower *(Emilia sonchifolia)* is similar but with smaller heads of lilac flowers.

STRAPLEAVED GUZMANIA
Guzmania monostachia (L.) Rusby ex Mez
Pineapple Family (Bromeliaceae)

Description: This epiphyte forms a rosette of strap-shaped leaves that measure 8"–12" long and ⅝"–1" wide. The lower bracts on the 6"–8" flower spike are green with brown stripes and the upper bracts are pink to scarlet. Small, white, tubular flowers emerge from behind the bracts.

Bloom Season: January–August

Habitat/Range: Hardwood forests and swamps of southern Florida and the Neotropics.

Comments: *Guzmania* honors Spanish naturalist Anastasio Guzmán who died in 1807 during an expedition in Ecuador searching for the lost gold of the Incas near Cordillera de los Llanganates. The name *monostachia* means "one spike," referring to the unbranched flower spike. This state-listed endangered species is locally common in the deep sloughs of the Fakahatchee Swamp but is threatened by an introduced Mexican weevil *(Metamasius callizona)* that kills the plants.

NORTHERN NEEDLELEAF

Tillandsia balbisiana Schult. & Schult. f.
Pineapple Family (Bromeliaceae)

Description: The gray-green leaves of this 4"–8" epiphyte are wide at the base but constrict near the top and twist downward. A narrow spike emerges from the center of the plant and small, tubular, purple flowers emerge from behind prominent red bracts.

Bloom Season: All year

Habitat/Range: Hardwood hammocks and wooded swamps from central and southern Florida to the Neotropics.

Comments: *Tillandsia* honors Swedish botanist Elias Tillands (1640–1693) who cataloged plants in Finland. The name *balbisiana* honors Italian botanist Giovanni-Batista Balbis (1765–1831). Like all bromeliads, this threatened species dies after flowering but in the process produces offsets from the base of the parent plant as well as wind-dispersed seeds that cling to tree bark. It is the principal host plant of the native Florida bromeliad weevil *(Metamasius mosieri).*

CARDINAL AIRPLANT

Tillandsia fasciculata Sw.
Pineapple Family (Bromeliaceae)

Description: This bromeliad forms a rosette of stiff, gray-green leaves from 8"–12" long, tapering to a pointed tip. The showy floral bracts vary in color but the lower bracts are usually red with greenish-yellow upper bracts. Some plants have uniformly red, green, or pink bracts. Tubular, purple (rarely white) flowers emerge from behind the bracts.

Bloom Season: All year

Habitat/Range: Hardwood forests and wooded swamps from central Florida south to the Neotropics.

Comments: The name *fasciculata* means "a bundle," referring to the rosette of leaves. Hummingbirds visit the flowers. Another common name is wild pine, referring to the related pineapple. Although still very common in parts of Florida, this species is endangered due to the larvae of an introduced Mexican weevil *(Metamasius callizona)* that is killing this and other native bromeliads throughout South Florida.

SCARLET CREEPER
Ipomoea hederifolia L.
Morning-Glory Family (Convolvulaceae)

Description: The leaf blades of this weedy, twining vine measure ¾"–4" long and are usually 3-lobed but may be entire. The trumpet-shaped flowers average 1"–1¾" long and ½"–⅝" wide with a slightly curved tube.

Bloom Season: June–December

Habitat/Range: Disturbed sites, fencerows, and hammock margins throughout most of Florida. Pantropical.

Comments: *Ipomoea* is Greek for "wormlike," alluding to the twining growth habit. The name *hederifolia* refers to the resemblance of the leaves to those of *Hedera helix,* a species of Ivy (Araliaceae). Bees, butterflies (especially skippers), and hummingbirds visit the flowers by day and moths seek nectar from them at night. This species has become globally widespread through cultivation. It is a common weedy vine in parts of Florida and is frequently seen growing on fences surrounding agricultural lands and natural areas.

MAN-IN-THE-GROUND
Ipomoea microdactyla Griseb.
Morning-Glory Family (Convolvulaceae)

Description: The ovate or lanceolate leaves measure 2"–4" long and may be entire or palmately lobed. The trumpet-shaped flowers measure about 1½" long and 1"–1½" wide and range in color from rosy pink to carmine.

Bloom Season: April–December

Habitat/Range: Pine rocklands of Florida (southern Miami-Dade County) to the Bahamas and Cuba.

Comments: The name *microdactyla* means "small fingers," alluding to the fingerlike projections on the tuberous root. This is a spectacular flowering vine, especially after fire when it twines over burnt stems of other plants and shows off its eyecatching blossoms. The common name refers to the large root tuber that is similar to the related sweet potato *(Ipomoea batatas).* Native-plant enthusiasts in southern Florida sometimes cultivate this state-listed endangered species. Skipper butterflies crawl down the floral tube for nectar.

PAINTED LEAF
Poinsettia cyathophora (Murray) Barl.
Spurge Family (Euphorbiaceae)

Description: This weedy species reaches 8"–24" tall with toothed leaves that range from entire to lobed and from very narrowly linear to broadly ovate. The uppermost floral bracts are typically bright red at the base. There is only 1 oval-shaped cyathial (floral) gland. All parts exude milky sap when broken.

Bloom Season: All year

Habitat/Range: Dunes, pinelands, and disturbed sites of the southern United States and the Neotropics.

Comments: *Poinsettia* honors Joel R. Poinsette (1775–1851) who introduced the cultivated Christmas poinsettia to the United States in 1833. The name *cyathophora* refers to the cyathia (false flowers). Narrow-leaved forms of this plant can easily be mistaken for the Florida endemic pineland poinsettia *(Poinsettia pinetorum)* but it produces 3–4 cyathial glands. This and other members of the genus are larval host plants of the Ello sphinx moth.

ALYCE CLOVER
Alysicarpus vaginalis (L.) DC
Pea Family (Fabaceae)

Description: The leafy stems of this low-growing annual (or short-lived perennial) are trailing or sometimes ascending. The leaflets are extremely variable in shape but are typically narrowly elliptic and measure 1"–2" long and ⅜"–½" wide. Flowers are in terminal clusters and each flower measures about ³⁄₁₆" wide.

Bloom Season: All year

Habitat/Range: Disturbed sites of southern Florida. Native to the Old World.

Comments: *Alysicarpus* is Greek for "chain fruit," alluding to the shape of the legume. The name *vaginalis* means "sheathed." It is also called buffalo clover and white moneywort. It was introduced into the United States for pasture improvement and erosion control. Cattle grazing on fields of alyce clover gain more weight than when feeding on Bermuda grass *(Cynodon dactylon)*. It is common along firebreak roads in Everglades National Park and elsewhere in the Everglades region.

FLORIDA COASTAL INDIGO
Indigofera miniata Ortega var. *florida* Isley
Pea Family (Fabaceae)

Description: The appressed hairs give the stem and leaves of this scrambling species a grayish appearance. The ¾"–1¼" leaves are compound with 5–9 narrow leaflets. Red or salmon-pink flowers appear on axillary stems and each flower measures about ⅜" long. The legume is straight.

Bloom Season: All year

Habitat/Range: Endemic to sandy pinelands and hammock margins from north-central Florida to the Florida Keys.

Comments: *Indigofera* is Latin meaning "to bear indigo," in reference to the dye extracted from some species. The name *miniata* alludes to the red flower color. The name *florida* means "profusely flowering." Several members of this genus were historically used to produce indigo dye but it is now mostly produced synthetically. Botanist Duane Isely (1918–2000), Professor Emeritus at Iowa State University, first described this endemic variety in 1981.

TRAILING INDIGO
Indigofera spicata Forssk.
Pea Family (Fabaceae)

Description: The leaves of this trailing species are divided into 3–5 ovate leaflets ranging from ⅜"–⅝" long and ³⁄₁₆"–½" wide. Coral-colored (rarely white) flowers are in erect, compact clusters. Individual flowers measure about ⅛" wide.

Bloom Season: All year

Habitat/Range: Pinelands, lawns, and disturbed sites through much of Florida. Native to the Old World.

Comments: The name *spicata* refers to the spike of flowers. This species can be fatal to horses if it amounts to 50 percent of the ingested feed. Horse deaths attributed to trailing indigo have occurred in South Florida as a result of overgrazing. Even dog food made from animals that have grazed on this plant can cause serious liver damage. It is a pernicious lawn, pasture, and roadside weed in South Florida and is extremely difficult to control. Perhaps its only attribute is as a larval host plant of the ceraunus blue butterfly.

FLORIDA HOARYPEA
Tephrosia florida (F. Dietr.) C. E. Wood
Pea Family (Fabaceae)

Description: This is a trailing species with loosely pubescent, opposite leaves that are divided into 7–13 linear-oblong to narrowly elliptic leaflets. Flowers can be red, pink, purple, or white and measure about ⅜" long.

Bloom Season: April–October

Habitat/Range: Pinelands, sandhills, and other dry, open habitats of the southeastern United States.

Comments: *Tephrosia* means "hoary" or "ash-colored" and relates to the grayish pubescence on the leaves of some species. The name *florida* means "profusely flowering." There are 8 species in this genus in Florida with 3 species, 1 variety, and 1 naturally occurring hybrid being endemic to the state. Some species have been used medicinally as a vermifuge to expel intestinal worms. The related goat's rue *(Tephrosia virginica)* contains rotenone and has been used as a natural poison by Native Americans to harvest small fish.

TROPICAL SAGE
Salvia coccinea Buc'hoz ex Etl.
Mint Family (Lamiaceae)

Description: The stems reach 3'–5' tall with scalloped, hairy, very fragrant leaves that average ½"–2" long and ⅜"–1" wide. Flowers vary from ½"–1" and are typically bright red.

Bloom Season: All year

Habitat/Range: Forest margins, canopy gaps, and disturbed sites of the southeastern United States and the Neotropics.

Comments: *Salvia* is Latin for "safe" or "well," in reference to the medicinal values bestowed upon some species. The name *coccinea* means "red." The flowers of this well-known cultivated species are irresistible to hummingbirds and an array of butterflies, plus the seeds are a favorite food of painted buntings. It is also called Texas sage, blood sage, and hummingbird sage. It spreads readily in cultivation and some cultivars may have pink, salmon, white, or bi-colored flowers. It is widespread but infrequently encountered in the wild in Florida.

PINE LILY
Lilium catesbaei Walter
Lily Family (Liliaceae)

Description: In flower, pine lily reaches 20"–30" tall with lanceolate leaves from 2"–3" long and ⅜" wide, becoming smaller up the stem. Typically, a single flower terminates the stem. The flowers have 3 spreading petals and 3 similar-looking sepals ranging from 3"–4" long.

Bloom Season: June–January

Habitat/Range: Moist flatwoods and savannas from North Carolina to Louisiana south in Florida to Collier County.

Comments: *Lilium* is Latin for "lily." The name *catesbaei* honors English author and naturalist Mark Catesby (1682–1749) who collected plants in Virginia and the Carolinas. Catesby is known for publishing the first account of the flora and fauna of North America, entitled *Natural History of Carolina, Florida and the Bahama Islands*. The lily family is well known in cultivation and herbalists have used the blossoms and bulbs medicinally, especially for improving the memory and to sooth coughs and irritated eyes. It is also called Catesby's lily and is a state-listed threatened species. Underground bulbs may lie dormant for years but then flower within weeks after fire. It is one of the most eyecatching flowers in the Everglades region but is absent from Everglades National Park.

SCARLET ROSEMALLOW
Hibiscus coccineus Walter
Mallow Family (Malvaceae)

Description: The smooth stems die back in winter and then resprout from the base in springtime, reaching up to 10' tall. The palmate leaves are 4"–8" long and deeply cut into 5 lobes. The bright red (rarely white) flowers are axillary on long petioles and measure about 6" wide.

Bloom Season: May–August

Habitat/Range: Freshwater swamps from Georgia and Alabama south in Florida to Palm Beach and Collier Counties.

Comments: *Hibiscus* is an ancient Greek name for "mallow." The name *coccineus* means "red," in reference to the flowers. This very attractive species can be easily seen from the elevated boardwalk that winds through Corkscrew Swamp Sanctuary in Collier County. Scarlet rosemallow can be successfully cultivated in pots submerged in water or grown in water gardens but explanations might be in order for inquisitive neighbors or the police because the leaves very closely resemble those of marijuana *(Cannibis sativa)*. Hummingbirds visit the flowers in their breeding range. In Corkscrew Swamp it grows in the company of swamp rosemallow *(Hibiscus grandiflorus)* with showy, light pink blossoms.

FAIRY HIBISCUS
Hibiscus poeppigii (Spreng.) Garcke
Mallow Family (Malvaceae)

Description: The leaves of this 2'–4' shrub are ovate and coarsely toothed along the margins with stiff hairs that give the leaf blades a rough texture. The leaves range from ¾"–2" long and half as wide. Pendent flowers are solitary from the leaf axils and average ¾" long.

Bloom Season: All year

Habitat/Range: Hardwood forests and coastal rock barrens of southern Florida to the West Indies and Mexico.

Comments: The name *poeppigii* commemorates botanist Eduard Friedrich Poeppig (1798–1868). In Florida, this species is found only in Miami-Dade and Monroe Counties and is a state-listed endangered species. A tea brewed from the flowers is used in the West Indies to treat colds and a wash made from crushed leaves is used to treat skin conditions. It adapts readily to cultivation and is grown by native-plant enthusiasts. It is also called Poeppig's rosemallow.

FLORIDA ADDERSMOUTH ORCHID
Malaxis spicata Sw.
Orchid Family (Orchidaceae)

Description: This species averages about 2½"–6" tall and often grows semiepiphytically on mossy stumps, logs, or tree bases. There are 2 (rarely 3) succulent, ovate leaves from 1"–3½" long and ½"–2" wide. The flower spike stands well above the leaves and bears greenish orange flowers, each measuring about ¼" wide. Plants may flower successively for several months.

Bloom Season: Principally December–February in the Everglades region

Habitat/Range: Wooded swamps of the Carolinas, Virginia, and Georgia to southwest Florida and the West Indies.

Comments: *Malaxis* is Greek for "softening" and alludes to the soft texture of the leaves. The name *spicata* refers to the erect spike of flowers. This orchid can be overlooked when growing among ferns, mosses, and even other orchids on stumps and floating logs. Green addersmouth *(Malaxis unifolia)* occurs farther north in Florida.

LEAFLESS BEAKED LADIES'-TRESSES

Sacoila lanceolata (Aubl.) Garay
(Also *Spiranthes lanceolata* [Aubl.] Léon)
Orchid Family (Orchidaceae)

Description: The large lanceolate leaves form a basal rosette and can reach 8" long and 2" wide but are not present when flowering. A stout, erect, fleshy spike, to 12" tall or more, is topped with a compact arrangement of coral red (or green), pubescent, 1" flowers.

Bloom Season: April–July

Habitat/Range: Open meadows, pastures, and roadsides of mainland Florida and the Neotropics.

Comments: *Sacoila* alludes to the sac-shaped projection formed by the sepals and base of the column. The name *lanceolata* refers to the lance-shaped leaves. Some plants produce green flowers and have been referred to as var. *luteoalba* or forma *albidaviridis*. This state-listed threatened species ranges south into Corkscrew Swamp and the CREW Marsh in Collier County and can form large, roadside colonies. Butterflies visit the flowers.

SCARLET LADIES'-TRESSES

Sacoila lanceolata (Aubl.) Garay var. *paludicola* (Luer) Sauleda et al
(Also *Spiranthes lanceolata* [Aubl.] Léon var. *paludicola* Luer)
Orchid Family (Orchidaceae)

Description: The large lanceolate leaves form a basal rosette and are usually present when flowering. The flowers are slightly smaller and brighter red (rarely yellow) than the previous species and there are also habitat, range, and bloom season differences.

Bloom Season: February–April

Habitat/Range: Swamps and hardwood forests from central and southern Florida south to Cuba.

Comments: The name *paludicola* means "swamp dweller." This terrestrial orchid is rare and localized in Florida, especially on old railroad beds in the Fakahatchee Swamp (Collier County). It was first described in 1971 and is a state-listed threatened species. Unlike the typical variety it can produce viable seeds without the presence of a pollinator (auto-pollination).

MULE-EAR ORCHID

Trichocentrum undulatum (Sw.) Ackerman & M. W. Chase
(Also *Oncidium luridum* Lindl.)
Orchid Family (Orchidaceae)

Description: The stiff, keeled, green or maroon leaves of this epiphytic orchid reach 3' long and 6" wide and are shaped like a mule's ear. The flower spike is 2'–4' long with an open spray of very ornamental, 1¼" flowers.

Bloom Season: March–May

Habitat/Range: Coastal forests of Everglades National Park, Bahamas, Cuba, and Jamaica.

Comments: *Trichocentrum* relates to the nectar-less spur of the flowers. The name *undulatum* refers to the undulating sepals and petals. This impressive orchid was first discovered in Florida by botanists Alvah Augustus Eaton (1865–1908) and John J. Soar (1869–1951) in Miami-Dade County in 1903. It is a state-listed endangered species that has recently become threatened by the larvae of an orchid fly *(Melanagromyza miamensis)* that cause the flowering stems to abort. Because of its striking flowers collectors have sought it out for more than 100 years in Florida. One photo taken in the early 1920s of a horse-drawn wagon piled high with mule-ear orchids attests to the pillage. It is also threatened by scale insects, hurricanes, and sea level rise due to global warming. It is one of the genuine treasures of the Everglades and is a thrill to see in flower in its native haunts.

WORMVINE ORCHID
Vanilla barbellata Rchb. f.
Orchid Family (Orchidaceae)

Description: The green or orange stems of this leafless, vining orchid are smooth, ⅜"–½" thick, and root to trees at the nodes. The flowers measure 2"–2½" wide, the lip partly rimmed with white, and brownish orange sepals and petals that are somewhat cupped.

Bloom Season: April–July

Habitat/Range: Coastal forests of southern Florida, Bahamas, and Cuba.

Comments: *Vanilla* is from the Spanish *vainilla*, or "small pod," in reference to the beanlike seed capsules. The name *barbellata* means "somewhat bearded," referring to the small bristles on the lip of this state-listed endangered species. Despite periodic hurricanes that ravage southern Florida's coastlines this orchid remains a locally common species in mangrove-buttonwood associations around the Flamingo area of Everglades National Park and through much of the Florida Keys. It is quite exciting to be paddling a canoe quietly along mangrove-lined creeks in the Everglades and come across a flowering wormvine orchid. The sweltering heat, thick humidity, deer flies, and hordes of saltmarsh mosquitoes will be briefly forgotten. The flowers are highly perfumed if you can pause long enough to take in their delightful fragrance. Screaming is optional.

DILLON'S VANILLA
Vanilla dilloniana Correll
Orchid Family (Orchidaceae)

Description: This vining orchid sometimes produces persistent fleshy leaves to 1½" long and ⅜" wide. The inflorescences are axillary with up to 15 flower buds that open a few at a time. The 3" flowers have green, flaring sepals and petals with a fluted lip that is mostly purplish red.

Bloom Season: May–July

Habitat/Range: Coastal hammocks of southern Florida (Miami-Dade and Monroe Counties) and the West Indies.

Comments: The name *dilloniana* honors Gordon Winston Dillon (1912–1982), a botanical illustrator at the Orchid Herbarium of Oakes Ames. This orchid was first collected in Brickell Hammock (Miami-Dade County) in 1928 and again in Madeira Hammock east of Flamingo in Everglades National Park in 1944. Brickell Hammock has long ago been destroyed but there is a good chance that this imperiled orchid still exists in remote, mostly unexplored coastal forests of the Everglades.

ORANGE MILKWORT
Polygala lutea L.
Milkwort Family (Polygalaceae)

Description: Orange milkwort is a biennial that averages 4"–8" tall with thick ovate leaves ranging from ¾"–1½" long and half as wide. The somewhat cylindrical, ¾"–1" flower heads are in compact arrangements of orange to yellow flowers subtended by bracts of the same color.

Bloom Season: February–November

Habitat/Range: Flatwoods, bogs, and cypress pond margins along the eastern seaboard from New York to Florida west to Louisiana.

Comments: *Polygala* means "much milk," in the fanciful belief that milkworts could increase milk flow in cattle. The name *lutea* means "yellow," alluding to the yellow flower heads produced on some plants. Most plants have orange flowers and bracts, hence the common name. It is also called yellow milkwort and yellow bachelor's button in parts of its range. It ranges into the Corkscrew Swamp and Big Cypres Swamp regions but does not occur in Everglades National Park.

YELLOW FLOWERS

Coreopsis leavenworthii

This section includes flowers from pale cream to bright, golden yellow. Some species have two-colored flowers, such as yellow and pink or yellow and white. If the predominant color is yellow, they are included here. Many species with yellow flowers also have green or orange flower variations or turn red as they age. You may need to check those sections if the flower you are searching for is not found here.

PINELAND ALLAMANDA
Angadenia berteroi (A. DC.) Miers
(Also *Angadenia sagraei* [A. DC.] Miers)
Dogbane Family (Apocynaceae)

Description: Pineland allamanda reaches 6"–30" tall, often branching near the top. The leaves are opposite, linear oblong with curled margins, and each measuring 1"–2" long and ⅜"–½" wide. Bright yellow, trumpet-shaped flowers are produced singly or a few at a time at the tips of the branches. The flowers measure ¾"–1¼" long and ¾" wide.

Bloom Season: All year

Habitat/Range: Pinelands of southern Florida, Bahamas, Cuba, and Hispaniola.

Comments: *Angadenia* refers to "gland" and "vessel," alluding to the enclosed stigma. The name *berteroi* honors Italian botanist Carlo Luigi Guiseppe Bertero (1789–1831), who explored the American tropics. The sap of this state-listed threatened species can causes severe eye irritation as well as a blistering skin rash. In the Bahamas it is called lice-root and has been used to ward off "intercourse taboo."

WILD ALLAMANDA
Pentalinon luteum (L.) B. F. Hansen & Wunderlin
(Also *Urechites lutea* [L.] Britton)
Dogbane Family (Apocynaceae)

Description: Wild allamanda is a semi-woody vine with glossy, opposite leaves that curl under along the margins. The leaves are 1"–3" long and ½"–1" wide. Trumpet-shaped, 2" flowers appear from clusters of buds at the branch tips.

Bloom Season: April–November

Habitat/Range: Coastal and inland habitats from central Florida south into the Florida Keys and West Indies.

Comments: *Pentalinon* is Greek for "five" and "rope," alluding to the anther appendages. The name *lutea* means "yellow." Consuming the latex in the plant causes burning of the mouth and throat, nausea, diarrhea, and convulsions, and may lead to heart failure and death. The sap burns sensitive skin and has been used as an arrow poison. This showy vine can be seen climbing over roadside vegetation between Mahogany Hammock and Flamingo in Everglades National Park.

OPPOSITELEAF SPOTFLOWER
Acmella oppositifolia (Lam.) R. K. Jansen var. *repens* (Walter) R. K. Jansen
Aster Family (Asteraceae)

Description: This low-growing species has opposite leaves on hairy, purple stems. The leaves are ovate with slightly toothed margins and measure ½"–1" long and ⅜" wide. The flower heads are about ½" wide.

Bloom Season: All year

Habitat/Range: Marshes and floodplains from North Carolina to Missouri and Texas south through mainland Florida.

Comments: *Acmella* means "a point" and somehow alludes to the taste of the leaves. The name *oppositifolia* refers to the opposite leaves and the name *repens* means "creeping." Eating the flowers causes a tingling sensation of the mouth that lasts about ten minutes. In Brazil it is called *abecedária* (alphabet plant) because it is thought to make babies speak more easily. It is eaten in Brazil as a mouth-tingling salad herb and chewed to relieve toothache. It occurs throughout the Everglades region.

COASTAL PLAIN HONEYCOMBHEAD
Balduina angustifolia (Pursh) B. L. Rob.
Aster Family (Asteraceae)

Description: This biennial reaches 2'–5' tall when flowering in its second year. Basal leaves are linear and eventually disappear as the plant grows, with only the upper leaves remaining. Upper leaves are very narrow and range from ½"–2" long. Bright yellow flower heads are 1½"–2" in diameter and produced in showy clusters.

Bloom Season: June–November but all year in southern Florida

Habitat/Range: Scrub, dunes, pinelands, and sandhills of mainland Florida, Georgia, Alabama, and Mississippi.

Comments: *Balduina* honors American botanist William Baldwin (1779–1819). John Torrey and Asa Gray attempted to change *Balduina* to *Baldwinia* in 1840 but the name was not accepted. The name *angustifolia* refers to the narrow leaves. This is a plant of dry, sunny habitats and ranges south in Florida into Collier County. Butterflies visit the disk flowers.

FLORIDA GREENEYES
Berlandiera subacaulis (Nutt.) Nutt.
Aster Family (Asteraceae)

Description: Florida greeneyes has alternate, deeply lobed or scalloped leaves that form a basal rosette. The leaves are mostly 1"–4½" long and downy beneath. The flower heads are held singly on a hairy stem from 6"–20" tall. The disk is green with conspicuous disk flowers arranged in a circle. The ray flowers are rather short with a notched tip.

Bloom Season: All year

Habitat/Range: Endemic to sandy pinelands nearly throughout Florida.

Comments: *Berlandiera* honors Jean Louis Berlandier (1805–1889), a Belgian botanist who explored Texas and New Mexico. The name *subacaulis* means "without much of a stem," referring to the short stem of this species. The genus is comprised of only 4 species indigenous to the southern United States and Mexico. This is an easy and attractive plant to grow in dry soils. The disk flowers attract nectar-seeking bees and small butterflies.

MARSH BEGGARTICKS
Bidens mitis (Michx.) Sherff
Aster Family (Asteraceae)

Description: This attractive species reaches 12"–48" tall with ovate or lanceolate leaves that are sometimes divided into narrow, unequal, pointed segments. The leaves average 1"–2" long and up to ⅜" wide. The flower heads measure 2" wide and are in flat-topped arrays.

Bloom Season: September–November

Habitat/Range: Marshes, swamps, and ditches from New Jersey to Missouri and Texas south in Florida to Collier County.

Comments: *Bidens* is Latin for "two toothed," referring to the 2 teeth on the dry, 1-seeded achene. The name *mitis* means "ripe," which is believed to relate to the original specimen bearing mature fruits (achenes). This species can turn acres of its habitat into fields of golden yellow when in flower. It is also called smallfruit beggarticks. It closely resembles bur marigold *(Bidens laevis),* which has sessile leaves. Butterflies frequent the flowers.

SEA OXEYE

Borrichia frutescens (L.) DC.
Aster Family (Asteraceae)

Description: Sea oxeye is a semi-woody shrub with grayish leaves, spreading by rhizomes to form dense colonies. The lanceolate leaves are 1"–2" long and ½"–¾" wide and covered with soft, gray hairs. Flower heads measure ⅝"–1" wide with yellow ray and disk flowers. The disk flowers are stiff to the touch.

Bloom Season: All year

Habitat/Range: Coastal strand and saltmarshes of the southeastern United States, Bahamas, Bermuda, and Mexico.

Comments: *Borrichia* honors Danish botanist Ole Borch (1628–1690), who Latinized his name to Olaus Borrichius. The name *frutescens* means "shrubby." A similar native species, *Borrichia arborescens*, has glossy, dark green leaves and is a taller, solitary shrub with soft disk flowers. Both species are often found growing together in coastal habitats of southern Florida but this species is the most common. Both are used in urban landscapes.

MOSIER'S FALSE BONESET

Brickellia mosieri (Small) Shinners
(Also *Brickellia eupatorioides* [L.] Shinners var. *floridana* [R. W. Long] B. L. Turner)
Aster Family (Asteraceae)

Description: The 12"–36" stems are finely pubescent with widely spaced alternate leaves to 1" long. The leaves are linear, typically drooping or twisted with revolute (rolled under) margins. The flower heads are in open, branched clusters.

Bloom Season: April–September

Habitat/Range: Endemic to pine rocklands of southern Miami-Dade County, Florida.

Comments: *Brickellia* honors Irish-born physician and naturalist John Brickell (1748–1809) who lived in Georgia. The name *mosieri* commemorates naturalist Charles A. Mosier (1871--1936) who was the first warden of Royal Palm State Park (now a part of Everglades National Park). It is a rare, state-listed endangered species. The name "boneset" relates to healing broken bones or treating dengue (breakbone) fever.

LEAVENWORTH'S TICKSEED
Coreopsis leavenworthii Torr. & A. Gray
Aster Family (Asteraceae)

Description: Tickseed averages 10"–24" tall with narrow, opposite leaves that average ½"–4" long and 1⁄16"–¼" wide (sometimes divided into narrow segments). Flower heads range from ½"–1" wide ray flowers that are regularly lobed at the tip.

Bloom Season: All year

Habitat/Range: Wet flatwoods of Florida and Alabama

Comments: *Coreopsis* means "ticklike," alluding to the seeds that resemble ticks. The name *leavenworthii* honors American botanist Melines Conklin Leavenworth (1796–1862). This species is a larval host plant of the common tan wave moth and is the only *Coreopsis* in the Everglades. All Florida native *Coreopsis* species are the state wildflower but, in a major boondoggle, the rendition on the Florida state wildflower license plate is golden tickseed *(Coreopsis tinctoria)*, a nonnative naturalized species with red bases on the yellow ray flowers.

SLENDER GOLDENTOP
Euthamia caroliniana (L.) Greene ex Porter & Britton
Aster Family (Asteraceae)

Description: This is a much-branched perennial from 10"–36" tall. The linear, very narrow leaves are deflexed or erect and measure 1"–2¾" long. The flower heads are in rounded or flat-topped arrangements.

Bloom Season: August–December

Habitat/Range: Open, moist, sandy soils from Nova Scotia across the eastern United States from Michigan south to Louisiana and Florida.

Comments: *Euthamia* means "well crowded," referring to either the branching pattern or the flower clusters. Another interpretation is that it means "pretty." The name *caroliniana* means "of the Carolinas." Native Americans used the roots and flowers of this species medicinally to treat chest pains from respiratory problems. The plants were also smoked in the belief that the odor of the smoke attracted deer. Bees swarm around flowering plants. It is also called slender flattop goldenrod.

COASTAL PLAIN YELLOWTOPS
Flaveria linearis Lag.
Aster Family (Asteraceae)

Description: Profusely branching, herbaceous perennial with narrowly linear, sessile, 1-veined leaves to about 4" long and ⅛"–¼" wide. The stems are often reddish purple with a flat-topped, spreading cluster of small disk flowers (5–10 per head; sometimes with a single ray flower) covering the plant like a flat umbrella.

Bloom Season: All year

Habitat/Range: Coastal and inland habitats from Florida to the West Indies and the Yucatan Peninsula in Mexico.

Comments: *Flaveria* means "yellow" and refers to the yellow dye extracted from some species. The name *linearis* refers to the narrow leaves. Florida gardeners cultivate this species because butterflies and bees are common sights around flowering plants. Four members of the genus are native to Florida but this is easily the most commonly seen species, especially in recently burned prairies and along roadways that border its habitat.

BLANKETFLOWER
Gaillardia pulchella Foug.
Aster Family (Asteraceae)

Description: Firewheel is an annual although it sometimes persists in cultivation. It typically reaches 8"–14" tall with oblong or spatula-shaped leaves that are usually entire but may be toothed, measuring about 2"–4" long and ⅜"–½" wide. The ray flowers are usually yellow to orange at the tips and reddish to purplish at the base.

Bloom Season: All year

Habitat/Range: Dunes, sandhills, and disturbed sites discontinuously from Maine to South Dakota south to Arizona and through the southeastern states.

Comments: *Gaillardia* honors 18th-century French magistrate Gaillard de Merentonneau (apparently in error as Charentonneau). The name *pulchella* means "beautiful" and aptly describes the blossoms. It is also called firewheel and Indian blanket. This species is widely cultivated for its cheery flowers and is even available in seed packets from mainstream garden centers.

SPANISH DAISY
Helenium amarum (Raf.) H. Rock
Aster Family (Asteraceae)

Description: The narrowly linear leaves of Spanish daisy are smooth or sparsely hairy and sometimes deeply dissected. The arrays of flower heads are held above the leaves and each head measures about ⅝"–1¼" wide with toothed ray flowers.

Bloom Season: May–November

Habitat/Range: Sandy pinelands and open disturbed sites of the eastern United States and northern Mexico.

Comments: *Helenium* honors Helen of Troy, a Greek heroine and queen of Sparta whose abduction by prince Paris of Troy brought about the Trojan War. The name *amarum* refers to the bitter leaves. This gave rise to the common name bitterweed in parts of its range. This is a common species that begins flowering in late spring. It is mostly associated with disturbed sandy soils so look for it in abandoned fields or along trails that bisect its habitat, especially along the Cypress Dome Trail at the CREW Marsh in Collier County.

PURPLEHEAD SNEEZEWEED
Helenium flexuosum Raf.
Aster Family (Asteraceae)

Description: The sparsely hairy stems are strongly winged with grooved flower stems. Oblong to lanceolate sessile leaves are 1"–5" long and average ¼"–½" wide. The plant reaches about 3" tall and is often branched in the upper half. The floral head measures about ⅝" wide. This species does not produce ray flowers in the Everglades population.

Bloom Season: February–October

Habitat/Range: Wet flatwoods and floodplains across the eastern half of North America.

Comments: The name *flexuosum* refers to the flexible stems. This species ranges south through central Florida with a disjunct population on Long Pine Key in Everglades National Park. It has been suggested that this species may be of hybrid origin. As is true of other members of the genus the leaves taste bitter and neither deer nor rabbits will eat the plant. Small bees and butterflies visit the disk flowers. It is also called Hélénie nudiflore.

SOUTHEASTERN SNEEZEWEED
Helenium pinnatifidum (Nutt.) Rydb.
Aster Family (Asteraceae)

Description: The basal leaves are pinnately divided partway to the midrib and are 2"–6" long. The flower heads are solitary on tall stems that rise from the center of the leafy rosette and stand 1'–2' tall or more. The flower heads average 1"–1½" wide with ray flowers notched twice at the tips.

Bloom Season: All year

Habitat/Range: Freshwater wetlands and flatwoods of mainland Florida to Mississippi and North Carolina.

Comments: The name *pinnatifidum* means "pinnately cut," in reference to the leaves. It is also called Everglades daisy and Glades sneezeweed in southern Florida. It commonly flowers in standing water or along wet roadsides and trails that bisect its habitat. The plant is toxic to livestock and is a principal cause of "spewing sickness" in cattle. The name sneezeweed derives from Native Americans drying and powdering certain species to use as snuff.

SOUTHEASTERN SUNFLOWER
Helianthus agrestis Pollard
Aster Family (Asteraceae)

Description: The stems of this annual may reach 8' tall with basal leaves that usually wither before flowering. The lanceolate stem leaves are mostly alternate and toothed with long white hairs on the petiole and leaf base. The larger leaves are 4" long to 1" wide. The flower heads are 2" wide or more with yellow ray flowers and reddish brown disks.

Bloom Season: August–November

Habitat/Range: Marshes and wet flatwoods from Georgia south in Florida to Collier County.

Comments: *Helianthus* is Greek for "sun flower" and relates to the flower heads that mostly face east after opening. There is a popular misconception that sunflowers track the sun from east to west across the sky. The name *agrestis* means "growing in the fields." This species can cover open marshes in a blaze of color and is especially abundant following a summer fire. Butterflies visit the small disk flowers for nectar.

SWAMP SUNFLOWER
Helianthus angustifolius L.
Aster Family (Asteraceae)

Description: The stems of this perennial species are usually hairy and reach 2'–5' tall. The leaves are linear and measure 3"–6" long with strongly revolute (rolled under) margins. The disk flowers can be yellow (pictured) or purplish brown. The flower heads measure about 2½" across.

Bloom Season: May–December

Habitat/Range: Marshes and wet flatwoods from New Jersey to Indiana south to Texas and Florida.

Comments: The name *angustifolius* refers to the narrow leaves. Another common name is narrowleaf sunflower. This species typically grows in standing water or saturated soil. In the Everglades region it occurs in Corkscrew Swamp and the CREW Marsh but not in the adjacent Big Cypress National Preserve or Everglades National Park. It is sometimes cultivated for its flamboyant flowers but requires regular watering. The flowers are a showstopper when it blooms in mass along roadsides.

EAST COAST DUNE SUNFLOWER
Helianthus debilis Nutt.
Aster Family (Asteraceae)

Description: This common sunflower has decumbent, mostly glabrous stems that form mounds along coastal dunes. The deltoid leaf blades are entire to shallowly toothed, averaging 2"–4" long and half as wide. The flower heads are 2"–2½" wide on long stems (peduncles) from 4"–8" long.

Bloom Season: All year

Habitat/Range: Endemic to coastal dunes from St. Johns County, Florida, southward along the east coast.

Comments: The name *debilis* means "weak" and perhaps refers to the decumbent stems. It is exceptionally drought and salt tolerant and is extensively cultivated in Florida. It has been inappropriately used in landscaping along Florida's central west coast where an endemic subspecies (subsp. *vestitus*) with coarsely toothed leaves occurs. This may likely cause the West Coast dune sunflower to become extinct from gene pool contamination through hybridization.

CAMPHORWEED

Heterotheca subaxillaris (Lam.) Britton & Rusby
Aster Family (Asteraceae)

Description: Camphorweed is well branched above and typically about 2'–4' tall with ovate to elliptic leaves ranging from ½"–2¾" long and ⅜"–2" wide. The larger basal leaves wither away before flowering. The leaf blades are entire or coarsely toothed and either flat or undulating. The flower heads average 1" wide.

Bloom Season: All year

Habitat/Range: Sandhills, dunes, and pinelands from Delaware to Texas south into Mexico and throughout mainland Florida.

Comments: *Heterotheca* means "different container," alluding to the dissimilar achene-like fruits called *cypselae*. The name *subaxillaris* refers to the floral heads being produced near the leaf axils. Yellow-flowered composites are to wildflower enthusiasts what warblers are to birdwatchers, in that they can be frustrating to identify. A key to identifying this species is that the leaves smell strongly of camphor when crushed.

COASTAL PLAIN HAWKWEED

Hieracium megacephalon Nash
Aster Family (Asteraceae)

Description: The leaves are elliptic to inversely egg-shaped (obovate) and range from 1⅜"–3" long and about half as wide. The leaves and flowering stems are covered with coarse hairs (the leaves are sometimes reddish purple). The heads of flowers are about ¾" wide and are produced on stems to 18" tall.

Bloom Season: All year

Habitat/Range: Sandhills, flatwoods, and pinelands of Florida, Georgia, and South Carolina.

Comments: *Hieracium* comes from *heirakos*, an ancient Greek word for "hawk," and relates to the fanciful belief by Pliny (AD 23–79) that hawks ate the plants to improve their vision. The name *megacephalon* means "large head" and refers to the heads of flowers that are larger than those of other species in the genus. Some species possess antibiotic properties and have been used medicinally to heal wounds. Members of this genus can reproduce asexually (apomixis).

BUTTERWEED

Packera glabella (Poir.) C. Jeffrey
(Also *Senecio glabellus* Poir.)
Aster Family (Asteraceae)

Description: The main leaves of this succulent, herbaceous annual are deeply and irregularly cut. The leaves have toothed margins and reduce in size up the stem. The fragrant, butter-yellow flower heads are produced in showy clusters and each flower head is about ⅜"–½" wide.

Bloom Season: March–July

Habitat/Range: Open, wet areas (including lawns and roadsides) of the eastern United States.

Comments: *Packera* honors John G. Packer, Professor Emeritus, University of Alberta, Canada. The name *glabella* means "glabrous," in reference to the smooth leaves. This is a large genus of about 1,250 species, many of which have been used medicinally by herbalists for a number of gynecological ailments. The leaves contain high levels of alkaloids and can cause severe liver damage in humans if eaten. This and other species are toxic to grazing livestock.

SANDDUNE CINCHWEED

Pectis glaucescens (Cass.) D. J. Keil
(Also *Pectis leptocephala* [Cass.] Urb.)
Aster Family (Asteraceae)

Description: This low-growing species has leaves that emit a lemonlike aroma when crushed. The leaves are opposite, sessile, and narrowly linear to 1¼" long and ³⁄₁₆" wide with 2 rows of oil glands on the lower surface. The flower heads are distinctly stalked.

Bloom Season: All year

Habitat/Range: Pinelands, beaches, and disturbed sites of central and southern Florida to the West Indies.

Comments: *Pectis* is Latin for "comb," alluding to the comblike bristles along the leaf margins. The name *glaucescens* refers to the glaucous leaves of this species. It is also called tea blinkum in Florida and has been used medicinally in Jamaica to treat colds and tuberculosis. It is called *chinche hierba* (bedbug herb) in Puerto Rico from its use to repel bedbugs. The related spreading cinchweed (*Pectis prostrata*) has wider leaves and sessile flowers.

SILK-GRASS
Pityopsis graminifolia (Michx.) Nutt.
(Also *Heterotheca graminifolia* [Michx.] Shinners)
Aster Family (Asteraceae)

Description: The lower leaves of silk-grass are 4"–8" long and ³⁄₁₆"–⁵⁄₁₆" wide with smaller leaves up the stem. The flower heads are 1 to many, with bright yellow ray and disk flowers. The flower heads are ⁵⁄₈"–³⁄₄" in diameter.

Bloom Season: All year

Habitat/Range: Pinelands and dry prairies across the eastern United States to the Bahamas.

Comments: *Pityopsis* means "resembling a pine," alluding to the narrow leaves of the type species that resemble a seedling pine *(Pinus)*. The name *graminifolia* refers to the grasslike leaves of this species. When not in flower it can easily be mistaken for a silky-leaved grass. It is also called fever-grass, silky golden aster, and gopher-grass. The plant is used medicinally to reduce fever and also to treat boils, colds, and rheumatism. It is common throughout the Everglades region.

BLACKEYED SUSAN
Rudbeckia hirta L.
Aster Family (Asteraceae)

Description: Blackeyed Susan produces a rosette of coarse-haired, toothed leaves with the upper leaves slightly clasping the stem. The ray flowers can radiate outward from the conelike central disk but they commonly arch downward.

Bloom Season: February–November

Habitat/Range: Sandhills and flatwoods across the eastern United States south in Florida to the Big Cypress and Corkscrew Swamp regions.

Comments: *Rudbeckia* honors botany professor Olaus Rudbeck (1660–1740), whose most famous student was Carolus Linnaeus. The name *hirta* refers to the coarsely hairy stems and leaves. The symbolic meaning of blackeyed Susan is "justice." Native Americans gave it names that translate to deer's eye daisy and black eyeballs. It is a larval host plant of the camouflaged looper and common pug moth. It is one of America's most well-known wildflowers and can grow in profusion along roadsides.

LEAVENWORTH'S GOLDENROD
Solidago leavenworthii Torr. & A. Gray
Aster Family (Asteraceae)

Description: Good field characteristics of this species are its lack of basal leaves and its pointed, non-twisted, serrate stem leaves. The stem leaves average 2"–3" long and ⅜"–½" wide and are bundled near the stem tip on young plants but line the stem on flowering specimens. Flowering plants average 2'–4' tall with flowers in a somewhat pyramidal array.

Bloom Season: May–December

Habitat/Range: Flatwoods, dunes, and disturbed sites of the southeastern United States.

Comments: *Solidago* means "to strengthen" and refers to medicinal uses to treat wounds. The name *leavenworthii* honors botanist Melines Conklin Leavenworth (1796–1862) who served as an Army surgeon in the Civil War and became one of the more important plant collectors in the southern United States. Goldenrods are used medicinally to treat impotence and conditions of the kidneys and urinary tract.

CHAPMAN'S GOLDENROD
Solidago odora Aiton var. *chapmanii* (A. Gray) Cronquist
Aster Family (Asteraceae)

Description: The anise-scented leaves of this species have entire margins and the stems on this variety are uniformly covered with soft hairs with smaller leaves than the typical variety. The stem leaves measure 1¼"–2¾" long and ⅜"–⅝" wide and are often slightly twisted.

Bloom Season: June–December

Habitat/Range: Sandhills and pine flatwoods of Florida and Georgia.

Comments: The name *odora* refers to the anise-scented leaves. The name *chapmanii* honors botanist Alvan Wentworth Chapman (1809–1899). After the Boston Tea Party, American colonists brewed the leaves of goldenrods instead of costly English tea and found it to be so pleasant tasting that they exported it to overseas markets. This and other goldenrods are larval host plants of a number of moths, including the asteroid, blackberry looper, dark-spotted palthis, and confused eusarca.

SEASIDE GOLDENROD
Solidago sempervirens L.
Aster Family (Asteraceae)

Description: This species reaches heights of 5'–6' tall when in flower. The fleshy, ovate to oblanceolate basal leaves measure 4"–16" long and 1½"–2½" wide and are present when flowering. Floral heads are packed along a tall, branched stem with leaves that are gradually reduced upward.

Bloom Season: August–December

Habitat/Range: Coastal dunes and brackish and freshwater marshes along the coastal plain from Massachusetts to Florida and west to Texas and Mexico.

Comments: The name *sempervirens* means "evergreen." This species is common throughout the Everglades region, particularly in the Big Cypress Swamp. The large basal leaves help tell it apart from other goldenrods in the region. The plant described here is treated as subsp. *mexicana* in the *Flora of North America*. The medicinal virtues of goldenrods have been known since the civilizations of ancient Rome and Greece.

WAND GOLDENROD
Solidago stricta Aiton
Aster Family (Asteraceae)

Description: Wand goldenrod has a simple, straight, grooved stem with the main leaves forming a basal rosette. The leaf blades are spatulate, to 6" long and 1" wide, tapering toward the base to a long petiole. The sessile, scalelike stem leaves are appressed to the stem. The flower spike is usually unbranched.

Bloom Season: All year

Habitat/Range: Pinelands, wet prairies, and margins of salt marshes from the eastern United States south to Cuba.

Comments: The name *stricta* means "erect" or "upright," in reference to the flower stem. This is a common species in the Everglades region, especially in Everglades National Park where it grows in abundance along the edges of wet prairies. Ragweed *(Ambrosia artemisiifolia)* has airborne pollen (unlike goldenrods) and has caused goldenrods to be wrongfully maligned as a source of allergies because they flower at the same time of year.

CREEPING OXEYE
Sphagneticola trilobata (L.) Pruski
(Also *Wedelia trilobata* [L.] Strother)
Aster Family (Asteraceae)

Description: The dark green, 3-lobed leaves are rough to the touch and average 1"–1¾" long and half as wide. The flower heads are bright yellow and range from 1"–1¼" in diameter. The ray flowers are notched at the apex.

Bloom Season: All year

Habitat/Range: Pinelands, coastal dunes, and disturbed sites of southern and central Florida. Native to the Neotropics.

Comments: *Sphagneticola* means "peat-bog dweller," in reference to the habitat of some species. The name *trilobata* refers to the 3-lobed leaves. This plant is an aggressive weed in tropical, subtropical, and warm temperate regions around the world. It is a popular ornamental ground cover in Florida but is regarded as a pest plant by resource managers and is listed by the Florida Exotic Pest Plant Council. Many gardeners know it simply as wedelia. Small butterflies visit the flowers.

COATBUTTONS
Tridax procumbens L.
Aster Family (Asteraceae)

Description: The opposite leaves of this hairy perennial are often 3-lobed and average 1"–3" long and half as wide. The flower heads are borne singly on erect stems that stand 3"–6" tall. The flower heads measure about ½"–⅝" wide with white or creamy yellow ray flowers that are 2- or 3-lobed at the tip.

Bloom Season: All year

Habitat/Range: Pinelands and disturbed sites, including cracks in sidewalks, of central and southern Florida. Native to the Neotropics.

Comments: *Tridax* refers to the 3-lobed ray flowers. The name *procumbens* refers to the procumbent growth habit. Butterflies visit the flowers but due to its weedy tendencies it is never purposely cultivated. This species is listed as a noxious weed in parts of the United States. Studies have shown that it has antiviral, antibiotic, insecticidal, and wound-healing properties. The leaves are used as an insecticide in Hawaii.

ORIENTAL FALSE HAWKSBEARD
Youngia japonica (L.) DC.
Aster Family (Asteraceae)

Desription: The leaves form a basal rosette and range from 1½"–5" long and ¾"–1½" wide with deep, rounded lobes. The flower heads are congested at the top of a densely hairy 6"–12" stem, or the stem may be branched near the top. Seeds are wind dispersed.

Bloom Season: All year

Habitat/Range: Disturbed sites throughout Florida. A pantropical weed native to southeastern Asia.

Comments: *Youngia* honors poet Edward Young (1683–1765) and physician Thomas Young (1773–1829). The name *japonica* means "of Japan" where it was first collected in 1838 but it is believed to have originated in China. The young leaves can be eaten raw or cooked as a potherb and the plant is also used medicinally in a decoction to reduce inflammation and to treat boils and snakebite. It is an extraordinarily common weed in disturbed sites throughout the Everglades region. Small butterflies and bees visit the flowers.

PINELAND HELIOTROPE
Heliotropium polyphyllum Lehm.
(Also *Heliotropium leavenworthii* Torr.)
Borage Family (Boraginaceae)

Description: Pineland heliotrope has ascending, radially spreading stems with narrow, alternate, elliptic leaves that are mostly ⅜"–¾" long and no more than ³⁄₁₆" wide. The leaves are smooth above and densely hairy beneath. The terminal flower spike curls under at the tip with 5-lobed yellow or white flowers, each about ³⁄₁₆"–¼" wide.

Bloom Season: All year

Habitat/Range: Pinelands and prairies from the Bahamas to Florida.

Comments: *Heliotropium* means "turning toward the sun," in reference to the flowers of some species that respond to the direction of the sun (heliotropism or phototropism). The name *polyphyllum* means "many leaves." The flowers of this species in Everglades National Park are yellow but are commonly white in Corkscrew Swamp and the CREW Marsh in Collier County. The roots are used medicinally in parts of its range.

EASTERN PRICKLY PEAR
Opuntia humifusa (Raf.) Raf.
Cactus Family (Cactaceae)

Description: This low-growing cactus has round to oblong, succulent pads (stems) that are connected together. The pads reach 2"–8" long and 1"–3" wide and bear wickedly sharp spines that range from ½"–1¼" long (sometimes absent). Very showy pale yellow or yellowish orange flowers range from 2"–2½" wide and are followed by cone shaped, reddish purple, 1"–2" fruits (berries).

Bloom Season: March–July

Habitat/Range: Dry, sandy habitats of the southeastern United States.

Comments: Greek philosopher Theophrastus (372–287 BC) used the name *Opuntia* for a plant found near the ancient city of Opus in Greece and it was later applied to this group of cacti in 1754 by Scottish botanist Philip Miller (1691–1771). The name *humifusa* means "sprawling" in reference to its growth habit. It is also called Indian fig. A South American moth *(Cactoblastis cactorum)* appeared in Florida in 1989 and its larvae bore through cactus pads, causing entire populations to die out. It is feared it could eradicate Florida native cacti if left unchecked. The stems are edible when peeled but will cause red urine. Cactus fruits are called "tuna" in Mexico and are made into jam, marmalade, and a paste called *queso de tuna*. The sharp spines can cause serious and painful injuries.

ERECT PRICKLY PEAR
Opuntia stricta (Haw.) Haw.
Cactus Family (Cactaceae)

Description: This cactus grows to 6' tall with large, flattened, obovate pads from 8"–12" long and 5"–8" wide. Sharp, ½"–1" spines are arranged in scattered clusters (or absent). Flowers average 2" wide and the reddish purple, pear-shaped fruits are 2"–2½" long.

Bloom Season: April–August

Habitat/Range: Coastal habitats from South Carolina to Texas south through Florida and the Neotropics.

Comments: The name *stricta* means "upright," in reference to its growth habit. In Everglades National Park this species grows along the edges of coastal hammocks, especially on shell mounds created by Calusa and Tequesta Indians. Small hairlike spines (glochids) often surround the stiff, needlelike spines on cacti. These can be irritating and should never be conveyed to your mouth or eyes. They should be removed from skin with tweezers or by placing duct tape over them and then pulling it off.

BANDANA-OF-THE-EVERGLADES
Canna flaccida Salisb.
Canna Family (Cannaceae)

Description: The broadly lanceolate leaves of this succulent herb range from 8"–24" long and 3"–6" wide, alternating along a fleshy 2'–4' stem. The showy, symmetric flowers are short-lived. The fruits are 3-parted capsules, 1"–2" wide, with hard, black seeds.

Bloom Season: March–November

Habitat/Range: Freshwater wetlands from South Carolina through mainland Florida.

Comments: *Canna* is Greek for "reed." The name *flaccida* refers to the lax flowers. Larvae of the Brazilian skipper butterfly often defoliate native and cultivated species of *Canna*. The larvae cut two slits on the leaf blade and fold the flap over themselves as a shelter to escape predators. Seminoles use the hard seeds in turtle shells to make ceremonial rattles and the hard seeds have been used to load shotgun shells for bird hunting. Indian shot *(Canna indica)* is naturalized and has small red flowers.

PINEBARREN FROSTWEED
Crocanthemum corymbosum (Michx.) Britton
(Also *Helianthemum corymbosum* Michx.)
Rockrose Family (Cistaceae)

Description: This species forms compact mounds and rarely stands more than about 10" tall. The leaves are linear lanceolate and range from 1"–1¾" long and ¼"–⅜" wide. The flowers are about ⅝" wide with petals that are squared off at the tip.

Bloom Season: March–August

Habitat/Range: Sandhills and dunes of the southeastern United States.

Comments: *Crocanthemum* means "saffron-yellow flower." The name *corymbosum* refers to the arrangement of the flowers in a corymb, a flat-topped inflorescence with flowers that open from the outside inward. This species ranges south in Florida to Collier and northern Miami-Dade Counties. The genus is centered in the Mediterranean but there are 6 species native to Florida. This is the most common species in the state and because it grows in sandy soils it would lend itself well as an attractive drought-tolerant plant in sandy gardens.

ROUNDPOD ST. JOHN'S-WORT
Hypericum cistifolium Lam.
Mangosteen Family (Clusiaceae)

Description: This species is shrubby (14"–36" tall) with 4-angled stems that bear linear-oblong, sessile leaves with underturned edges. The leaves measure 1"–3" long and about ⅓" wide. The stalked, 5-petaled flowers are in loose corymbs and each flower measures about ½" wide.

Bloom Season: June–September

Habitat/Range: Wet flatwoods and freshwater marshes of the southeastern United States from North Carolina to Texas south through mainland Florida.

Comments: *Hypericum* relates to an idol or apparition believed to be capable of warding off evil. The name *cistifolium* refers to the resemblance of the leaves to those of a *Cistus* (Cistaceae). Several species of St. John's-wort are used as herbal treatments for various forms of depression and were once used as a charm against witchcraft and demons. Common names of other species include demon chaser and devil's scourge.

MARSH ST. JOHN'S-WORT
Hypericum fasciculatum Lam.
Mangosteen Family (Clusiaceae)

Description: This shrubby species reaches 4' tall with peeling, reddish or gray bark. The leaves are needlelike, ⅜"–⅞" long, and formed in bundles. The yellow flowers average ⅝" wide with 5 pinwheel-like petals.

Bloom Season: All year

Habitat/Range: Flatwoods and freshwater wetlands of the southeastern United States.

Comments: The name *fasciculatum* means "bundled," referring to the leaves. Members of this genus contain a chemical that reacts with light so exposure to sun after drinking tea brewed from the flowers can result in burns on fair-skinned persons. The name St. John's-wort relates to picking the flowers on St. John's Day (June 24) to foretell marriage for maidens. In Christian tradition, Saint John baptized Jesus along the bank of the River Jordan and he was a major religious figure mentioned in both the Christian Bible and the central religious text of Islam, the Quran.

ST. ANDREW'S CROSS
Hypericum hypericoides (L.) Crantz
Mangosteen Family (Clusiaceae)

Description: This species is usually diffusely branched with reddish brown stems that are erect or decumbent. Leaves are linear to somewhat egg-shaped, opposite, and measure about ⅜"–1" long and up to half as wide. The flowers measure about ¾"–1" long with petals that form an X.

Bloom Season: May–December

Habitat/Range: Wet flatwoods and floodplains from New Jersey to Illinois south through Mexico to Honduras, West Indies, and the Bahamas.

Comments: When Linnaeus first described this species he placed it in the genus *Ascyrum* and gave it the specific epithet *hypericoides* because he thought it resembled a *Hypericum*. The common name refers to the resemblance of the flowers to the diagonal cross (a saltire) on which Saint Andrew was martyred by crucifixion in the 1st century. St. Andrew became the patron saint of Scotland with a saltire proudly represented on the national flag.

FOURPETAL ST. JOHN'S-WORT
Hypericum tetrapetalum Lam.
Mangosteen Family (Clusiaceae)

Description: The dull-green clasping leaves are broadly ovate and paired in 2 sizes. The X-shaped flowers have 4 petals with 2 outer sepals that resemble leaves, and 2 narrower inner sepals. The flowers are about 1" wide and appear singly at the branch tips and leaf axils.

Bloom Season: All year

Habitat/Range: Wet flatwoods from southern Georgia through mainland Florida to Cuba.

Comments: The name *tetrapetalum* means "four petals." Early Christians made St. John's-worts a symbol of St. John the Baptist because they flowered around June 24, St. John's Day. Members of the genus have long been used medicinally to promote healing of wounds because of their anti-biotic properties. Flower extracts are antiviral so researchers are testing their effectiveness against the virus that causes acquired immunodeficiency syndrome (AIDS). This species is common in the CREW Marsh.

CREEPING CUCUMBER
Melothria pendula L.
Gourd Family (Cucurbitaceae)

Description: The 3–5-lobed leaves of this tendriled vine range from 1"–1½" wide. Male and female flowers are produced separately on the same plant and average ¼" wide. The fruits are about ½"–⅝" long and ⅜" wide (mottled green but ripening black).

Bloom Season: March–November

Habitat/Range: Floodplain forests, sandhills, flatwoods, and fencerows from Pennsylvania to Missouri south through Texas, Florida, and the West Indies.

Comments: *Melothria* means "a melon," alluding to the immature fruits that resemble miniature watermelons. The name *pendula* relates to the pendent fruits. The fruits are edible when green but become strongly purgative once they have ripened and may cause diarrhea. The unripe fruits are pickled in the West Indies. The vine is considered to be excellent for grazing livestock because it is high in protein. It is also called Guadeloupe cucumber.

BALSAM PEAR
Momordica charantia L.
Gourd Family (Cucurbitaceae)

Description: The alternate, ill-smelling leaves of this slender, herbaceous, annual vine are divided into 5–7 lobes. The solitary, yellow, ¾" flowers have 5 petals. The fruits average 1½" long and ¾" wide with orange, warty skin, splitting open to reveal seeds encased in a red, sticky aril.

Bloom Season: All year

Habitat/Range: Hammocks, pinelands, and disturbed sites of Florida. Native to the Old World tropics.

Comments: *Momordica* means "to bite," alluding to the jagged seeds that look as if they have been bitten. The name *charantia* is a pre-Linnaean name. The red aril is safe to eat but the seeds and skin of ripe fruits are poisonous and can be fatal to dogs. The unripe fruits are soaked in salt water, then cooked as a vegetable in Asia and the Caribbean. It is sold as bitter melon in marketplaces and is used to treat malaria, leukemia, influenza, obesity, and Type 2 diabetes. It is very weedy.

WATER TOOTHLEAF
Stillingia aquatica Chapm.
Spurge Family (Euphorbiaceae)

Description: This attractive species has toothed, narrowly lanceolate leaves from 1"–3" long, often with bright red stems. Flower stalks reach 4" tall and produce male flowers above and female flowers below. All parts exude milky sap if broken and can irritate the mouth and eyes.

Bloom Season: All year

Habitat/Range: Freshwater wetlands and wet prairies of the southeastern United States.

Comments: *Stillingia* honors English naturalist Benjamin Stillingfleet (1702–1771). The name *aquatica* means "of wetlands." It is also called corkwood because the stems float and were used as fishing corks. The similar queen's delight *(Stillingia sylvatica)* is common in dry pinelands and sandhills. The erect inflorescence has been fancifully compared to male genitalia, hence the name queen's delight. Both species were used medicinally to treat syphilis, spasms, boils, and liver ailments.

STICKY JOINTVETCH
Aeschynomene viscidula Michx.
Pea Family (Fabaceae)

Description: The leaves of this prostrate species are divided into ovate leaflets that average ½"–⅝" long and ¼"–⅜" wide. The flowers are solitary and typically widely spaced along the stems. The jointed, hairy fruits are flattened on one side.

Bloom Season: May–December

Habitat/Range: Sandhills, scrub, and pinelands from Georgia to Texas south through Florida and the Neotropics.

Comments: *Aeschynomene* is Greek for "ashamed" and relates to the sensitive leaflets of some species that fold when touched. The name *viscidula* refers to the viscid, or sticky, hairs on the stems and leaves. This species occurs through northern and central Florida down the east coast to mainland Miami-Dade County east of Everglades National Park. The young leaves serve as larval food of the barred yellow butterfly. The related shyleaf *(Aeschynomene americana)* has narrow, feathery leaflets.

GRAY NICKER
Caesalpinia bonduc (L.) Roxb.
Pea Family (Fabaceae)

Description: The spiny stems of this vining species have evenly bipinnate leaves that are armed beneath with wickedly sharp recurved thorns. The leaflets are ¾"–1½" long and ½"–¾" wide. Fragrant, ⅜" flowers are crowded on erect stalks. The pods are covered with short spines and contain 1–2 marblelike, hard, gray seeds.

Bloom Season: All year

Habitat/Range: Coastal areas worldwide.

Comments: *Caesalpinia* honors Italian botanist Andrea Caesalpino (1519–1603). The name *bonduc* is Arabic and means "little ball," alluding to the round seeds. The seeds have been used in the tropics to treat malaria and are referred to as "poorman's quinine." The seeds are buoyant in seawater and are carried long distances on ocean currents. It is a larval host of the martial scrub-hairstreak, nickerbean blue, ceraunus blue, and the imperiled Miami blue butterfly. Yellow nicker *(Caesalpinia major)* has yellow seeds.

DEERING'S PARTRIDGE PEA
Chamaecrista deeringiana Small & Pennell
Pea Family (Fabaceae)

Description: This perennial species averages 6"–9" tall. The compound leaves bear small leaflets in pairs of 20 or less. Solitary, flaccid, yellow flowers are produced from the leaf axils, with 5 unequal, ½" petals and prominent red anthers. The petals are red at the base.

Bloom Season: All year

Habitat/Range: Endemic to pine rocklands of southern Florida.

Comments: *Chamaecrista* means "on the ground" and "a crest." The name *deeringiana* honors philanthropist Charles Deering (1852–1927) who funded many of the botanical excursions made by John Kunkel Small (1869–1938) in Florida. Some botanists relegate this endemic species as a synonym of the annual, bushy, yellow-anthered *Chamaecrista fasciculata* that ranges across the eastern United States. Both are larval host plants of the little yellow, cloudless sulphur, gray hairstreak, and ceraunus blue butterflies.

SENSITIVE PEA

Chamaecrista nictitans (L.) Moench var. *aspera* (Muhl. ex Elliott) H. S. Irwin & Barnaby
Pea Family (Fabaceae)

Description: This variety of sensitive pea is covered with soft, shaggy hairs, usually with 3 or more stems to about 4' tall. The compound leaves are 1¼"–2¾" long and ⅜"–¾" wide with 7–32 small, hairy leaflets. The yellow flowers are less than ⅜" wide. The narrow pods average ¾" long and ⅛" wide and are covered with white hairs when young.

Bloom Season: Sporadically all year but principally from March to November

Habitat/Range: Pinelands along the coastal plain from Florida to South Carolina.

Comments: The name *nictitans* means "blinking" or "moving," relating to the leaves that fold against the rachis at night. The name *aspera* means "rough," in reference to the coarse hairs on the stems and pods. The typical variety is nearly glabrous. The leaves serve as larval food for the cloudless sulphur, gray hairstreak, and ceraunus blue butterflies.

SMOOTH RATTLEBOX

Crotalaria pallida Aiton var. *obovata* (G. Don) Polhill
Pea Family (Fabaceae)

Description: This weedy species stands 2'–5' tall with compound leaves divided into 3 obovate leaflets that range from 1"–2¾" long and ¾"–1½" wide. The stem terminates in an erect spike crowded with ½" yellow flowers bearing thin, reddish stripes. The pods are 1½" long and covered with short hairs.

Bloom Season: All year

Habitat/Range: Disturbed sites of the southeastern United States. Native to Africa.

Commments: *Crotalaria* refers to "a rattle," in reference to the seeds that rattle inside the mature pods. The same Greek word gave rise to the rattlesnake genus *Crotalus*. The name *pallida* relates to the pale pods and *obovata* refers to the obovate leaflets. This species is frequent in disturbed areas throughout the Everglades region. It resembles showy rattlebox *(Crotalaria spectabilis)* but differs by its 3 leaflets and narrower flowers with reddish stripes.

LOW RATTLEBOX
Crotalaria pumila Ortega
Pea Family (Fabaceae)

Description: Low rattlebox forms low mounds of stems to 12" tall. The compound leaves are divided into 3 leaflets from ¼"–⅜" long that are inversely egg shaped. The flower standard is oval and has thin red lines on a yellow background. The corolla is yellow with a keel that is bent at a sharp right angle.

Bloom Season: All year

Habitat/Range: Pinelands and grassy open areas from central and southern Florida to the Bahamas, and from the southwestern United States to South America.

Comments: The name *pumila* means "little," referring to the small stature of this species. This is a larval host plant of the bella moth, a day-flying moth with orangish pink forewings marked with white bands and black spots. The bright pink hind wings create a flash of color when the moth takes flight. Adult bella moths exude a toxic, frothy spit to defend against predators. Low rattlebox is common on Long Pine Key in Everglades National Park.

RABBITBELLS
Crotalaria rotundifolia J. F. Gmel
Pea Family (Fabaceae)

Description: Rabbitbells has prostrate (or slightly ascending) hairy stems with oval or oblong, alternate leaves that measure ½"–1¼" long and ¼"–½" wide. The leaves are hairy on the upper surface. The ⅜" flowers are often solitary on long stems. The pods are ¾"–1" long.

Bloom Season: All year

Habitat/Range: Flatwoods and sandhills from Maryland to Arkansas south through Florida and the Neotropics.

Comments: The name *rotundifolia* refers to the oval (round) leaves produced by some plants. Botanist John Kunkel Small (1869–1938) discovered this species on Big Pine Key in the Lower Florida Keys in 1913. It is occasional to frequent in the proper habitat throughout the Everglades region. Small bees are attracted to the flowers. The small, usually solitary flowers and round or oblong simple leaves combine to help tell this species apart from other members of the genus that share its habitat.

SHOWY RATTLEBOX
Crotalaria spectabilis Roth.
Pea Family (Fabaceae)

Description: Showy rattlebox is a 3' tall annual with simple, obovate leaves from 3"–6" long. The erect flower spike produces showy flowers averaging ¾" long and wide. Pendent, 1½" pods are green, turning brown at maturity.

Bloom Season: All year

Habitat/Range: Pinelands and dry disturbed sites throughout Florida. Native to the Indo-Malaysia region.

Comments: The name *spectabilis* means "spectacular" or "showy." Eating the seeds will cause intense abdominal pain combined with vomiting, bloody diarrhea, and liver damage. The plant poisons grazing livestock and the seeds can be fatal to poultry. It was purposely introduced in 1921 as a forage crop before its poisonous properties were realized. It is a ubiquitous roadside weed in Florida and is sometimes grown as green manure for its nitrogen fixing properties. In herbal medicine it is used to treat contagious skin infections.

TROPICAL PUFF
Neptunia pubescens Benth.
Pea Family (Fabaceae)

Description: This low, creeping plant has compound leaves divided into 3–4 pairs of segments that divide again into many tiny leaflets. The complex, tightly arranged ½" clusters of flowers are terminal on stalks averaging 2"–3½" tall and bear many stamens. The hairy pods are about 1" long and ⅜" wide.

Bloom Season: April–November

Habitat/Range: Flatwoods, margins of salt marshes, and disturbed sites from Texas to Florida and the Neotropics.

Comments: *Neptunia* honors Neptune, the mythological Greek god of the sea, and relates to members of the genus that grow in coastal habitats. The name *pubescens* alludes to the soft hairs (pubescence) covering the stems and leaves of this species. The leaflets fold together at night and also close quickly when touched. Small bees are attracted to the flowers for pollen and are effective pollinators. Some species are eaten as pot herbs in tropical Asia.

DOLLARLEAF
Rhynchosia reniformis DC.
Pea Family (Fabaceae)

Description: Dollarleaf bears a single rounded leaflet (rarely 3) that is about 1" in diameter with netted veins, resinous dots, and long, hairy petioles. Small, pealike, ¼" flowers are in axillary clusters. The oblong pods are ½"–¾" long with soft hairs along the sutures.

Bloom Season: January–September

Habitat/Range: Dry, sandy pinelands from North Carolina to Texas south through Florida.

Comments: *Rhynchosia* is Greek for "a beak," and alludes to the beaklike keel petals. The name *reniformis* means "kidney shaped," referring to the leaflet shape. The common name also relates to the leaflet, which is about the size of a silver dollar. Only 1 other member of this genus in Florida has 1 leaflet and it has a trailing or twining growth habit. Other species have 3 leaflets. Dollarleaf frequently flowers in burned areas long before other plants have resprouted. It is also called snoutbean.

CHEESYTOES
Stylosanthes hamata (L.) Taub.
Pea Family (Fabaceae)

Description: This ground-hugging species has a line of silky hairs on the stem and its compound, alternate leaves are divided into 3 narrow leaflets from ¼"–¾" long and ¼" wide. The ³⁄₁₆" flowers are pale yellow, sometimes partly red. The small pods have 2 fertile segments and a hooked beak on the tip.

Bloom Season: All year

Habitat/Range: Dry pinelands, coastal strand, and disturbed sites of central and southern Florida to the Neotropics.

Comments: *Stylosanthes* is Greek for "column flower," referring to the columnlike calyx tube of the flower. The name *hamata* means "hooked," referring to the beak on the pods. The leaves serve as larval food for the barred yellow butterfly. Although seldom cultivated it would make a great trouble-free, drought-tolerant ground cover. Pencilflower *(Stylosanthes calcicola)* differs by typically having a straight beak on the pods and only 1 fertile segment.

COWPEA
Vigna luteola (Jacq.) Benth.
Pea Family (Fabaceae)

Description: Cowpea is a weedy vine with alternate, compound leaves on long petioles. There are 3 lanceolate leaflets, each about 1½" long and ⅝" wide. The ¾" flowers are produced in few-flowered clusters at the tops of tall, angled stalks that stand well above the foliage.

Bloom Season: All year

Habitat/Range: A wide variety of habitats including disturbed sites of the southern United States, Bermuda, and the Neotropics.

Comments: *Vigna* honors Italian professor Dominicus Vigna (1581–1647) who wrote a commentary on Theophrastus in 1625. The name *luteola* means "yellow," in reference to the flower color. This is a larval host plant of the gray hairstreak, cassius blue, ceraunus blue, and long-tailed skipper butterflies. The plant is used in Polynesia to cure "ghost sickness," a perceived ailment caused by supernatural powers. It is sometimes grown as a green manure in croplands.

CAROLINA REDROOT
Lachnanthes caroliana (Lam.) Dandy
Bloodwort Family (Haemodoraceae)

Description: The leaves of redroot are mostly basal, spreading in a fan like an iris. A flowering plant is typically 12"–24" tall. The inflorescence is yellowish and covered with copious soft hairs. Flowers are yellow to reddish brown.

Bloom Season: May–September

Habitat/Range: Wet soils of swamps, savannas, and flatwoods from Nova Scotia south to Florida and Cuba.

Comments: *Lachnanthes* means "wool flower" and alludes to the wooly inflorescence. The name *caroliana* refers to the Carolinas. Native Americans used redroot to produce mental stimulation and to develop "a heroic attitude." A tonic made from the roots was said to cause "brilliancy and fearless expression of the eye." The common name relates to a red dye extracted from the roots and used to color hair and clothing, noted by William Bartram (1739–1823) in 1789 during his travels across the southern states.

FRINGED YELLOW STARGRASS
Hypoxis juncea Sm.
Yellow Stargrass Family (Hypoxidaceae)

Description: The rushlike leaves of this species are rolled inward (involute). The leaves rarely exceed 8" long and ⅛" wide and have long hairs on the undersurface with a wide midrib. The erect flower stalk is usually finely pubescent and topped by a single (rarely 2), starlike, ½" flower.

Bloom Season: All year

Habitat/Range: Flatwoods and low depressions from North Carolina to northeastern Texas south in Florida to the Big Cypress Swamp and into the West Indies.

Comments: *Hypoxis* is a Greek name originally used for a plant with sour leaves. The name *juncea* means "rushlike," referring to the leaves that somewhat resemble those of a species of rush *(Juncus)*. Bristleseed yellow stargrass *(Hypoxis wrightii)* is the only species that occurs in Everglades National Park and it has basal flowers with flattened, hairy leaves that are longer and wider than this species.

HORNED BLADDERWORT
Utricularia cornuta Michx.
Bladderwort Family (Lentibulariaceae)

Description: Horned Bladderwort is a delicately branched, aquatic species with creeping stems and thin, filamentous leaves. Tiny, bladderlike traps are produced on the leaf margins. The erect, wiry, 4"–16" raceme is topped with 1–8 yellow flowers. Each flower measures about ⅝" and bears a prominent spur.

Bloom Season: All year

Habitat/Range: Freshwater wetlands from Newfoundland and Quebec to Texas and Florida.

Comments: *Utricularia* is Latin for "little bag," alluding to the small, baglike traps on the leaves of all species. When a tiny aquatic organism triggers a trap it is sucked inside where digestive enzymes absorb nutrients from the prey. The name *cornuta* means "horned," in reference to the curved spur of the flower. Although aquatic it frequently flowers while stranded in mud. This is a common species that can form spreading colonies in shallow water.

LEAFY BLADDERWORT

Utricularia foliosa L.
Bladderwort Family (Lentibulariaceae)

Description: This free-floating, submerged, carnivorous plant has a mucilaginous coating on the stems and filamentous leaves. The leafless flowering stems stand above the water surface and bear yellow flowers that measure ⅝"–¾" wide. It reproduces by seeds and fragmentation. The small bladderlike traps are visible along the stems.

Bloom Season: Principally June–November

Habitat/Range: Freshwater lakes, ponds, and swamps of Africa, North America, and South America.

Comments: The name *foliosa* means "leafy." In the Everglades region look for this common species in open water, especially around culvert pipes, lake margins, and deep, open areas in sloughs and marshes. This is 1 of 7 members of the genus in Everglades National Park and 1 of 9 species in Corkscrew Swamp. It is sometimes cultivated in home water gardens. Fish and turtles graze on the leaves and stems of all species.

FRINGED BLADDERWORT

Utricularia simulans Pilg.
(Also *Utricularia fimbriata* Kunth, misapplied)
Bladderwort Family (Lentibulariaceae)

Description: This petite carnivorous species has small traps underground or along its tiny threadlike leaves in shallow water. The inflorescence is erect from 1"–4" tall with 1–5 flowers congested on top of the frail stem. The calyx lobes are deeply divided into pointed teeth. The flowers are ³⁄₁₆" wide or slightly wider.

Bloom Season: June–January, peaking in late October

Habitat/Range: Sandy flatwoods of central and southern Florida, the Neotropics, and tropical Africa.

Comments: The name *simulans* means "resembling," in reference to its similarity to other species. In the Bear Island area of the Big Cypress Swamp it grows in wet, sandy soil in openings surrounded by saw palmetto *(Serenoa repens)*. It is not in Everglades National Park. Photographing it requires lying flat on the ground with the ticks and chiggers.

ZIGZAG BLADDERWORT
Utricularia subulata L.
Bladderwort Family (Lentibulariaceae)

Description: The delicate, threadlike stems of this minuscule plant creep along the bottom in shallow water or may be terrestrial in moist sand. Leaflike segments are either absent or narrowly linear to ⅜" long. The thin, erect raceme averages 1"–3" tall and is most often topped by a single blossom (or 2–8) that measures about ⅛"–³⁄₁₆" wide.

Bloom Season: April–December

Habitat/Range: Cosmopolitan in shallow water or moist soils. It ranges south in Florida into Everglades National Park.

Comments: The name *subulata* means "awl-shaped," in reference to the spur. Although small in stature, flowering colonies are quite attractive. When a plant produces numerous flowers the stem zigzags to help support the weight, hence the common name. The diminutive traps capture nematodes and other tiny organisms that live in the soil.

SMALL'S FLAX
Linum carteri Small var. *smallii* C. M. Rogers
Flax Family (Linaceae)

Description: Small's flax has narrow, glabrous, alternate leaves ranging from ½"–¾" long. The 6"–12"-tall stems are sparingly branched with forked flower spikes. The ¾" flowers have slightly jagged, squared-off petals.

Bloom Season: Mostly February–April

Habitat/Range: Endemic to pinelands and open, sandy sites of central and southern mainland Florida.

Comments: *Linum* is an ancient Latin name for flax. The name *carteri* honors Pennsylvania botanist Joel Jackson Carter (1843–1912) who explored southern Florida with his botanist friend John Kunkel Small (1869–1938), whom the variety name *smallii* honors. This endangered species is locally common in the Everglades region and can be confused with pitted stripeseed *(Piriqueta cistoides)* but it has much wider leaves. The similar Carter's flax *(Linum carteri* var. *carteri)* is endemic to Miami-Dade County and has hairy leaves.

FLORIDA YELLOW FLAX
Linum floridanum (Planch.) Trel.
Flax Family (Linaceae)

Description: This wiry species ranges from 8"–24" tall with narrow, alternate, overlapping leaves facing upward on the stems. The leaves measure ½"–⅝" long and ⅛" wide. The ⅜" flowers are produced at or near the tips of the stems with only 1 to several flowers open at a time.

Bloom Season: All year

Habitat/Range: Sandhills and flatwoods of the southeastern United States.

Comments: The name *floridanum* means "of Florida." The similar but very rare sand flax *(Linum arenicola)* is endemic to Miami-Dade County and the Lower Florida Keys (Monroe County) and has a pair of red glands at the leaf bases. Stiff yellow flax *(Linum medium* var. *texanum)* is also similar but has conspicuous glands on the margins of the inner sepals. Linen and linseed oil are derived from European and Mediterranean members of this genus. Larvae of the variegated fritillary butterfly feed on this and other members of the genus.

POORMAN'S PATCH
Mentzelia floridana Nutt.
Stick-Leaf Family (Loasaceae)

Description: This rather weedy species has ascending branches with hairy, ovate, alternate leaves that measure ¾"–2" long and half as wide. Yellow, 5-petaled flowers are solitary in the upper leaf axils and measure about 1" wide.

Bloom Season: January–April

Habitat/Range: Coastal sandy areas of Florida and the islands of New Providence and Eleuthera in the Bahamas.

Comments: *Mentzelia* honors German botanist Christian Mentzel (1622–1701). The name *floridana* means "of Florida." The leaves of this species cling tightly to clothing and are difficult to remove. The barbed hairs can cut off the feet and legs of insects that alight on the leaves, which may be a ploy by the plant to utilize dead insects as a natural fertilizer. The common name refers to downtrodden people who walk through fields of this plant, resulting in their clothing being covered by the leaves, like patches.

SLIPPERY BURR
Corchorus siliquosus L.
Mallow Family (Malvaceae)

Description: This is a bushy species to 4' tall with hairy stems and toothed, pointed, oblong-lanceolate leaves from ½"–3" long. The axillary flowers are usually solitary and average about ½" wide with many stamens.

Bloom Season: May–December

Habitat/Range: Hammock margins and disturbed sites of Florida, Alabama, Mississippi, and the Neotropics.

Comments: *Corchorus* is from the ancient Greek word *korkoros*. Carolus Linnaeus (1707–1778) used the name for this group of plants in 1753. The name *siliquosus* refers to a silique, which are fruits that measure at least 3 times longer than their width. It was formerly in the basswood family (Tiliaceae). The dried leaves and seeds will thicken soups and stews, causing the water to become mucilaginous, hence the common name. The health benefit in eating the leaves is said to exceed that of spinach, collards, and other cooked greens.

COMMON FANPETALS
Sida ulmifolia Mill.
(Also *Sida acuta* Burm. f.)
Mallow Family (Malvaceae)

Description: This ubiquitous weed stands 1'–3' tall with alternate, toothed leaves that average ¾"–1" long and ½"–¾" wide. The ½"–⅝" flowers are axillary on short stalks.

Bloom Season: All year

Habitat/Range: Pinelands and disturbed sites of the southeastern United States. Circumtropical.

Comments: *Sida* is an ancient Greek name. The name *ulmifolia* means the leaves resemble a species of elm *(Ulmus)*. Indian hemp *(Sida rhombifolia)* is similar but has rhomboid leaves with flowers on longer stalks. Elliott's fanpetals *(Sida elliottii)* is low growing with narrowly linear leaves and larger flowers. Spreading fanpetals *(Sida abutifolia)* is prostrate and has ⅜" orange flowers. Members of the genus are larval host plants of the gray hairstreak, mallow scrub-hairstreak, common checkered-skipper, white checkered-skipper, and tropical checkered-skipper butterflies.

SLEEPY MORNING

Waltheria indica L.
Mallow Family (Malvaceae)

Description: Sleepy morning is a shrubby species to 6' tall. The ovate to oblong leaves are alternate, about 2" long and ⅝" wide, and covered with soft, white, wooly hairs. The 5-petaled, ¼" flowers are crowded together in axillary clusters.

Bloom Season: All year

Habitat/Range: Pinelands, hammock margins, and disturbed sites of central and southern Florida. Cosmopolitan.

Comments: *Waltheria* honors German professor Augustin Friedrich Walther (1688–1746). The name *indica* means "of India." This is a relative of the well-known hibiscus and the cacao tree *(Theobroma cacao),* which is the source of cocoa powder and chocolate. It is used medicinally in some cultures to treat acne, sore throat, asthma, painful menstruation, and unwanted pregnancy. The common name refers to the habit of the flowers to open long after sunrise. It is a larval host plant of the mallow scrub-hairstreak butterfly.

YELLOW COLICROOT

Aletris lutea Small
Bog Asphodel Family (Nartheciaceae)

Description: The basal rosette of leaves resembles a miniature species of agave. The leaves are broadly linear, ranging from 1½"–6" long and ⅜"–⅞" wide. The raceme stands 12" tall or more with yellow flowers spaced along the top half. Each flower is about ⅜" long and ⅛" wide and covered with mealy bumps.

Bloom Season: February–September

Habitat/Range: Flatwoods, prairies, and open cypress depressions of the southeastern United States.

Comments: *Aletris* means "to grind," alluding to the cornmeal-like texture of the flowers. Aletris was a legendary Greek slave who ground corn. The name *lutea* means "yellow." The common name relates to its use by Native Americans and settlers as a bitter tea to treat colic, dysentery, and other ailments. The leaves were also dried into a powder and mixed with whiskey to treat backaches and sore breasts or brewed into a tea to treat diarrhea and stomach problems.

SPATTERDOCK

Nuphar advena (Aiton) Aiton f.
(Also *Nuphar lutea* [L.] Small)
Waterlily Family (Nymphaeaceae)

Description: Spatterdock leaf blades typically stand above the water and measure 8"–12" long and 6"–8" wide with a deep notch at the base. The flowers have 6–9 yellow sepals that form a cup. The true petals are small and scalelike, crowded among the stamens.

Bloom Season: All year

Habitat/Range: Widespread in freshwater habitats from the United States to Eurasia.

Comments: *Nuphar* comes from *nîlûfar,* an Arabic name for the plant. The name *advena* means "adventive" and relates to using any means to spread from one place to another. Spatterdock is an aggressive colonizer, sometimes covering the entire water surface of ponds and roadside canals. It is generally found in much deeper water than waterlilies (*Nymphaea* spp.). The seeds are an important food source for waterfowl and the leaves provide cover for fish and other aquatic life in its habitat.

YELLOW WATERLILY

Nymphaea mexicana Zucc.
Waterlily Family (Nymphaeaceae)

Description: The leaf blades of this species are deeply notched, green above, red below, and may reach up to 10" wide. The showy, 3"–4" flowers bear 12–30 petals and are open from midday to late afternoon, closing at night. They may be floating or held just above the water surface.

Bloom Season: May–October

Habitat/Range: Ponds and streams of the southern United States south through mainland Florida and Mexico.

Comments: *Nymphaea* is Greek for "water nymph." The name *mexicana* refers to Mexico, where it was first collected in 1832. In the Everglades region this species occurs in freshwater habitats of southwest Florida. The bananalike root tubers are an important food item for canvasback ducks in their winter range. It hybridizes with the native scented waterlily *(Nymphaea odorata)* to form a vigorous, sterile cross known as *Nymphaea* x *thiona.* The hybrid is intermediate in all aspects.

SEASIDE PRIMROSEWILLOW

Ludwigia maritima R. M. Harper
Evening Primrose Family (Onagraceae)

Description: Stems of this species are simple or with a few branches near the top. Stems range from 2'–3' tall and are usually reddish to golden with coarse hairs. Leaves are alternate, ovate to lanceolate, and average 1"–3" long and ½" wide (sometimes red). The showy, 1" flowers are axillary.

Bloom Season: May–November

Habitat/Range: Flatwoods and moist habitats of the southeastern United States.

Comments: *Ludwigia* honors German botanist and professor of medicine Christian Gottlieb Ludwig (1709–1773). The name *maritima* refers to "growing by the sea," where this species often occurs. There are 25 native *Ludwigia* species in Florida. Mexican primrosewillow *(Ludwigia octovalvis)* is a common shrub of the Everglades region with 2" yellow flowers. Creeping primrosewillow *(Ludwigia repens)* is a trailing succulent herb that often grows underwater.

CUTLEAF EVENING PRIMROSE

Oenothera laciniata Hill
Evening Primrose Family (Onagraceae)

Description: This trailing species has lobed leaves to 2" long and ⅜"–¾" wide. The flowers are ¾"–1" wide with 4 petals and 4 petal-like sepals. The seed capsule is narrowly cylindrical measuring ¾"–1½" long.

Bloom Season: All year

Habitat/Range: Sandy woods and fields from Vermont to South Dakota through Texas and Florida.

Comments: One translation of *Oenothera* is that it was taken from *oinos* (wine) and *thera* (imbibing), relating to its use in making wine "to make the heart merry." Other translations involve wine in one way or another. The name *laciniata* means "formed into narrow divisions," alluding to the leaves. The flowers open before dusk and close by late morning. Evening primroses are a natural source of gamma-lineolic acid that promotes women's health, especially for premenstrual syndrome. The leaves are larval food of the galium sphinx moth.

SPIDER ORCHID
Brassia caudata (L.) Lindl.
Orchid Family (Orchidaceae)

Description: This epiphytic orchid has pseudo-bulbs covered by sheathing bracts with 1–2 leaves that average 4"–6" long and ¾"–1" wide. The spindly flowers are about 2" long.

Bloom Season: March–July

Habitat/Range: Hardwood forests of southern Florida (Miami-Dade County) and the Neotropics.

Comments: *Brassia* honors 18th-century British botanical illustrator William Brass. The name *caudata* refers to the long tails on the flowers. In Florida this orchid was first discovered in Nixon-Lewis Hammock (Miami-Dade County) in 1915 but was taken by collectors. It was rediscovered in an Everglades hammock on Long Pine Key in 1917. The last known plant there was killed by the January 1977 freeze that brought snow to Miami. It is doubtful that it still exists in Florida but there is always the chance of a natural reintroduction. The flowers mimic spiders and are pollinated by wasps that attack them.

RIBBON ORCHID
Campylocentrum pachyrrhizum (Rchb. f.) Rolfe
Orchid Family (Orchidaceae)

Description: The leafless ribbon orchid is comprised of flattened roots radiating outward from an indistinct stem. The grayish-green roots are about ³⁄₁₆" wide with orange growing tips. From 12–25 flowers are in ½"–2", pendent, 2-ranked clusters. The ¼" pale yellow flowers are sometimes marked with pink.

Bloom Season: September–November

Habitat/Range: Hardwood swamps of southern Florida (Collier County) and the Neotropics.

Comments: *Campylocentrum* is Greek for "crooked spur," in reference to the bent spur of the flowers in this genus. The name *pachyrrhizum* is Greek for "thick root." When not in flower it can be confused with the ghost orchid *(Dendrophylax lindenii)* but it has white-flecked roots with green growing tips. In the Fakahatchee Swamp this orchid can sometimes be found growing on the moss-covered trunks of native royal palms *(Roystonea regia)*.

PARANÁ CIGAR ORCHID
Cyrtopodium flavum Link & Otto ex Rchb.
Orchid Family (Orchidaceae)

Description: The pseudobulbs of this terrestrial orchid can reach 2'–2½' long with linear leaves that are held on one plane. The leaves average 6"–14" long and 1"–2" wide. Flowers are about ¾" wide on erect stalks.

Bloom Season: February–May

Habitat/Range: Pinelands, cypress swamps, and disturbed sites of southern Florida. Native to eastern Brazil.

Comments: *Cyrtopodium* is Greek for "curved foot," alluding to the curved column foot. The name *flavum* means "yellow," in reference to the flower color. It was described from plants collected in the Brazilian state of Paraná in 1830 (as *Cyrtopodium paranaense*). Botanist George Newton Avery (1922–1983) made the first collection of this handsome orchid in Florida (Miami-Dade County) in 1972. It has since been found in several locations in Broward and Collier Counties. Some populations harbor thousands of plants.

COWHORN ORCHID
Cyrtopodium punctatum (L.) Lindl.
Orchid Family (Orchidaceae)

Description: This impressive epiphytic orchid has long, cigar-shaped pseudobulbs with linear, pleated leaves that spread in a single plane. The leaves wither away in winter leaving sharp-tipped sheaths that peel away with age. One flower spike can produce 30–50 blossoms, each about 1⅛" wide.

Bloom Season: March–May

Habitat/Range: Hardwood swamps, hammocks, and mangroves of southern Florida and the Neotropics.

Comments: The name *punctatum* refers to the spotted flowers. Abram Paschell Garber (1838–1881) discovered this orchid in Florida near Miami in 1867. It was once common in the Everglades but is now restricted to secluded areas. In 1923 botanist John Kunkel Small (1869–1938) wrote about collecting a specimen that had 201 pseudobulbs that took 6 men to carry it. He then planted it at the Biscayne Bay estate of his wealthy industrialist friend, Charles Deering (1852–1927). It occurs from Everglades National Park to the Big Cypress National Preserve west to Corkscrew Swamp (Collier, Lee, Miami-Dade, and Monroe Counties). This state-listed endangered species is also called cigar orchid and beeswarm orchid. The latter name relates to the flowers resembling a swarm of bees hovering above the plant.

FLORIDA DANCING LADY ORCHID
Oncidium ensatum Lindl.
(Also *Oncidium floridanum* Ames)
Orchid Family (Orchidaceae)

Description: This orchid is usually terrestrial with long, linear leaves that are ½"–1" wide and up to 4' long, often spreading fanlike. The branched flower spike bears many ¾"–1" flowers and may exceed 7' tall.

Bloom Season: April–August

Habitat/Range: Hardwood forests of southern Florida (Miami-Dade and Collier Counties) and the Neotropics.

Comments: *Oncidium* is Greek for "little swelling," referring to the warty calluses on the surface of the lip. The name *ensatum* means "sword-like," referring to the leaves. This state-listed endangered species was first discovered in Florida in 1903 and is now mostly restricted to Everglades National Park. Members of this genus offer no pollinator reward but mimic nectar-producing flowers in the malpighia family (Malpighiaceae) to lure small bees and other potential pollinators through deceit.

DOLLAR ORCHID
Prosthechea boothiana (Lindl.) W. E. Higgins var. *erythronioides* (Small) W. E. Higgins
(Also *Encyclia boothiana* [Lindl.] Dressler)
Orchid Family (Orchidaceae)

Description: This epiphyte is recognizable by its round, flattened pseudobulbs that are the size of a silver dollar. The 1–3 glossy, lanceolate leaves measure 2"–4" long and ½"–1" wide. The flower spike bears 1–12 waxy flowers to about ⅞" wide.

Bloom Season: August–October

Habitat/Range: Epiphytic in coastal forests of southern Florida, Bahamas, and the Neotropics.

Comments: *Prosthechea* refers to the appendage on the back of the column. The name *boothiana* honors British botanist William Beattie Booth (1804–1874). The name *erythronioides* refers to the similarity of the leaves to an *Erythronium* (Liliaceae). It is a state-listed endangered species due to collecting and habitat loss but is locally common in coastal forests of Everglades National Park and the Florida Keys.

PRICKLY POPPY
Argemone mexicana L.
Poppy Family (Papaveraceae)

Description: Prickly poppy is a wickedly spiny annual that averages 1'–3' tall. The deeply lobed, alternate leaves are sessile, ranging from 3"–8" long with sharp tips terminating each lobe and with sharp spines along the bottom of the midvein. The flowers have 6 bright yellow petals that form a tuliplike cup, averaging 1¼"–1½" wide. The stems and leaves exude yellow sap if broken.

Bloom Season: January–June

Habitat/Range: Disturbed soils of the United States and Mexico. Widely naturalized.

Comments: *Argemone* means "cataract," a name originally used for another poppylike plant believed to cure cataract of the eye. The name *mexicana* means "of Mexico." The seeds and latex are poisonous to grazing animals. It is used medicinally to treat warts, malaria, and migraine headaches as well as to cleanse the body following birth. Poisoning from consuming the latex causes extreme swelling of the legs.

PITTED STRIPESEED
Piriqueta cistoides (L.) Griseb. subsp. *caroliniana* (Walter) Arbo.
Passionflower Family (Passifloraceae)

Description: This frequently encountered species averages 4"–8" tall and has toothed, linear to elliptic-ovate leaves that can be pubescent or smooth. The leaves range from ¾"–2" long and ¼"–⅝" wide. The flowers average ¾" wide with 5 stamens and 3 bushy-tipped stigmas. Pitted seeds are in 3-valved fruits.

Bloom Season: All year

Habitat/Range: Marshes and pinelands of the southeastern United States, Bahamas, and West Indies.

Comments: *Piriqueta* is a Guiana name of an African member of the genus. The name *cistoides* relates to the resemblance of the flowers to rock-roses in the genus *Cistus*. The subspecies *caroliniana* means "of Carolina." Gulf fritillary butterflies readily use this species as a larval host plant. It is also called morning buttercup and piriquet. It can be confused with members of the genus *Linum*, which do not have bushy-tipped stigmas.

RAMGOAT DASHALONG
Turnera ulmifolia L.
Passionflower Family (Passifloraceae)

Description: Ramgoat dashalong is a bushy species to about 3' tall with dark green, oblong-elliptic, coarsely toothed leaves that reach 2" long and 1" wide. The flowers are about 1½" wide and close at night.

Bloom Season: All year

Habitat/Range: Dunes and disturbed sites of central and southern Florida. Native to the Neotropics.

Comments: *Turnera* honors Protestant physician and herbalist William Turner (1508–1568). The name *ulmifolia* relates to the resemblance of the leaves to elms *(Ulmus)*. The common name relates to male goats in Jamaica that become sexually frisky after eating the plant. It is also called buttercups and yellow alder. It is used medicinally as an aphrodisiac and to treat depression, diabetes, and Parkinson's disease. The turnera family (Turneraceae) was recently moved into the passionflower family (Passifloraceae) by molecular taxonomists.

CANDYROOT
Polygala nana (Michx.) DC
Milkwort Family (Polygalaceae)

Description: This biennial is only ¾"–2" tall with spatulate, ¾"–2⅜" leaves that form a small rosette. The compact raceme measures about ⅜"–¾" long and ⁵⁄₁₆"–½" wide. The flowers are lemon yellow with elliptic wings that are rolled inward at the tip. Seeds are less than 1 millimeter long.

Bloom Season: All year

Habitat/Range: Flatwoods, seepage bogs, and coastal swales from New York to Pennsylvania along the coastal plain to Louisiana and Florida (south to Broward and Collier Counties).

Comments: *Polygala* means "much milk," in the fanciful belief that milkworts could increase milk flow in cattle. The name *nana* refers to its small stature. The common name refers to the licorice-like flavor of the roots. The very similar Small's milkwort *(Polygala smallii)* is a Florida endemic ranging along the east coast from Miami-Dade County north to Indian River County. It has seeds longer than 1 millimeter.

LOW PINEBARREN MILKWORT
Polygala ramosa Elliott
Milkwort Family (Polygalaceae)

Description: The racemes of this species reach 12" tall with a basal rosette of spatulate leaves, mostly ⅜"–¾" long, but may not be present when flowering. The erect raceme is branched at the top. The flowers are in tight clusters and each flower is about ³⁄₁₆" long.

Bloom Season: February–September

Habitat/Range: Pine savannas, flatwoods, and pond margins from New Jersey to Texas south in Florida to Corkscrew Swamp and the Big Cypress National Preserve.

Comments: The name *ramosa* means "branched." This species is very similar to tall pinebarren milkwort *(Polygala cymosa)*, which does not occur in the Everglades region. The roots of some milkworts have been fermented to make alcoholic beverages and are important medicinal herbs used principally for respiratory ailments and to stimulate clearing of phlegm in the lungs. They are also used to reduce wheezing and to treat pneumonia.

YELLOW MILKWORT
Polygala rugelii Shuttlew. ex Chapm.
Milkwort Family (Polygalaceae)

Description: The basal leaves of this annual or biennial (sometimes perennial) species are in an irregular rosette and often not present when flowering. The leaves are spatulate (spatula-shaped), narrow at the base, and range from 1¼"–2¼" long and ¼"–½" wide. The rounded flower clusters are ⅜"–1¼" long and 1" wide, held on stems that may exceed 24" in height. The flowers are lemon yellow.

Bloom Season: March–November

Habitat/Range: Endemic to wet flatwoods of peninsular Florida to the eastern panhandle.

Comments: The name *rugelii* honors German-born botanist Ferdinand Rugel (1806–1879), a professional field botanist who collected in Florida, Cuba, and the southern Appalachians. Yellow milkwort ranges south into the Big Cypress and Corkscrew Swamp region (absent from Everglades National Park) where it typically grows in the company of other members of the genus.

GROUNDCHERRY
Physalis walteri Nutt.
Nightshade Family (Solanaceae)

Description: Gray hairs cover the stems and leaves of this 6"–20"-tall species. The ovate to lanceolate leaves are 1½"–4" long with entire margins. The pendent, trumpet-shaped flowers are solitary, ranging from ½"–¾" long and wide. The round, yellow fruits are encased in a lanternlike, papery calyx.

Bloom Season: All year

Habitat/Range: Coastal strand and pinelands of the southeastern United States to the Neotropics.

Comments: *Physalis* is Greek for "bladder," alluding to the inflated calyx. The name *walteri* honors botanist Thomas Walter (1740–1789). Some species are cultivated for their fruits and sold under the name husk tomato in markets and were an important food source long before the debut of the related tomato. Another species *(Physalis philadelphica)* is the popular *tomatillo* in Mexico. This and other species are larval food of the tomato hornworm and Carolina sphinx moths.

ROCKLAND LANTANA
Lantana depressa Small
Verbena Family (Verbenaceae)

Description: This is a low-spreading shrub to 12" tall with elliptic leaves ranging from ⅜"–1" long and ¼"–⅜" wide. The stems lack prickles. The leaves are shiny, roughly hairy, and toothed. The clustered flowers are tubular and measure ³⁄₁₆"–¼" long and ⅛" wide. The flowers open yellow and turn tawny orange.

Bloom Season: All year

Habitat/Range: Endemic to pine rocklands of southern Miami-Dade County, Florida.

Comments: *Lantana* is a name that relates to *Viburnum lantana* but was later applied to this group of plants. The name *depressa* refers to the low growth habit. It is listed as endangered mostly because its gene pool is being compromised by hybridization with the naturalized exotic *Lantana camara*. Hybrids are bushier with leaves that are more squared off at the base. Most all nursery-grown plants sold as *Lantana depressa* are low-growing cultivars or hybrids of *Lantana camara*.

ELLIOTT'S YELLOWEYED GRASS
Xyris elliottii Chapm.
Yelloweyed Grass Family (Xyridaceae)

Description: This species grows in dense, low tufts with narrow, flattened, fanlike leaves that resemble a miniature iris. The leaves range from 4"–10" tall and about ¼" wide. The narrow scape is 1–2 ribbed and is topped by an ovoid to elliptic conelike spike that bears 1–3 flowers, each with 3 petals that unfold in the morning.

Bloom Season: All year in the Everglades region

Habitat/Range: Wet flatwoods, savannas, and bogs from South Carolina to Alabama south through Florida, West Indies, and Central America.

Comments: *Xyris* comes from a Greek word meaning "razor" and refers to a species with 2-edged leaves that resemble swords. The name *elliottii* honors American legislator, banker, and botanist Stephen Elliott (1771–1830) of South Carolina. There are 24 *Xyris* species that are native to Florida (4 are endemic) with 11 species that range south into the Everglades region.

PUNCTURE VINE
Tribulus cistoides L.
Caltrop Family (Zygophyllaceae)

Description: This global traveler has stems that radiate outward from the base. The opposite, compound leaves are evenly pinnate with 5–10 pairs of softly hairy, elliptic leaflets from ⅜"–½" long and ¼" wide. The 5-petaled flowers are 1"–1½" wide. The ⅝"-wide fruits are armed with 4 stout, ¼" spines.

Bloom Season: All year

Habitat/Range: Sandy soils of beaches and disturbed sites of the southeastern United States and the Neotropics. Native to the Old World.

Comments: *Tribulus* is a Latinized form of the Greek word *tribolos*, or "caltrop," in reference to the spiny fruits. A caltrop is a metal ball with 4 sharp iron spikes used on battlefields in the 16th-century to thwart advancing foot soldiers. The name *cistoides* alludes to the similarity of the flowers to the genus *Cistus*. The spiny fruits can puncture feet, sandals, and bicycle tires. Airplane tires transport the fruits long distances.

BROWN AND GREEN FLOWERS

Epidendrum anceps

This section includes flowers that range from pale green to purplish brown. You may want to check the White and Yellow sections for very pale green or pale yellowish flowers if you cannot find what you are looking for here.

EASTERN POISON IVY
Toxicodendron radicans (L.) Kuntze
Cashew Family (Anacardiaceae)

Description: This well-known woody vine bears compound leaves with 3 entire or variously lobed leaflets that average 1"–4" long and ½"–3" wide. The flowers are in axillary clusters and measure ¼" wide. The ⅛" round fruits ripen white.

Bloom Season: January–July

Habitat/Range: Hardwood forests, swamps, and pinelands of eastern North America.

Comments: *Toxicodendron* means "poison tree." The name *radicans* refers to its habit of rooting along the stem. The sap contains *urushiol* that causes a blistering rash on sensitive people after a 24-hour or more delay and may require hospitalization. Smoke from burning poison ivy can cause severe and sometimes fatal respiratory difficulty. Birds eat the fruits without harm. It is related to mango, cashew, and pistachio. The related poisonwood *(Metopium toxiferum)* is a tree in the southern Everglades region that should also be avoided.

GREEN ANTELOPEHORN
Asclepias viridis Walter
Dogbane Family (Apocynaceae)

Description: This highly ornamental species may reach 2' tall but is usually sprawling. The leaves are narrowly oblong from 2½"–5" long and ½"–⅝" wide with yellow or reddish midveins. The flower clusters are showy with green, ⅜"–½" flowers. The 5 petals are not reflexed as in other species and there are 5 purplish stamens.

Bloom Season: February–September

Habitat/Range: Sandy pinelands from southern Florida to Texas, Tennessee, and Nebraska.

Comments: *Asclepias* was named for Aesculapius, the legendary Greek god of medicine. The name *viridis* refers to the green flower color. In the Everglades region this fire-dependent species is found in sandy pinelands on the Miami Rock Ridge east of Everglades National Park. The common name is a fanciful allusion to the resemblance of the pods to the horns of an antelope. It is a larval host plant of monarch, queen, and soldier butterflies in Florida.

POWDERY CATOPSIS

Catopsis berteroana (Schult. f.) Mez
Pineapple Family (Bromeliaceae)

Description: Powdery catopsis is easily identified by its light green, vaselike rosette of 12"–16" leaves that are covered with chalky powder at the base. The erect, branching, yellow flower spike may reach 3' in height and bears inconspicuous, white, tubular flowers.

Bloom Season: October–January

Habitat/Range: Hardwood swamps, hammocks, and mangroves from southern Florida and Mexico to Brazil.

Comments: *Catopsis* means "view," alluding to growing on tree branches. The name *berteroana* honors Italian botanist Carlo Luigi Giuseppe Bertero (1789–1831). According to the International Code of Botanical Nomenclature the older spelling of the species name *(berteroniana)* is invalid. The chalky powder on the leaf bases of this state-listed endangered species causes insects to slip into the leafy rosette where they drown, decompose, and supply nutrients to the plant.

SPANISH MOSS

Tillandsia usneoides (L.) L.
Pineapple Family (Bromeliaceae)

Description: This rootless epiphyte produces slender, elongated stems covered with silvery gray hairs. The threadlike strands hang in long clumps from trees, especially oaks and cypress. The leaves are 1"–2" long and ¹⁄₁₆" wide. Inconspicuous, fragrant flowers appear in the leaf axils.

Bloom Season: April–August

Habitat/Range: A variety of habitats of the southeastern United States and the Neotropics.

Comments: *Tillandsia* honors Swedish botanist Elias Tillands (1640–1693). The name *usneoides* refers to the resemblance of the leaves to the lichen genus *Usnea*. It has the widest natural range of all bromeliads and is sometimes used for bedding and packing material or dampened and tossed on campfires to smoke out mosquitoes. It is the larval host plant of the black-winged dahana moth and provides the preferred habitat of a species of jumping spider *(Pelegrina tillandsiae)*.

DELTOID SPURGE

Chamaesyce deltoidea (Engelm. ex Chapm.) Small
subsp. *deltoidea*
Spurge Family (Euphorbiaceae)

Description: This fire-dependent species forms small, dense mats across sandy pockets in pine rocklands. The leaves are ³⁄₃₂"–⅛" wide with inconspicuous, solitary, yellowish-green flowers measuring about ¹⁄₁₆" wide.

Bloom Season: All year

Habitat/Range: Endemic to pine rocklands on the Miami Rock Ridge in southern Miami-Dade County east of Everglades National Park.

Comments: *Chamaesyce* means "on the ground" and "fig," and alludes to the prostrate growth with figlike fruits. The name *deltoidea* refers to the deltoid (triangular) leaves. This is a federal and state-listed endangered species because its entire global range is restricted to remnant pine rockland parcels between SW 72 Street and SW 264 Street in southern Miami-Dade County. Mature plants measure about 8" across and resemble spilled green paint. It is also called wedge sandmat.

PINELAND SPURGE

Chamaesyce deltoidea (Engelm. ex Chapm.) Small
subsp. *pinetorum* (Small) A. Herndon
Spurge Family (Euphorbiaceae)

Description: This low-growing subspecies is conspicuously hairy with reddish, ascending stems to 4" long. The opposite leaves are triangular or ovate and measure about ⅛"–³⁄₁₆" wide. Inconspicuous yellowish-green flowers are about ¹⁄₁₆" wide.

Bloom Season: All year

Habitat/Range: Endemic to pine rocklands on the Miami Rock Ridge in southern Miami-Dade County.

Comments: The name *pinetorum* refers to its pineland habitat. This state-listed endangered subspecies of the deltoid spurge is currently a candidate for federal listing. It occurs from about SW 300 Street to Long Pine Key in Everglades National Park. The pine rockland habitat where it occurs is listed by the Florida Natural Areas Inventory as globally imperiled. A third imperiled subspecies (subsp. *serpyllum*) is endemic to Big Pine Key in the Lower Florida Keys.

COASTAL BEACH SPURGE
Chamaesyce mesembrianthemifolia (Jacq.) Dugand
Spurge Family (Euphorbiaceae)

Description: This coastal species is either prostrate or bushy to 30" tall with somewhat fleshy, ovate or elliptic leaves averaging ¼"–⅜" long with entire margins. The greenish-white axillary flowers are about ⅛" wide.

Bloom Season: All year

Habitat/Range: Coastal dunes and rocky shorelines from Florida to Bermuda and the Neotropics.

Comments: The cumbersome name *mesembrianthemifolia* means that the leaves resemble those of a member of the genus *Mesembryanthemum* (Aizoaceae). The sap has been used in the Caribbean to treat stab wounds from sea urchins. All parts of the plant are toxic and can be lethal if eaten by humans and livestock. It is a common constituent of beach dune vegetation along both coasts of mainland Florida and is sometimes used in coastal landscaping. James Cosmo Dobres Melvill (1845–1929) first reported it from Key West in 1884.

BEACH TEA
Croton punctatus Jacq.
Spurge Family (Euphorbiaceae)

Description: The leaves and stems of this bushy species (to 3') are densely covered with star-shaped hairs. The leaves are entire, elliptic to ovate, and range from ⅝"–2" long and ½"–1" wide. Greenish male and female flowers are produced on the same plant, and measure about ⅛" wide.

Bloom Season: All year

Habitat/Range: Beach dunes from North Carolina to Texas south through Florida and the Neotropics.

Comments: *Croton* comes from *kroton*, a Greek name for ticks, and is used for this group of plants because of the resemblance of the seeds to the blood-sucking parasites. The name *punctatus* means "spotted" or "marked with dots," in reference to the dots that cover the leaves. Members of this genus are the source of croton oil, once used as a purgative but now abandoned because overdoses caused coma and death. A tea from the leaves has been used in home remedies and is said to help remedy colds, fevers, and cramps.

RATTAIL ORCHID
Bulbophyllum pachyrachis (A. Rich.) Griseb.
Orchid Family (Orchidaceae)

Description: From 1–3 oblong leaves emerge from angled pseudobulbs with ¼" flowers arranged along a pendent, thickened spike that measures about 6"–7" long, resembling a rat's tail.

Bloom Season: October–December

Habitat/Range: Fakahatchee Swamp in Collier County, Florida, and the Neotropics.

Comments: *Bulbophyllum* refers to the leafy pseudobulb of the type species. The name *pachyrachis* alludes to the thick flower stem. Fred Fuchs Jr. (1923–1990) discovered this species in Florida while exploring the Fakahatchee Swamp in 1956. By 1962 collectors had found the slough and it has not been seen in Florida since. A methodical 3-day search in 1977 by the author using a detailed map provided by Carlyle Luer (1922–) proved fruitless but the Fakahatchee Swamp has a long history of hiding rare botanical gems in unexplored sloughs deep in the interior.

SPECKLED LADIES'-TRESSES
Cyclopogon cranichoides (Grisb.) Schltr.
(Also *Spiranthes cranichoides* [Grisb.] Cogn.)
Orchid Family (Orchidaceae)

Description: The basal rosette of 4–6 glistening leaves wither in winter before flowering. The leaves are ovate, purplish beneath, from ¾"–2" long and ⅜"–1" wide. The flower spike is 4"–10" tall and lined with 10–30 speckled, ³⁄₁₆" flowers.

Bloom Season: March–April

Habitat/Range: Hardwood forests of peninsular Florida and the Neotropics.

Comments: *Cyclopogon* means "circular beard," and may refer to the hairs on the base of the sepals of the type species. The name *cranichoides* refers to the similarity of this species to a member of the orchid genus *Cranichis*. It has a spotty distribution in Florida but is locally common in several shady hammocks of Miami-Dade County east of Everglades National Park. It is exceptionally difficult to find because it blends in perfectly with the leaf litter on the forest floor.

TALL NEOTTIA
Cyclopogon elatus (Sw.) Schltr.
Orchid Family (Orchidaceae)

Description: The rosette of light green, elliptic-lanceolate leaves average 1½"–3½" long and ⅜"–1¼" wide with long petioles. The erect, hairy flower spike reaches 8"–24" tall with nodding, ⁵⁄₁₆" flowers.

Bloom Season: February–March

Habitat/Range: Rocky hammocks and hardwood swamps of Florida and the Neotropics.

Comments: The name *elatus* means "tall" and relates to the flower spike. This state-listed endangered orchid is extremely rare and is currently known only from the Fakahatchee Swamp in Collier County where it was discovered in 2009. It was first discovered in Florida in 1881 in Hernando County and was not known elsewhere for 80 years until it was found in Miami-Dade County in 1961 and again in 1978. A March 2013 survey of the Fakahatchee Swamp population revealed a total of 13 plants growing on 4 moss-covered logs in a remote slough protected by miles of trackless swamp.

BUTTERFLY ORCHID
Encyclia tampensis (Lindl.) Small
Orchid Family (Orchidaceae)

Description: The butterfly orchid resembles a bunch of scallions attached to a tree. The pseudobulbs are topped by 1–3 linear-lanceolate leaves from 3"–12" long and ⅜"–¾" wide. Fragrant, ¾" flowers are on branching spikes. Albino forms with pure white lips are rare.

Bloom Season: Principally May–July

Habitat/Range: Hardwood forests, wooded swamps, and mangroves from northern Florida through the Florida Keys to the Bahamas.

Comments: *Encyclia* means "to encircle," alluding to the lateral lobes of the lip that encircle the column. The name *tampensis* refers to the Tampa Bay area where it was first discovered in 1846. Orchid growers use it to create attractive hybrids and to breed cold tolerance into tropical orchids. Although exploited illegally by collectors it remains relatively abundant. Flower color is extremely variable in the southernmost Florida counties.

DINGY STAR ORCHID
Epidendrum anceps Jacq.
Orchid Family (Orchidaceae)

Description: The leafy stems of this epiphytic orchid average 12"–24" long. The alternate, elliptic leaves measure 1½"–6" long and ⅜"–1½" wide. The leaves are usually green but may be burgundy colored. The flowers form a ball of ⅜" greenish-yellow to dingy brown flowers and are produced on a terminal spike.

Bloom Season: November–July

Habitat/Range: Hardwood swamps of central and southern Florida and the Neotropics.

Comments: *Epidendrum* is Greek for "on tree," referring to the epiphytic habit of many members of the genus. The name *anceps* means "two-edged," alluding to the flattened peduncle. This orchid was first discovered in Florida at Gobbler's Head (Collier County) in 1904. The flowers smell like overripe vegetables at night and are pollinated by male nocturnal moths. It is a state-listed endangered species but can be locally common in wooded swamps of the Everglades.

STIFF STAR ORCHID
Epidendrum rigidum Jacq.
Orchid Family (Orchidaceae)

Description: The creeping rhizomes of this epiphyte can form large colonies on tree branches. The leathery leaves are elliptic and measure 1"–3¼" long and ¼"–⅜" wide, produced near the tip of the stem. The green flowers reach about ¼" wide and alternate along a zigzagging, sheathed spike.

Bloom Season: October–May

Habitat/Range: Epiphytic in hardwood forests and wooded swamps from southern mainland Florida to the Bahamas and the Neotropics.

Comments: The name *rigidum* refers to the somewhat rigid flowers. This orchid is locally common but is often hidden on the host tree by resurrection fern *(Pleopeltis polypodioides)*. Botanist Allan Hiram Curtiss (1845–1907) first discovered this species near Miami in 1877. In hardwood hammocks it prefers to grow on live oak *(Quercus virginiana)* but in swamps it is often found on pond-apple *(Annona glabra)* and pop ash *(Fraxinus caroliniana)* trees.

WILD COCO

Eulophia alta (L.) Fawc. & Rendle

Orchid Family (Orchidaceae)

Description: Wild coco produces erect, lanceolate leaves that arise from a bulbous corm. The leaves are typically 1'–2' long and 1"–2" wide. The tall flower spike is lined with 20–50 flowers with green to purple sepals and petals. The crested, 3-lobed lip is maroon.

Bloom Season: September–November

Habitat/Range: Swamps, marshes, and roadside ditches from central and southern Florida through the Neotropics and across much of Africa.

Comments: *Eulophia* refers to the crest on the lip of the flower. The name *alta* means "tall." Wild coco was first discovered in Florida by botanist Alvan Wentworth Chapman (1809–1899) in 1875. It can be locally common along roadsides that bisect freshwater wetlands but the pleated leaves can easily be mistaken for those of immature palms or even some grass species. The flowers have been described as resembling a German shepherd with erect ears and panting tongue.

CRESTLESS PLUME ORCHID

Eulophia ecristata (Fernald) Ames

(Also *Pteroglossaspis ecristata* [Fernald] Rolfe)

Orchid Family (Orchidaceae)

Description: Flowering stems of this species can reach 5' tall with erect, linear-lanceolate leaves that reach 6"–30" long and ½"–1¼" wide, arising from a corm. The odd-shaped flowers measure about ⅝" across and the sepals and petals form a hood over the lip.

Bloom Season: August–September

Habitat/Range: Pinelands, oak barrens, and scrub from North Carolina to Louisiana through peninsular Florida, Cuba, and Colombia.

Comments: The name *ecristata* means "without a crest," relating to the crestless lip of the flower. There is a population in southern Miami-Dade County with flowers that do not open because they become pollinated while in bud (cleistogamous). Recent DNA work at the Royal Botanical Gardens, Kew, has reinstated this species into the genus *Eulophia* from *Pteroglossaspis*. Habitat loss is its principal threat in Florida.

CHINESE CROWN ORCHID
Eulophia graminea Lindl.
Orchid Family (Orchidaceae)

Description: The grasslike leaves of this terrestrial orchid average 6"–12" tall and ⅜" wide, emerging from 1"–3" spherical pseudobulbs. The fragrant flowers are on erect stalks and measure ¾"–1" wide.

Bloom Season: April–October

Habitat/Range: Pinelands and disturbed sites of Florida. Native to southern Asia.

Comments: The name *graminea* refers to the grasslike leaves. It was first collected in Singapore in 1833 and the common name in its native China is Mei Guan Lan, which translates to "beautiful crown orchid." It was first observed in Florida in 2007 (Miami-Dade County) and in 5 years has spread through the Florida Keys and well into Central Florida, presumably from seeds contaminating commercial mulch. Some regions within its native range in Asia are cold temperate (USDA Zone 9) so it is expected to spread across the lower southeastern United States in relatively short order.

TOOTHPETAL ORCHID
Habenaria floribunda Lindl.
(Also *Habenaria odontopetala* Rchb. f.)
Orchid Family (Orchidaceae)

Description: This common terrestrial orchid produces a rosette of succulent, elliptic leaves from 3"–6" long and ¾"–1¼" wide. Green, ⅜" flowers are on a 10"–24" erect stem. There is a toothlike projection at the base of each petal, including the lip.

Bloom Season: September–February

Habitat/Range: Hardwood forests and swamps of Florida, West Indies, and Mexico to Central America.

Comments: *Habenaria* means "rein," alluding to the reinlike spurs on the lip. The name *floribunda* refers to the abundant flowers. This may be Florida's most common terrestrial orchid and it can form large colonies in forests or grow semi-epiphytically on rotting stumps and floating logs in swamps. The blossoms emit a very sweet nocturnal fragrance. Seminoles used the plant in funeral processions to help ward off evil spirits and "to strengthen medicine men."

WATER SPIDER ORCHID
Habenaria repens Nutt.
Orchid Family (Orchidaceae)

Description: The fleshy, lanceolate leaves of this terrestrial or semiaquatic orchid are 3"–6" long and ½"–1" wide. Spindly, ⅜" green flowers are crowded on an erect, terminal spike. The dorsal sepal is shallowly concave with thin, spreading lateral sepals and the lip is greenish with a descending central lobe.

Bloom Season: Primarily June–October but sporadically all year

Habitat/Range: Freshwater wetlands, edges of ponds, and roadside ditches of the southeastern United States and the Neotropics.

Comments: The name *repens* means "creeping," in reference to its growth habit. This relatively common native orchid can be found growing among floating vegetation, especially among rafts of invasive water hyacinth *(Eichhornia crassipes),* or it may form floating mats on its own. It is similar to Michaux's orchid *(Habenaria quinqueseta)* that has mostly white sepals and petals.

COPPER LADIES'-TRESSES
Mesadenus lucayanus (Britton) Schltr.
Orchid Family (Orchidaceae)

Description: The pale to grayish-green, elliptic to oblanceolate leaves form a small rosette and measure ½"–4" long and ⅜"–1⅛" wide. Flower stalks average 8"–10" tall with the upper half lined with coppery, ⅛" flowers.

Bloom Season: December–March

Habitat/Range: Hardwood forests of Florida (Citrus, Duval, and Miami-Dade Counties), Bahamas, West Indies, and Mexico.

Comments: *Mesadenus* means "middle gland." The name *lucayanus* refers to the Lucayans, the original inhabitants of the Bahamas before the arrival of Europeans. Charles Mosier (1871–1936) and John Kunkel Small (1869–1938) first discovered this species in Florida in 1915 on Elliott Key (Miami-Dade County). Orchid taxonomist Ruben Sauleda (1946–) collected 2 herbarium specimens from Everglades National Park in 1988. Although it has not been reported from the park since, it is very difficult to find.

YELLOWSPIKE ORCHID
Polystachya concreta (Jacq.) Garay & H. R. Sweet
Orchid Family (Orchidaceae)

Description: From 2–4 narrowly oblong to elliptic leaves arise from a thickened stem that is hidden by leaf sheaths. The leaves average 4"–8" long and ⅝"–1¼" wide. The hooded, green to yellowish, ¼" flowers are on terminal spikes, often with numerous branchlets.

Bloom Season: July–December

Habitat/Range: Epiphytic in wooded swamps, hammocks, and mangrove forests of southern Florida, Bahamas, West Indies, and South America to tropical Africa and Asia.

Comments: *Polystachya* means "many spikes" and refers to the many branchlets on the inflorescence. The name *concreta* is Latin for "grown together" in reference to the flower parts. This state-listed endangered orchid is locally common and often grows on limbs of live oak *(Quercus virginiana)* but can be found on other trees as well, especially buttonwood *(Conocarpus erectus)* in coastal forests.

MRS. BRITTON'S SHADOW WITCH
Ponthieva brittoniae Ames
Orchid Family (Orchidaceae)

Description: Flowering plants of this terrestrial orchid average 4"–8" tall with elliptic to ovate leaves that measure 2"–4" long and ½"–1" wide but may be leafless when flowering. The flowers measure about ⁷⁄₁₆" wide.

Bloom Season: January–March

Habitat/Range: In and around limestone sinks in pine rocklands of Miami-Dade County, Florida, and the Bahamas.

Comments: *Ponthieva* honors Henri de Ponthieu, an 18th-century West Indian Huguenot merchant who sent botanical specimens to Sir Joseph Banks in 1778. The name *brittoniae* honors Elizabeth Gertrude Britton (1858–1934), wife of Nathaniel Lord Britton (1859–1934), who helped found the New York Botanical Garden in 1891. In Florida this orchid is restricted to Long Pine Key in Everglades National Park and is a critically imperiled state-listed endangered species. It is extraordinarily rare and exceptionally hard to find.

HAIRY SHADOW WITCH

Ponthieva racemosa (Walter) C. Mohr
Orchid Family (Orchidaceae)

Description: The elliptic to oblanceolate leaves of this terrestrial orchid measure 2"–4" long and ½"–1" wide and are present at flowering. From 20–35 green and white hairy flowers are arranged on a softly hairy spike, each measuring about ¼" wide and held nearly horizontal.

Bloom Season: Principally December–January in South Florida

Habitat/Range: Shady forests, tree islands, swamps, and pine flatwoods from North Carolina to Texas, south to Florida and the Neotropics.

Comments: The name *racemosa* refers to the raceme of flowers. This orchid ranges south in Florida to Everglades National Park where it grows in and around small tree islands surrounded by prairie habitat. It looks very much like the preceding species but the habitats are different and the stalks holding the flowers are not canted up as high. Small halictid bees pollinate the flowers in Florida.

LEAFLESS BEAKED LADIES'-TRESSES

Sacoila lanceolata (Aubl.) Garay forma *albidaviridis* Catling & Sheviak
(Also *Spiranthes lanceolata* [Aubl.] Léon)
Orchid Family (Orchidaceae)

Description: The large lanceolate leaves form a basal rosette and can reach 8" long and 2" wide but are not present when flowering. A stout, erect, fleshy spike, to 12" tall or more, is topped with a compact arrangement of green, pubescent, 1" flowers.

Bloom Season: April–July

Habitat/Range: Open meadows, pastures, and roadsides of mainland Florida and the Neotropics.

Comments: *Sacoila* alludes to the sac-shaped projection formed by the sepals and base of the column. The name *lanceolata* refers to the lance-shaped leaves and *albidaviridis* means "whitish green," in reference to the flower color. This is a rare color form that can sometimes occur among colonies of red-flowered plants. Large populations of this species can be found along road swales, including turnpikes.

DUSKY VANILLA
Vanilla phaeantha Rchb. f.
Orchid Family (Orchidaceae)

Description: The ½" thick, usually zigzagging stems of this vining orchid may exceed 20' in length. The oblong leaves reach 5" long and 1½" wide and clusters of 3"–4" flowers emerge from the leaf axils. Only 1 or 2 flowers open at a time.

Bloom Season: April–July

Habitat/Range: Mixed hardwood and cypress swamps of southern Florida and the West Indies.

Comments: The name *phaeantha* means "dusky flower," alluding to the shadowy cast of the flower. Its population is centered in the Fakahatchee Swamp in Collier County but it also occurs in Everglades National Park. This is Florida's largest-flowered native orchid but is only observed by the most dedicated wildflower enthusiasts. To see it in flower usually requires early morning slogs through deep sloughs while accompanied by tormenting heat, humidity, and clouds of summertime mosquitoes. It is a state-listed endangered species.

VANILLA ORCHID
Vanilla planifolia Andrews
Orchid Family (Orchidaceae)

Description: The oblong leaves are 4"–6" long and 2" wide with flowers that open 1 or 2 at a time in axillary clusters. The flowers open at night and close by midday. Cylindrical capsules are 4"–10" long and ½" wide.

Bloom Season: March–May

Habitat/Range: Hardwood forests of southern Florida. Native to the Neotropics.

Comments: The name *planifolia* refers to the flat leaves. The dried capsule is the source of vanilla flavoring. A Spanish officer under Cortez observed the Aztec emperor Montezuma drink *chocolatl*, a beverage of ground cacao seeds mixed with "beans" called *tlilxochitl*. This was the first European account of chocolate and vanilla. This rambunctious vining orchid is usually found around middens once inhabited by indigenous Florida tribes, the Calusa and Tequesta. Vanilla ranks as one of the world's most expensive crops because each flower must be pollinated by hand.

CORKYSTEM PASSIONFLOWER
Passiflora suberosa L.
Passionflower Family (Passifloraceae)

Description: This petite herbaceous vine has corky outgrowths on mature stems and climbs by tendrils. The alternate leaves are extremely variable in size and shape, ranging from ⅜"–4" long and linear, lanceolate, or variously lobed. The flowers are about ⅜" wide. The round fruits are about ⅜" wide and ripen purple.

Bloom Season: All year

Habitat/Range: Hammocks, pinelands, and coastal strand of Florida and the Neotropics.

Comments: *Passiflora* is Latin for "passion flower" or "crucifixion flower" and relates to the crucifixion of Jesus. The name *suberosa* means "corky," alluding to the corky bark. Varying leaf shape is believed by lepidopterists to be a ploy to avoid being recognized by butterflies. This is a preferred larval host plant of the zebra longwing, Julia, and gulf fritillary butterflies and is commonly cultivated by butterfly enthusiasts in Florida.

EARLEAF GREENBRIER
Smilax auriculata Walter
Smilax Family (Smilacaceae)

Description: This wickedly thorny vine scrambles across other vegetation with long stems. The leaves typically have earlike basal lobes, often with pale white mottling. The fragrant flowers are clustered and measure ¼"–⁵⁄₁₆" wide.

Bloom Season: All year

Habitat/Range: Wet flatwoods, hammocks, and thickets of the southeastern United States and the Bahamas.

Comments: *Smilax* comes from *smilakos,* a name used by Pliny (AD 23–79) for a twining plant. Smilax was also a mythological Greek nymph who fell hopelessly in love with a mortal so the gods changed her into a brambly vine. The name *auriculata* refers to the earlike lobes on the leaves. The young stems can be eaten raw or cooked and the rhizomes of *Smilax* are the source of sarsaparilla and root beer. This species makes travel through its habitat a difficult and painful task, especially if you are foolish enough to wear shorts.

WHITE FLOWERS

Passiflora pallens

This section is for either pure white flowers or flowers with white as the dominant color. Be advised that some flowers produce albino morphs so you may need to check other color sections if you do not find what you are looking for here.

CAROLINA SCALYSTEM
Elytraria caroliniensis (J. F. Gmel.) Pers. var. *angustifolia* (Fernald) S. F. Blake
Acanthus Family (Acanthaceae)

Description: There is a basal rosette of pubescent, linear, spatulate leaves that measure 4"–6" long and no more than ⅜" wide. The thick, prominent midvein is white to pinkish, wide at the base and becoming obscure near the tip. The erect 6"–12" flower spike is covered with small scales, becoming conelike at the apex with a single 5-petaled, ⅜" flower.

Bloom Season: February–November

Habitat/Range: Endemic to wet prairies and pinelands from Lee and Martin Counties southward in Florida.

Comments: *Elytraria* is Greek for "sheath" or "vagina," in reference to the flowers and fruits enclosed by bracts. The name *caroliniensis* means "of Carolina" and *angustifolia* means "narrow leaved." This endemic variety can be locally common in wet marl prairies or along edges of depression marshes throughout the Everglades region.

GRASSY ARROWHEAD
Sagittaria graminea Michx.
Water Plantain Family (Alismataceae)

Description: This wetland perennial has narrow, grasslike leaves that average 4"–10" long and ⅛"–⁵⁄₁₆" wide. The leaves are sometimes submerged. The 3-petaled flowers are on erect, unbranched, fleshy stalks and measure about ½"–⅝" wide. Male and female flowers are borne separately on the same stalk.

Bloom Season: All year

Habitat/Range: Freshwater wetlands and roadside ditches from Newfoundland and Ontario south to Texas, Florida, and Cuba.

Comments: *Sagittaria* is Latin for "an arrow," referring to the leaf shape of some species. The name *graminea* alludes to the grasslike leaves of this species. A variety of this species (var. *chapmanii*) also occurs in the region and differs by having a branched inflorescence. Grassy arrowhead occurs in Corkscrew Swamp and the Big Cypress Swamp but not in Everglades National Park. Its flowers are smaller than other species in the region.

LANCELEAF ARROWHEAD
Sagittaria lancifolia L.
Water Plantain Family (Alismataceae)

Description: The lanceolate leaves spread fanlike, usually from standing water. The leaf blade can reach 16" long and 4" wide (leaf blades sometimes absent). Tall stalks produce flowers in whorls of 3, each with 3 prominent petals. The pistils of the female flowers form a yellow dome. Whorls of male flowers are produced above the females.

Bloom Season: February–October

Habitat/Range: Freshwater wetlands from Delaware and Maryland to Florida, Texas, Oklahoma, and the Neotropics.

Comments: The name *lancifolia* means "lance leaved." The common name duck potato relates to ducks that eat the corms on the rhizome tips. The corms, roots, and base of the plant can be blanched and eaten but are rather bland, which proves there is a big difference between edible and eatable. Seminoles used the plant medicinally to treat trauma resulting from alligator bites with little known effect.

SEVEN SISTERS
Crinum americanum L.
Amaryllis Family (Amaryllidaceae)

Description: The succulent straplike leaves of this amaryllis emerge from a deep-rooted bulb and average 1'–2' long and 1"–2" wide, becoming flat near the tip. The showy, fragrant flowers (2–6, usually 4) are radially symmetrical with reflexed sepals and petals that measure 2½"–5½" long.

Bloom Season: All year

Habitat/Range: Freshwater wetlands from Texas to Georgia and Florida.

Comments: *Crinum* is a Greek name for "lily." The name *americanum* means "of America." It is called seven sisters because the flower clusters resemble the Pleiades, a star cluster known as Seven Sisters. Sphinx moths dust their wings with pollen while sipping nectar and are effective pollinators. It is also called string-lily and is common throughout the Everglades region, adorning sunny prairies mostly in spring and summer. The leaves are a favorite food of the flightless lubber grasshopper.

BEACH SPIDERLILY
Hymenocallis latifolia (Mill.) M. Roem.
Amaryllis Family (Amaryllidaceae)

Description: The straplike leaves range from 2'–4' long, 2"–4" wide, and are boat shaped in cross section. The flower stalk is 2'–4' tall and is topped by 6–10 or more fragrant, funnel-shaped flowers, each with 3 petals and 3 petal-like sepals. A thin, cuplike, white membrane connects the lower portion of the 6 stamens.

Bloom Season: May–September

Habitat/Range: Beach dunes and other coastal habitats of central and southern Florida to the West Indies.

Comments: *Hymenocallis* means "beautiful membrane," referring to the hymenlike membrane attached to the stamen filaments. The name *latifolia* means "broad leaved." Sphinx moths serve as effective pollinators by visiting the flowers for nectar after dark and transferring pollen on their wings. This species is widely cultivated for its fragrant flowers, salt and drought tolerance, and ease of care.

ALLIGATORLILY
Hymenocallis palmeri S. Watson
Amaryllis Family (Amaryllidaceae)

Description: This species has strap-shaped leaves from 6"–16" long and up to ½" wide. The flowers have 3 widely spreading, linear petals and 3 similar petal-like sepals measuring 2"–3" long and spread beneath a thin, cuplike, white membrane that connects the stamen filaments.

Bloom Season: May–September

Habitat/Range: Endemic to freshwater marshes and prairies of central and southern Florida.

Comments: The name *palmeri* honors botanist Edward Palmer (1829–1911). The flowers of this state-listed endangered species are very fragrant but smelling them will likely cause pollen to be transferred to your face. All members of the genus are larval host plants of the Spanish moth. This species is widespread in the Everglades region and is common in open prairies. The fruits and bulbs of all species contain the toxin lycorine and cause vomiting and diarrhea if eaten.

FLORIDA SPIDERLILY
Hymenocallis tridentata Small
Amaryllis Family (Amaryllidaceae)

Description: The strap-shaped leaves average 12"–24" long and 1" wide and usually emerge from standing water. The flowering stem typically stands 12"–14" tall and is forked at the top to produce paired flowers with one opening a day or two before the other. The flowers measure 8" across the spreading sepals and petals. A cuplike membrane connects the stamen filaments.

Bloom Season: April–June

Habitat/Range: Endemic to freshwater marshes and prairies of central and southern mainland Florida.

Comments: The name *tridentata* refers to the (usually) 3 teeth on the edge of the filament. This species is common in open marshes along the road leading to the Pa Hay Okee overlook in Everglades National Park. Of the 13 Florida native species in this genus, 7 are endemic to the state. The leaves and flowers of all species are a favorite food of the flightless lubber grasshopper.

SIMPSON'S ZEPHYRLILY
Zephyranthes simpsonii Chapm.
Amaryllis Family (Amaryllidaceae)

Description: The very narrow leaves measure 12"–20" long and ¹⁄₁₆"–³⁄₁₆" wide. The funnel-shaped flowers are white or pink-tinged with pink stripes on the backs of the sepals. The stigma is shorter than (or equal to) the anthers.

Bloom Season: April–August

Habitat/Range: Wet flatwoods discontinuously from North Carolina to Mississippi south in Florida to the Big Cypress Swamp.

Comments: Zephyrus is the mythological Greek god of the west wind so *Zephyranthes* translates to "west wind flower," alluding to the west wind that brings spring rains and flowers. The name *simpsonii* honors Illinois botanist Joseph Herman Simpson (1841–1918) who collected plants in Florida. Although this state-listed threatened species flowers in response to fire, zephyrlilies are widely planted as ornamentals and their habit of blooming shortly after rain gave rise to the name rain lily.

RATTLESNAKE MASTER
Eryngium yuccifolium Michx.
Carrot Family (Apiaceae)

Description: This species has weak bristles on the margins of narrowly linear leaves. The leaves are 6"–24" long and ½"–1" wide, becoming smaller up the flowering stem. Flower heads are on branched stalks that may reach 5' tall. The white flowers are in 1" balls with bracts that stick out to give the heads a prickly feel.

Bloom Season: May–September

Habitat/Range: Pinelands, prairies, and flatwoods from Georgia to Texas and south in Florida to the Big Cypress Swamp.

Comments: *Eryngium* is the Greek name for a related species. The name *yuccifolium* refers to the resemblance of the plant to a species of yucca (Agavaceae). A concoction prepared from the roots of this species was the ceremonial "black drink" of the Seminoles in Florida. The common name alludes to its unsuccessful use by Native Americans of the southeastern United States to treat bites from venomous rattlesnakes.

WATER DROPWORT

Tiedemannia filiformis (Walt.) Feist & S. R. Downie
(Also *Oxypolis filiformis* [Walt.] Britt.)
Carrot Family (Apiaceae)

Description: This sparsely branched plant averages 1'–3' tall. The leaves are reduced to rounded phyllodes (dilated petioles serving as a leaf blade) ranging from 4"–24" long. Although each flower is only about ⅛" wide, they are displayed in showy, terminal umbels that reach over 4" across.

Bloom Season: All year

Habitat/Range: Freshwater wetlands from Virginia to Florida and Texas to the Bahamas and Cuba.

Comments: *Tiedemannia* honors German physiologist Friedrich Tiedemann (1781–1861). The name *filiformis* means "threadlike," in reference to the filamentous leaflike petioles. This is a larval host plant of the black swallowtail butterfly. It is closely related to celery, parsley, carrot, dill, and fennel. The related mock bishopsweed *(Ptilimnium capillaceum)* is much smaller in all aspects.

BLODGETT'S SWALLOWWORT

Cynanchum blodgettii (A. Gray) Shinners
Dogbane Family (Apocynaceae)

Description: This petite vine twines through low vegetation and bears opposite, lanceolate leaves that measure about ½" long and ¼" wide. The small, 5-lobed flowers are in clusters along the stem, each flower measuring only about ³⁄₃₂" wide. The flowers have small hairs on the inner surfaces of the lobes.

Bloom Season: Sporadically all year

Habitat/Range: Pine rocklands of southern Florida (Miami-Dade and Monroe Counties) and the West Indies.

Comments: *Cynanchum* is a combination of words that mean "dog" and "to strangle," apparently referring to a species that is harmful to dogs. The name *blodgettii* commemorates John Loomis Blodgett (1809–1853), who was an important figure in the early botanical history of southern Florida. Four other members of the genus occur in Florida. Like all *Cynanchum* species the leaves and stems exude milky sap when broken.

WHITE TWINEVINE
Sarcostemma clausum (Jacq.) Roem. & Schult.
Dogbane Family (Apocynaceae)

Description: White twinevine forms entangle-ments of twining stems that reach 10' long or more. All parts exude milky sap if broken. The oblong to linear, dark green leaves are opposite and measure 1"–3" long and ⅜"–¾" wide. Fragrant, hairy, 5-lobed flowers measure ⅜" wide and form rounded clusters. The base of each lobe is reddish purple, forming a ring.

Bloom Season: June–January

Habitat/Range: Moist soils of coastal strand, cypress swamps, and mangroves of central and southern Florida to the Neotropics.

Comments: *Sarcostemma* refers to the stems that twine around each other like a wreath or a gar-land. The name *clausum* means "closed" or "shut," with unknown reference to this plant. This and other members of the family are larval host plants of the monarch, queen, and soldier butterflies. Toxins in the plant make their larvae distasteful to birds and other predators.

DEVIL'S POTATO
Echites umbellata Jacq.
Dogbane Family (Apocynaceae)

Description: The paired leaves of this twining vine are oblong-elliptic and range from 1½"–4" long and 1"–2" wide and are typically spaced far apart along the stem. Trumpet-shaped flowers are creamy white with 5 curved lobes that look as if they are twirling. The flowers are about 1½"–2" wide. The cylindrical, 6"–8" green pods are paired and extend outward from each other.

Bloom Season: All year

Habitat/Range: Pinelands and scrub of Florida and the Neotropics.

Comments: *Echites* is Greek for "a viper," alluding to the snakelike, twining stems and also to its toxic properties. The name *umbellata* refers to the umbels of flowers. The common name relates to the poisonous, tuberous root. This is a larval host plant of the faithful beauty, a stunning red-white-and-blue day-flying moth. The gaudy larvae are scarlet with iridescent blue spots meant to warn birds of their toxicity.

MANGROVE RUBBER VINE
Rhabdadenia biflora (Jacq.) Müll. Arg.
Dogbane Family (Apocynaceae)

Description: This is a high-climbing, twining vine with flexible stems and opposite, oblong leaves from 2"–4" long and ⅝"–1" wide, often with pinkish veins. The 5-lobed, trumpet-shaped flowers are about 1½" wide and are often in pairs. The yellow-centered flowers are white or lightly tinged with pink.

Bloom Season: All year

Habitat/Range: Mangrove and cypress swamps from central Florida into the Florida Keys and the Neotropics.

Comments: *Rhabdadenia* is Greek for "wand gland," alluding to the slender pods. The name *biflora* relates to the (usually) paired flowers. This is one of the few vines that inhabit mangrove forests. Many members of the dogbane family are poisonous to eat and symptoms of poisoning include dizziness, nausea, heart failure, and death. The sap is acrid and can cause severe blistering of the skin. It is related to such well-known plants as oleander and allamanda.

ARROW ARUM
Peltandra virginica (L.) Schott. & Endl.
Arum Family (Araceae)

Description: This wetland aroid has arrow-shaped leaf blades on long, fleshy petioles. The inflorescence is typical of the arum family, with a long, cylindrical spadix enveloped by a leaflike bract called a spathe. The spathe is green with white margins. The spadix is covered with minuscule, white to yellowish flowers. Female flowers are lowermost on the spadix.

Bloom Season: All year

Habitat/Range: Freshwater swamps, sloughs, and roadside ditches of the eastern United States and Canada.

Comments: *Peltandra* comes from the Greek words *pelte*, meaning "a shield," and *andros*, or "stamens," alluding to the shield (spathe) surrounding the spadix that bears the flowers. The name *virginica* means "of Virginia." Native Americans ate the roots but only after properly preparing them to remove toxins. Water garden enthusiasts sometimes cultivate this attractive wetland species.

SPANISH NEEDLES
Bidens alba (L.) DC.
Aster Family (Asteraceae)

Description: This weedy species has finely toothed leaves that are mostly opposite along angled stems. The simple or pinnately 3–7-lobed leaves average 1"–4" long and the flower heads are about 1" wide. The dry, needlelike seeds (achenes) cling to fur and clothing.

Bloom Season: All year

Habitat/Range: Disturbed sites from Canada south through Florida into the Neotropics.

Comments: *Bidens* is Latin for "two toothed," alluding to the 2 teeth on the achene. The name *alba* means "white," referring to the ray flowers. Bahamians use it as a tea for "cooling the blood," to cure a "sick stomach," and to rid children of worms. If applied to a small cut the clear sap will stop bleeding almost instantly. The leaves are high in iron but taste resiny. Although it is very weedy the flowers are highly prized by butterflies, plus it is the larval host plant of the dainty sulphur butterfly. It is a weed worth growing.

WHITE SUNBONNETS
Chaptalia albicans (Sw.) Vent ex B. D. Jacks
Aster Family (Asteraceae)

Description: The 1"–5½" basal leaves are typically wavy, obovate-elliptic with white pubescence on the underside. The creamy white flower heads are produced atop an erect 3"–6" stalk.

Bloom Season: November–May

Habitat/Range: Pinelands of southern Florida (Miami-Dade County), Bahamas, West Indies, Mexico, and Central America.

Comments: *Chaptalia* honors noted French chemist and statesman Jean-Antoine-Claude Chaptal (1756–1831) who developed the process of adding cane sugar to pressed grape juice to raise the alcohol content of wine. The name *albicans* means "off white," in reference to the creamy white florets. This is a state-listed endangered species that is rare in pine rockland habitat of Miami-Dade County, including Long Pine Key in Everglades National Park. It does not occur in the same region as the following species.

PINELAND DAISY
Chaptalia tomentosa Vent.
Aster Family (Asteraceae)

Description: The elliptic leaves of this species are densely white tomentose below. The leaves form a basal rosette and measure 1"–7" long and ¾"–1¼" wide with 1" flower heads at the top of a 4"–12" leafless stalk. The flower heads close and nod at night, becoming open and erect by midday.

Bloom Season: November–May

Habitat/Range: Wet flatwoods from North Carolina to Texas and south in Florida to the Big Cypress Swamp.

Comments: The name *tomentosa* refers to the densely wooly (tomentose) hairs on the undersides of the leaves. It is common in the Bear Island region of the Big Cypress Swamp and the CREW Marsh. It was first collected in Charleston County, South Carolina, in 1801 and named *Tussilago integrifolia* by French botanist André Michaux (1746–1802). Michaux introduced it to France where it is still cultivated. The leaves are used in a tea in the West Indies to invoke the Devil during séances.

OAKLEAF FLEABANE
Erigeron quercifolius Lam.
Aster Family (Asteraceae)

Description: The lobed, hairy leaves range from 2"–7" long and ⅝"–1½" wide, forming a rosette with smaller leaves up the flowering stem. The ⅜"–½" flower heads are in open clusters at the tops of branching stems. The ray flowers are narrowly linear and number 100 or more per head.

Bloom Season: All year

Habitat/Range: Pinelands, prairies, and disturbed sites of the southeastern United States, Bahamas, and Greater Antilles.

Comments: *Erigeron* is Greek for "wooly" and "old man," alluding to the wooly heads of some species. The name *quercifolius* relates to the leaves that resemble oaks in the genus *Quercus*. This is a common species in the Everglades region and often grows in large spreading colonies along roadsides. The ray flowers can vary from blue to pink but are commonly white. The flowers are similar to prairie fleabane *(Erigeron strigosus)* that occurs north of the Everglades region.

EARLY WHITETOP FLEABANE
Erigeron vernus (L.) Torr. & A. Gray
Aster Family (Asteraceae)

Description: The oblanceolate or spatulate leaves of this species form ground-hugging rosettes that spread by underground rhizomes. The flower heads measure about ⅝" wide with many narrow ray flowers and yellow disk flowers. The flowering stems reach 10"–20" tall and are branched near the top.

Bloom Season: March–August

Habitat/Range: Pine flatwoods, bogs, and savannas from Virginia to Louisiana south through most of mainland Florida.

Comments: The name *vernus* refers to the vernal equinox and relates to its early springtime flowering. In the proper habitat this species can be exceptionally abundant. In the Everglades region it ranges into Corkscrew Swamp, CREW Marsh, and the Big Cypress Swamp but is absent from Everglades National Park. It can easily be mistaken for a member of the genus *Symphyotrichum*. Small bees and butterflies visit the flowers.

FALSE FENNEL
Eupatorium leptophyllum DC.
Aster Family (Asteraceae)

Description: The narrowly linear stem leaves of this species are deeply dissected and average 1"–3" long and only about ⅟₁₆" wide. The leaves are strongly scented when crushed. Small heads of flowers are in panicles and the glabrous branches supporting them are recurved. The heads are all directed to one side of the axis.

Bloom Season: May–September

Habitat/Range: Moist to dry flatwoods of the southeastern United States.

Comments: *Eupatorium* was named to honor Mithridates Eupator (132–63 BC), King of Pontus (modern-day northeastern Turkey), who used a species in this genus medicinally, perhaps as an antidote for poison. The name *leptophyllum* means "with narrow leaves." It is not related to the fennel used as a culinary herb. Native Americans used members of the genus medicinally to treat dengue, typhus, and yellow fevers. This is a common species in the Everglades region.

SEMAPHORE THOROUGHWORT

Eupatorium mikanioides Chapm.
Aster Family (Asteraceae)

Description: The diamond-shaped leaves are opposite and held vertically on the stem, each measuring about 1"–1½" long and ½"–¾" wide. The flower heads are in showy, flat-topped clusters above the leaves.

Bloom Season: May–November

Habitat/Range: Endemic to coastal flatwoods, saltmarshes, and freshwater prairies of mainland Florida.

Comments: The name *mikanioides* refers to the resemblance of the flowers to a *Mikania* (Asteraceae). Of the 17 members of the genus in Florida this is the only endemic species. It is common in the open prairies of the Everglades region and is favored by butterflies when in bloom. "Thoroughwort" is a corruption of "through-wort," named because the stems on some species look like they go through the leaf blades. Some species are among the best butterfly attractors in Florida, especially lateflowering thoroughwort *(Eupatorium serotinum).*

SNOW SQUARESTEM

Melanthera nivea (L.) Small
(Also *Melanthera parvifolia* Small)
Aster Family (Asteraceae)

Description: This is a trailing or bushy plant (to 7') with square stems. The rough, coarsely toothed to entire, ¾"–1¼" leaves are arrow shaped with the basal lobes held at right angles to the midrib. Spherical ⅝" flower clusters are on long stems. Black anthers protrude from the flowers.

Bloom Season: All year

Habitat/Range: Pine flatwoods, prairies, and edges of moist to dry forests along the Gulf and Atlantic coastal plain to Illinois and Kentucky.

Comments: *Melanthera* means "black anther." The name *nivea* means "snow white," referring to the flowers. Some botanists separate the low, sprawling plants found in the Everglades region as a Florida endemic species *(Melanthera parvifolia).* Taxonomic revisions now place it under synonymy with this wide-ranging and morphologically diverse species. The flowers attract an assortment of butterflies.

CLIMBING HEMPVINE
Mikania scandens (L.) Willd.
Aster Family (Asteraceae)

Description: This twining vine has angled stems and somewhat triangular, opposite leaves that are irregularly and sharply lobed. The leaves average ¾"–1¼" long but may be larger in shade. Cylindrical flower heads are in flat-topped clusters composed of small, fragrant, disk flowers. The flowers are white or rarely tinged with pink and measure about ½" long.

Bloom Season: All year

Habitat/Range: Hammocks, pinelands, prairies, and coastal strand from Canada through the eastern United States, Bahamas, and Mexico.

Comments: *Mikania* honors Austrian-Czech botanist and professor Joseph Gottfried Mikan (1743–1814). The name *scandens* means "climbing," in reference to the growth habit. Gardeners should take special note of this vine because butterflies swarm around flowering plants, plus it is a larval host plant of the little metalmark butterfly and the scarlet-bodied wasp moth.

FEAY'S PALAFOX
Palafoxia feayi A. Gray
Aster Family (Asteraceae)

Description: The leaf blades of this tall, somewhat lanky species are narrowly elliptic to ovate with heads of white to pinkish, dark-anthered, tubular flowers terminating the stems. The flowers average about ½" long and ⅛" wide.

Bloom Season: September–January

Habitat/Range: Endemic to sandhills and scrub of peninsular Florida.

Comments: *Palafoxia* honors Spanish patriot José Rebolledo de Palafox y Melci (1776–1847), the Duke of Saragossa, who fought against Napoleon's armies. The name *feayi* honors physician and botanist William T. Féay (1803–1879). The flowers of this attractive species are visited by an array of butterflies and other insects. It ranges south to the Corkscrew Swamp region and the Bear Island Unit of the Big Cypress Swamp and in sandy pockets of pine rocklands east of Everglades National Park in Miami-Dade County. This species was first described in 1877.

BLACKROOT
Pterocaulon pycnostachyum (Michx.) Elliott
Aster Family (Asteraceae)

Description: Blackroot has wooly, conspicuously winged stems that reach 8"–24" tall with alternate, often shallowly toothed, lanceolate leaves from 1½"–4" long. The leaves are green above, white wooly below with a white midvein. Flowers are creamy white and densely packed in cone-shaped, compact clusters along an erect or arching spike.

Bloom Season: All year

Habitat/Range: Flatwoods, pinelands, and disturbed sites from North Carolina and Mississippi through Florida.

Comments: *Pterocaulon* means "winged stem" and the name *pycnostachyum* refers to the densely packed flowers on the spike. The black, tuberous roots are poisonous to eat. Another common name in Florida is rabbit tobacco, which means "wild tobacco" and has nothing to do with a bunny. The plant contains a chemical called coumarin used in pipe tobacco as an aroma enhancer and as an anticoagulant in rat poison.

BAHAMA SACHSIA
Sachsia polycephala Griseb.
(Also *Sachsia bahamensis* Urb.)
Aster Family (Asteraceae)

Description: The toothed, spatulate leaves of this species typically lie flat on the ground and form a rosette with each leaf averaging 1"–2½" long and ½"–¾" wide. The flowering stems range from 8"–20" tall and are openly branched near the top. Flower heads measure about ⅜" long and ⅛" wide.

Bloom Season: Sporadically all year

Habitat/Range: Rocky pinelands of southern Florida (Miami-Dade and Monroe Counties), Bahamas, Cuba, Hispaniola, and Jamaica.

Comments: *Sachsia* commemorates German plant physiologist Julius von Sachs (1832–1897). The name *polycephala* refers to the many heads of flowers produced by this species. It was listed as endangered in 1998 but is now relegated as a state-listed threatened species. It is very local on Long Pine Key in Everglades National Park and in the lower Florida Keys. The only other 2 species in this genus are endemic to Cuba.

RICE BUTTON ASTER
Symphyotrichum dumosum [L.] G. L. Nesom
Aster Family (Asteraceae)

Description: This species is easily distinguished from other asters in the Everglades region by its sessile leaves that do not clasp the stem. The spatulate or lanceolate leaves are entire or slightly toothed. The ⅜" flower heads have white to pale blue rays with yellow disk flowers.

Bloom Season: All year

Habitat/Range: Pinelands and prairies of the eastern United States to the Greater Antilles.

Comments: *Symphyotrichum* is Greek for "junction" and "hair," perhaps alluding to the bristles on the European cultivar used to describe the genus. The name *dumosum* means "bushy," in reference to the growth habit. It is extremely variable and some botanists have attempted to separate it into more than one species. It is a good candidate for cultivation by butterfly enthusiasts because butterflies visit the flowers for nectar and it is a larval host plant of the pearl crescent butterfly.

WHITE CROWNBEARD
Verbesina virginica L.
(Also *Verbesina laciniata* [Poir.] Nutt.)
Aster Family (Asteraceae)

Description: The stems of this species are prominently winged and may reach 6' in height. The alternate 6"–8" leaves are rough to the touch, ovate, and irregularly lobed. The upper leaves are smaller. The ¾" flower heads are in terminal, branching clusters.

Bloom Season: May–November

Habitat/Range: Hammock margins, coastal strand, and disturbed sites of the eastern United States north to Pennsylvania.

Comments: *Verbesina* is a modification of the genus *Verbena*. The name *virginica* means "of Virginia." This plant dies back during winter and resprouts from the rootstock in spring. It is conspicuous because of its height and often forms large populations, especially in open, sandy areas. Another common name is frostweed. Seminoles used the plant to treat such ills as fever, headache, eye disease, chills, and hot flashes.

SCORPIONTAIL
Heliotropium angiospermum Murray
Borage Family (Boraginaceae)

Description: Scorpiontail is somewhat shrubby with lanceolate leaves measuring 1"–6" long and ½"–2" wide. The ¹⁄₁₆" flowers are in 2 ranks on terminal spikes that curl under at the tip then unfurl as the flowers open.

Bloom Season: All year

Habitat/Range: Coastal strand and shell mounds of the southern United States and the Neotropics.

Comments: *Heliotropium* means "turning toward the sun," in reference to the flowers of some species that respond to the direction of the sun. The name *angiospermum* means "with enclosed seeds." Adult male butterflies take alkaloids from the flower nectar that they turn into pheromones. The related seaside heliotrope *(Heliotropium curassavicum)* has similar flowers but is a prostrate species on beaches and salty flats. Seaside heliotrope is not safe to eat because alkaloids in the leaves are known to contribute to liver cancer.

COASTAL SEA ROCKET
Cakile lanceolata (Willd.) O. E. Schulz
Mustard Family (Brassicaceae)

Description: Sea rocket is a bushy seashore plant to 2' tall with cylindrical, corky pods. The fleshy, lanceolate leaves are usually coarsely toothed and average 2"–4" long and 7⁄16"–1⁄2" wide. The lower leaves may be much larger. The flowers are about 3⁄8" wide, each with 4 white petals.

Bloom Season: All year

Habitat/Range: Coastal sands of Florida and the Neotropics.

Comments: *Cakile* relates to the Arabic name for cardamom *(Elettaria cardamomum).* The name *lanceolata* refers to the lance-shaped leaves. The boiled leaves and green pods are cooked as a vegetable or eaten raw in salads and are high in vitamin C. It is called pork bush in the Bahamas and is served with pork dishes. It is also called ocean arugula. The name sea rocket relates to *rochette,* an Italian name for arugula, or garden rocket, commonly eaten in salads. It is a larval host plant of the great southern white butterfly.

SLENDERLEAF CLAMMYWEED
Polanisia tenuifolia Torr. & A. Gray
Mustard Family (Brassicaceae)

Description: The stems of this species are usually unbranched and are covered with glandular hairs. The leaves are green or sometimes purple and measure 1⁄2"–2" long and very narrowly linear. The reflexed sepals are pale yellow with white, oblong petals.

Bloom Season: March–September

Habitat/Range: Scrub, dry pinelands, sandhills, and lakeshores from Georgia, Alabama, and Mississippi south through mainland Florida.

Comments: *Polanisia* refers to the many unequal stamens. The name *tenuifolia* describes the slender leaves. It is called catchfly in parts of its range because insects stick to the viscid secretions of the leaves. It is not insectivorous but the dead insects offer nutrients for the plant when the leaves fall off. In the Everglades region this species is found in remnant pinelands along the western side of Biscayne Bay in southern Miami-Dade County.

BARBED-WIRE CACTUS

Acanthocereus tetragonus (L.) Hummelinck
Cactus Family (Cactaceae)

Description: The 3- or 4-angled stems of this vining cactus are armed with clusters of wickedly sharp, ⅜"–1" spines. The stems can reach 12' long or more, rambling across tree branches and shrubs. The fragrant flowers are 4" wide and are followed by 2", ovoid, scarlet fruits (berries).

Bloom Season: July–September

Habitat/Range: Coastal hammocks of southern Florida, Texas, and Mexico.

Comments: *Acanthocereus* means "thorny" and "waxy," referring to the armed, waxy stems. The name *tetragonus* refers to the stems with 4 angles. Other common names are triangle cactus and dildoe cactus. It creates formidable thickets in coastal hammocks and blooms late at night in the summer when mosquitoes are so thick they can drive the most dedicated wildflower photographers beyond the brink of insanity. The flowers attract sphinx moths as pollinators. Bats visit the flowers in Mexico.

PRICKLY APPLE

Harrisia fragrans Small ex Britton & Rose
(Also *Harrisia simpsonii* Small ex Britton & Rose)
Cactus Family (Cactaceae)

Description: This erect cactus has cylindrical, ribbed stems from 6'–16' tall that are covered with clusters of ⅜"–1½" sharp spines. The nocturnal flowers measure about 4" wide. The red, globose fruits average 2" wide.

Bloom Season: April–August

Habitat/Range: Historically endemic to coastal habitats of Volusia County south along the east coast to the Florida Keys. Now known only from St. Lucie and Monroe Counties.

Comments: *Harrisia* honors Irish botanist William H. Harris (1860–1920). The name *fragrans* refers to the floral scent. In the Everglades region this state-listed endangered species occurs in the coastal forests from the 10,000 Islands to Flamingo in Everglades National Park. It takes a lack of good judgment to admire the flower in its native habitat at night while covered with swarms of saltmarsh mosquitoes.

SWAMP LOBELIA
Lobelia paludosa Nutt.
Bellflower Family (Campanulaceae)

Description: The narrowly oblong leaves are mostly tufted near the base and measure 2"–6" long and 2"–3" wide. The few stem leaves are small and sessile. The flowers are white to very pale violet and measure ½"–⅝" with pubescence at the base of the lower lip.

Bloom Season: April–November

Habitat/Range: Wet flatwoods and marshes of Alabama, Georgia, and mainland Florida.

Comments: *Lobelia* commemorates Flemish herbalist Matthias de l'Obel (1538–1616). The name *paludosa* means "of the swamps," or "marsh loving," in reference to its habitat. It is also called white lobelia. It ranges south into the Big Cypress Swamp and Corkscrew Swamp region but does not occur within Everglades National Park. Members of this genus contain lobeline, used in anti-smoking medicines to lessen the withdrawal symptoms from nicotine. The plants also contain heart toxins if consumed. Butterflies occasionally visit the flowers.

HEAVENLY TRUMPETS
Calystegia sepium (L.) R. Br. subsp. *limnophila* (Greene) Brummitt
Morning-Glory Family (Convolvulaceae)

Description: The arrow-shaped leaves of this twining vine range from 1¼"–3" long and ⅜"–¾" wide (it always twines counter-clockwise). Trumpet-shaped flowers flare to about 2"–2¼" wide, often with thin, green stripes in the throat.

Bloom Season: March–September

Habitat/Range: Marshes and wet disturbed sites of the southeastern United States discontinuously west to California.

Comments: *Calystegia* means "calyx cover" and alludes to the bracts that cover the calyx. The name *sepium* means "growing in hedges," and *limnophila* means "pond" and "friend," alluding to its marsh habitat. It is also called hedge bindweed because of its propensity to aggressively cover cultivated hedges. Other common names are bugle vine and bellbind. There are many subspecies throughout its range and the leaves and rhizomes of one are eaten as a pot herb in Asia.

MOONFLOWER
Ipomoea alba L.
Morning-Glory Family (Convolvulaceae)

Description: The stems of this aggressive vine are smooth or with short, fleshy prickles. The rounded, alternate, heart-shaped leaves are either entire or with 3–5 lobes. Funnel-shaped flowers are 3"–4" wide and produced singly or 2–3 in a cluster. There are greenish nectar guides radiating into the throat.

Bloom Season: All year

Habitat/Range: Hardwood hammocks, mangroves, groves, and fencerows throughout Florida. Pantropical.

Comments: *Ipomoea* is Greek for "wormlike," alluding to the twining growth habit. The name *alba* means "white." The flowers open after dark and emit a heavy fragrance to attract sphinx moths as pollinators and then close shortly after sunrise, hence the common name. The young leaves are edible when cooked but the seeds are toxic and may cause hallucinations. The seeds were used in religious ceremonies in Mexico but with unpleasant side effects.

BEACH MORNING GLORY
Ipomoea imperati (Vahl) Griseb.
(Also *Ipomoea stolonifera* J. F. Gmel.)
Morning-Glory Family (Convolvulaceae)

Description: The rounded, alternate leaves of this trailing vine reach about 2" long and may be somewhat violin-shaped with 3–7 rounded lobes. The trumpet-shaped flowers are white with a yellow throat and reach about 2" wide. The flowers open in the morning and fade by midday.

Bloom Season: April–December

Habitat/Range: Sandy beaches of tropical and warm temperate regions worldwide (throughout Florida).

Comments: The name *imperati* honors Italian apothecary and naturalist Ferrante Imperato (1550–1625) who was among the first to correctly describe how fossils were formed. This vine is ecologically important as a dune stabilizer by trapping drifting sand. It seems to sense the high-tide line and will change its direction of growth back toward the dunes. It is used medicinally in Asia to treat jellyfish stings.

PINELAND CLUSTERVINE
Jacquemontia curtisii Peters ex Hallier f.
Morning-Glory Family (Convolvulaceae)

Description: This petite vinelike species has alternate, elliptic leaves that measure ½"–⅞" long and ¼"–⅜" wide. The flowers have rounded, essentially glabrous outer sepals and range from ⅝"–¾" wide, sometimes with a pinkish or violet tinge.

Bloom Season: All year

Habitat/Range: Endemic to pinelands and limestone outcroppings in prairies of central and southern Florida.

Comments: *Jacquemontia* honors French botanist Victor Jacquemont (1801–1832) who undertook a scientific survey of India in 1828 but succumbed to a tropical disease. The name *curtisii* honors Allan Hiram Curtiss (1845–1907), a prolific collector of plants throughout Florida. The imperiled beach clustervine *(Jacquemontia reclinata)* occurs from Key Biscayne (Miami-Dade County) to southern Broward County and differs principally by having sparsely pubescent outer sepals.

NOYAU VINE
Merremia dissecta (Jacq.) Hallier f.
Morning-Glory Family (Convolvulaceae)

Description: This weedy, twining vine has alternate leaves that are palmately divided nearly to the base with 7–9 toothed lobes. The leaves average 2"–4" wide. The trumpet-shaped flowers measure 1¼"–2" wide.

Bloom Season: May–November

Habitat/Range: Hammock margins, pinelands, and disturbed sites throughout Florida. Native to the Neotropics.

Comments: *Merremia* honors German naturalist and ornithologist Blasius Merrem (1761–1824). The name *dissecta* refers to the deeply dissected leaves. It is closely related to the woodrose *(Merremia tuberosa),* an invasive, yellow-flowered species with woody fruits used in dry floral arrangements. *Noyau* (pronounced *nwayoh*) means *nuts* or *kernels* in French and is also a French liqueur made from brandy flavored with nut kernels. Sphinx moths visit the flowers at night and skipper butterflies visit them during the day.

CHRISTMAS VINE
Turbina corymbosa (L.) Raf.
Morning-Glory Family (Convolvulaceae)

Description: The heart-shaped leaves of this twining vine average 1½"–3½" long. The bell-shaped, ¾" flowers bloom all at once in a sequence over a period of weeks, often at Christmastime.

Bloom Season: December–January

Habitat/Range: Hammock margins of southern Florida, Bahamas, and the Neotropics.

Comments: *Turbina* alludes to the similarity of the fruits to spinning tops. The name *corymbosa* refers to the corymbs of flowers. The seeds are called *ololiuqui* (round thing) in Nahuatl and contain hallucinatory principles. The seeds are still widely used in Mexico for psychedelic divinatory ceremonies and to communicate with the Devil. The use of *ololiuqui* dates back to Aztec priests who used the seeds to lose their fear when sacrificing young female virgins to their gods. A 16th-century Spanish missionary once wrote, "*Ololiuqui* deprives all who use it of their reason."

STARRUSH WHITETOP
Rhynchospora colorata (L.) H. Pfeiff.
(Also *Dichromena colorata* [L.] Hitchc.)
Sedge Family (Cyperaceae)

Description: Starrush whitetop spreads by rhizomes and has erect, linear leaves from 4"–12" long and about ⅛" wide. The erect flower spike is topped by 3–6 conspicuous, white, leafy bracts (involucres) tipped with green. Insignificant flowers are crowded in the center of the bracts.

Bloom Season: All year

Habitat/Range: Freshwater wetlands of the eastern United States, Bermuda, the West Indies, and Mexico.

Comments: *Rhynchospora* is Greek for "snout seed." The name *colorata* means "colored," in reference to the white bracts. The showy bracts help attract small insect pollinators to the tiny flowers. The very similar Florida whitetop *(Rhynchospora floridensis)* is a clumping species that is common in dry habitats throughout the Everglades region. Sandswamp whitetop *(Rhynchospora latifolia)* is larger and much taller.

TENANGLE PIPEWORT

Eriocaulon decangulare L.
Pipewort Family (Eriocaulaceae)

Description: The linear, basal leaves of this species are arranged in a spiral. The angled scape ranges from 12"–40" tall and is topped by a compact head of tiny flowers that form a rounded, white, somewhat compressed ball. The flower heads on this species are firm to the touch.

Bloom Season: May–October

Habitat/Range: Freshwater wetlands and flatwoods along the Atlantic Coastal Plain from New Jersey to Texas and Florida south to Mexico and Nicaragua.

Comments: *Eriocaulon* means "wooly stem" in reference to the wooly hairs that line the flowering stems. The name *decangulare* means "ten angled," referring to the typical number of angles on the flowering stem. It prefers strong sunlight so it benefits from fire by burning off competing vegetation. Flattened pipewort *(Eriocaulon compressum)* is similar but has soft, flattened flower heads and is typically found in deeper water.

YELLOW HATPINS

Syngonanthus flavidulus (Michx.) Ruhland
Pipewort Family (Eriocaulaceae)

Description: Narrowly linear, recurved, shiny leaves measure ¾"–1¼" long and form small tufts in moist, sandy soils. Minuscule flowers are borne in globose heads that appear as small, white buttons on slender stems held well above the leaves. The bracts below the heads are dull yellow and each head bears male and female flowers.

Bloom Season: February–July

Habitat/Range: Wet flatwoods, pond margins, and prairies along the coastal plain from North Carolina to Alabama south through mainland Florida.

Comments: *Syngonanthus* means "joined together" and "flower," alluding to the fused petals of the female flowers. The name *flavidulus* refers to the pale yellow floral bracts. It is also called bantam-buttons and is the only member of the genus in Florida. It ranges south into the Big Cypress and Corkscrew Swamp regions but does not occur within Everglades National Park.

BASTARD COPPERLEAF

Acalypha chamaedrifolia (Lam.) Müll. Arg.
Spurge Family (Euphorbiaceae)

Description: This prostrate species has ovate or lanceolate leaves with scalloped margins and range from ½"–1" long and ¼"–⅜" wide. The erect flower spike ranges from ½"–1¼" tall and is lined with minuscule flowers that require a hand lens to appreciate. Female flowers are toward the bottom of the spike.

Bloom Season: April–October

Habitat/Range: Pinelands of Florida (Hillsborough, Miami-Dade, and Monroe Counties) to the West Indies.

Comments: *Acalypha* is an ancient Greek word for "nettle" and was used for this genus because Linnaeus thought the leaves looked like a nettle. The name *chamaedrifolia* means "leaves resting on the ground," alluding to its low stature. In the Everglades region it inhabits pine rocklands from Biscayne Bay to Long Pine Key in Everglades National Park and also Big Pine Key in the Lower Florida Keys. It is locally common but easily overlooked.

CHESTNUTLEAF FALSE CROTON

Caperonia castaneifolia (L.) A. St.-Hil.
Spurge Family (Euphorbiaceae)

Description: The slightly hairy stems and spreading branches of this species have widely spaced, toothed, elliptic or narrowly lanceolate leaves from ¾"–2½" long. Male and female flowers are separate on the same plant. The petals on the male flowers are about ⅛"–³⁄₁₆" long, and slightly smaller on the female flowers.

Bloom Season: All year

Habitat/Range: Freshwater wetlands of central and southern Florida to the West Indies.

Comments: *Caperonia* honors Nöel Capperon, a 16th-century apothecary of Orléans, France. The name *castaneifolia* refers to the leaves resembling a *Castanea*, the sweet chestnut (Fagaceae). It is frequent in seasonally flooded habitats throughout the Everglades region. Butterflies visit the flowers. This is the only species in the genus native to Florida but sacatrapo *(Caperonia palustris)* is a Neotropical species that is naturalized in the state.

GRACEFUL SANDMAT
Chamaesyce hypericifolia (L.) Millsp.
Spurge Family (Euphorbiaceae)

Description: Graceful sandmat averages 12"–24" tall with finely toothed, oblong leaves that average ½"–1½" long and ⅜"–¾" wide. All parts exude milky sap if broken. White to pinkish, ⅛" flowers with conspicuous stipules are borne in round clusters.

Bloom Season: All year

Habitat/Range: Pinelands and disturbed sites of the southern United States to the Neotropics.

Comments: *Chamaesyce* means "on the ground" and "fig," and alludes to a prostrate species with figlike fruits. The name *hypericifolia* relates to the similarity of the leaves to those of a *Hypericum* (Clusiaceae). It is also called Yerba Niña. This species is common along roadsides and in disturbed natural areas. The similar Hyssopleaf Sandmat (*Chamaesyce hyssopifolia*) has narrower leaves and inconspicuous stipules. Both are common weeds in abandoned farm fields, along roadsides, and in urban landscapes.

STINGING NETTLE
Cnidoscolus stimulosus (Michx.) Engelm. & A. Gray
Spurge Family (Euphorbiaceae)

Description: Stinging hairs cover the stems and leaves of this species. It is usually less than 12" tall with 3- or 5-lobed leaves, often irregularly dissected, and typically 3"–6" long and 2"–4" wide. The ½" flowers are fragrant.

Bloom Season: All year

Habitat/Range: Sandy habitats of the southeastern United States.

Comments: *Cnidoscolus* is Greek for "sting nettle." The name *stimulosus* means "tormenting" or "stinging," in reference to the stinging hairs that cover the stems and leaves. Contact with the hairs will result in intense stinging that feels much like fire ants, followed by a persistent red rash that may leave the skin discolored for weeks. If left alone the stinging will dissipate in about a half hour but scratching only makes it worse. The root is also edible and the leaves taste like spinach when cooked. Another common name is tread-softly.

PINELAND CROTON
Croton linearis Jacq.
Spurge Family (Euphorbiaceae)

Description: This species averages 3'–4' tall with linear, alternate leaves. The leaves are ¾"–2" long and ⅛"–¼" wide, green above and covered with silvery or golden hairs below. Male and female flowers are produced on separate plants and measure ³⁄₁₆"–¼" wide.

Bloom Season: All year

Habitat/Range: Pinelands of southern Florida, the Bahamas, and Greater Antilles.

Comments: *Croton* means "tick," referring to the seed shape. The name *linearis* means "linear," referring to the leaves. This is the larval food plant of the Florida leafwing and Bartram's hairstreak. Both are state-listed endangered butterflies that occur on Long Pine Key in Everglades National Park, often near this plant. Plants in this genus contain poisonous alkaloids but are sometimes used medicinally. Vente conmigo *(Croton glandulosus)* has similar flowers but is a small herbaceous species of pinelands and beach dunes.

LESSER FLORIDA SPURGE
Euphorbia polyphylla Engelm. ex Chapm.
Spurge Family (Euphorbiaceae)

Description: This is a wiry plant from 8"–12" tall with numerous narrowly linear leaves measuring ¼"–⅝" long and ¹⁄₁₆" wide or less. The small flowers are less than ⅛" wide and have 5 lobes that are white along the outer edge and reddish purple at the base. All parts exude milky latex if broken.

Bloom Season: All year

Habitat/Range: Endemic to pine rocklands, sandhills, and flatwoods of central and southern Florida.

Comments: *Euphorbia* honors Trojan War hero Euphorbus, physician to the king of the ancient North African country of Mauretania and a contemporary of the Roman scholar Pliny (AD 23–79). The name *polyphylla* means "with many leaves." All members of this genus contain toxic latex that can cause a burning skin rash. If conveyed to the eyes the sap produces severe irritation and temporary blindness. Wasps visit the flowers for nectar and are effective pollinators.

FLORIDA PRAIRIECLOVER
Dalea carthagenensis (Jacq.) J. F. Macrb. var. *floridana* (Rydb.) Barneby
Pea Family (Fabaceae)

Description: The compound leaves of this bushy species have 11–23 oval, gland-dotted leaflets that measure ⅜"–⅝" long and half as wide. Flowers are about ⅜" wide and are in loose axillary clusters at the ends of hairy stalks.

Bloom Season: All year

Habitat/Range: Endemic to pinelands and edges of marl prairies in southern Florida.

Comments: *Dalea* commemorates English physician and amateur botanist Samuel Dale (1659–1739). The name *carthagenensis* relates to Cartagena, Colombia, where the species was first collected. The name *floridana* means "of Florida" where this rare variety was first collected in 1878. It is currently known from two preserves in Miami-Dade County and two locations in the Big Cypress National Preserve (Collier & Monroe Counties). It historically occurred in Everglades National Park and Palm Beach County.

ELLIOTT'S MILKPEA
Galactia elliottii Nutt.
Pea Family (Fabaceae)

Description: This twining or spreading species has leaves divided into 3–9 oblong leaflets with axillary flowers borne on long stems (peduncles). The pealike flowers are showy and measure ½"–⅝" wide. The narrow ½"–1" pods are densely covered with short appressed hairs.

Bloom Season: April–November

Habitat/Range: Pinelands and flatwoods of Florida, Georgia, and South Carolina.

Comments: *Galactia* means "milk-yielding," a name first used in 1756 to describe a species with milky sap. The name *elliottii* honors American legislator, banker, and botanist Stephen Elliott (1771–1830) of South Carolina. Elliott's milkpea ranges south into the Florida Keys but is surprisingly absent from Everglades National Park. It is a larval host plant of the zarucco duskywing and northern cloudywing butterflies in Florida and is the only white-flowered *Galactia* in the Everglades region.

WHITE CLOVER
Trifolium repens L.
Pea Family (Fabaceae)

Description: White clover produces flower stalks that arise from underground stolons (other species in Florida are not stoloniferous). The leaves have 3 oval leaflets, each measuring about ⅜"–½" wide. The heads of flowers average ¾"–1" wide on erect stalks that stand about 2½" tall.

Bloom Season: All year

Habitat/Range: Road swales, lawns, pastures, and other disturbed sites of Florida. Native to Eurasia.

Comments: *Trifolium* refers to the 3 leaflets and the name *repens* alludes to its creeping growth habit. The leaves form the shamrock that is the symbol of Ireland. It has been introduced worldwide as a forage crop for livestock but the leaves are also widely eaten as salad greens and are high in protein. It is also called Dutch clover and has been used to treat fevers and Bright's disease. Bees visit the flowers and it is a larval host plant of the orange sulphur and southern dogface butterflies in Florida.

SHORTLEAF ROSEGENTIAN
Sabatia brevifolia Raf.
Gentian Family (Gentianaceae)

Description: This annual typically reaches 4"–8" tall but may be much taller. The narrowly linear leaves are ascending and are sometimes appressed to the stem, reaching 1" long and barely ⅛" wide. The flowers are white (never pink) with a greenish-yellow center and average about ⅞" wide. The upper branches are alternate.

Bloom Season: March–September

Habitat/Range: Flatwoods and brackish marshes of the southeastern United States.

Comments: *Sabatia* honors 18th-century Italian botanist Liberato Sabbati who was the keeper of the botanical garden in Rome. The name *brevifolia* refers to the short leaves. Relating to its use to treat malaria it is also called quinine herb and quinine flower. This species lacks the jagged red line at the base of the corolla lobes found on white forms of rose of Plymouth *(Sabatia stellaris)*, which may share its habitat and bloom at the same time.

GHOSTPLANT
Voyria parasitica (Schltdl. & Cham.) Ruyters & Maas
Gentian Family (Gentianaceae)

Description: Ghostplant lacks chlorophyll and typically stands 3"–6" tall, branching near the top of the very frail beige stems. The flowers are about ¼" wide and are followed by cylindrical fruits with dustlike seeds.

Bloom Season: All year

Habitat/Range: Hammocks of Miami-Dade County and the Florida Keys south into the West Indies.

Comments: *Voyria* is a name from French Guiana. The name *parasitica* refers to the plant deriving all of its food from fungi that it parasitizes, called *myco-heterotrophy*. Ghostplant occurs in tropical hammocks throughout Miami-Dade County including Long Pine Key in Everglades National Park. It forms spreading colonies but can easily be overlooked because it blends in perfectly with the leaf litter where it is loosely rooted on the forest floor. Some members of the genus are used medicinally to treat chronic indigestion (dyspepsia).

INKBERRY
Scaevola plumieri (L.) Vahl.
Goodenia Family (Goodeniaceae)

Description: This shrubby, coastal species typically reaches about 2'–3' tall. The spatulate leaves are glossy and crowded at the tips of the stems, ranging from 2"–4" long and 1"–1¾" wide. The flowers are fan shaped. The ½" round fruits are black.

Bloom Season: All year

Habitat/Range: Beaches of central and southern Florida through the Neotropics.

Comments: *Scaevola* means "left hand" and relates to the half-flowers produced by these plants. The related beach naupaka *(Scaevola taccada)* from the Pacific Ocean region aggressively invades Florida's beach dunes. It differs by its light green leaves and white fruits. In Hawaiian legend two lovers got in an argument so she tore a naupaka flower in half. The angry gods then turned all naupaka flowers into half flowers. The name *plumieri* honors French Franciscan monk Charles Plumier (1646–1704) who explored the Neotropics. Gulls eat the fruits.

MUSKY MINT
Hyptis alata (Raf.) Shinners
Mint Family (Lamiaceae)

Description: This mint has square stems from 2'–3' tall or more and lanceolate, coarsely toothed, opposite leaves that measure 1½"–4" long and ½"–1½" wide. Round, compact, greenish heads are on long, axillary stems. The 5-lobed flowers are white, spotted with purple, and there are 5 white, hairy sepals.

Bloom Season: All year

Habitat/Range: Freshwater wetlands of the southeastern United States and the West Indies.

Comments: *Hyptis* is a Greek word meaning "resupinate" and refers to the reflexed lower lip of the flower that gives it an upside-down appearance. The name *alata* means "winged," in reference to the leaf blades that taper to the base and appear winglike. This species has a musky odor unlike the refreshing scent of other mints. Musky mint is the only native member of the genus in Florida and is common throughout the Everglades region. The flowers attract small butterflies.

LOVEVINE
Cassytha filiformis L.
Laurel Family (Lauraceae)

Description: This conspicuous parasitic vine is usually void of leaves or they appear scalelike. The threadlike stems are typically orange and attach to herbaceous and woody plants that it may weaken or kill. Tiny white flowers are followed by white, pearl-like fruits up to ¼" in diameter.

Bloom Season: All year

Habitat/Range: Coastal dunes, sandhills, and pinelands from Florida, Bahamas, and the West Indies.

Comments: *Cassytha* is Greek for a parasitic plant. The name *filiformis* means "threadlike," in reference to the stems. This plant superficially resembles the parasitic dodder *(Cuscuta)* in the morning-glory family (Convolvulaceae). Crushed stems of lovevine emit a spicy fragrance that typifies the laurel family. The common name relates to a tea brewed in the Bahamas that is said to "put the lead in a man's pencil." It is called *fideo* in Cuba, Spanish for "noodle" or "spaghetti."

LAX HORNPOD
Mitreola petiolata (J. F. Gmel.) Torr. & A. Gray
Logania Family (Loganiaceae)

Description: This annual, wetland species is typically 4"–12" tall, usually branched, with very short petioles on most leaves. The leaves are mostly narrowly lanceolate from ¾"–3" long and ⅜"–1½" wide. Smaller leaves may form at the axils of the main leaves. Flowers are about 3/32" wide.

Bloom Season: April–November

Habitat/Range: Freshwater wetlands throughout mainland Florida. Cosmopolitan.

Comments: *Mitreola* refers to the resemblance of the fruits to a bishop's mitre. The name *petiolata* refers to the small petioles of this species. It is also called stalked miterwort. Swamp hornpod *(Mitreola sessilifolia)* is similar but differs principally by its ovate, clasping, sessile leaves. Both are common and can form spreading colonies in shallow water or in wet soil along trails that bisect their habitat. This is the only genus in the logania family in Florida.

WHITE FENROSE
Kosteletzkya depressa (L.) O. J. Blanch. et al
Mallow Family (Malvaceae)

Description: The branches and leaves of this 3' semi-woody shrub are covered with bristly, starlike hairs. The leaves are narrowly oblong, ovate, or unequally triangular, mostly ¾"–2½" long with toothed or scalloped margins. The hibiscus-like, ⅜"–½" flowers have 5 white petals.

Bloom Season: All year

Habitat/Range: Salt marshes and borders of mangroves and coastal hammocks of the southwestern tip of mainland Florida and the West Indies.

Comments: *Kosteletzkya* commemorates Czechoslovakian botanist Vincenz Franz Kosteletzky (1801–1887). The name *depressa* means "flattened" or "pressed down," in reference to the growth habit of some plants. The hairs on the stems and leaves of this species are irritating and can inflame sensitive skin. This state-listed endangered species can be seen along the Snake Bight and Rowdy Bend trails in Everglades National Park.

FLOATING HEART
Nymphoides aquatica (J. F. Gmel.) Kuntze
Bogbean Family (Menyanthaceae)

Description: The floating, ovate leaves of this aquatic species measure 4"–6" wide and are conspicuously roughened on the lower surface. Thickened roots are often at the base of the flowering stalks that appear from the node just below the leaf blade. The ⅜"–½" flowers are held just above the water surface.

Bloom Season: All year

Habitat/Range: Swamps, ponds, lakes, and canals from New Jersey to Texas through mainland Florida.

Comments: *Nymphoides* refers to the similarity of this genus to *Nymphaea*, the waterlilies. The name *aquatica* refers to its aquatic habitat. This plant is sold in the aquarium trade as "banana lily" because of the banana-like clusters of swollen roots beneath the leaf blades. The similar *Nymphoides cristata* is naturalized from Asia and has a longitudinal crest on the corolla lobes with cordate leaves that are often blotched with maroon.

SOUTHERN COLICROOT
Aletris bracteata Northr.
Bog Asphodel Family (Nartheciaceae)

Description: The rosette of leaves of this species resembles a miniature agave. The leaves are linear lanceolate, gray green, and range from 2½"–4" long and ¼"–⅜" wide. The erect flower stalk is 12"–24" tall, bearing small, leaflike bracts. The floral bracts are about ³⁄₁₆"–¼" long, almost equaling the length of the mealy, somewhat cylindrical, creamy white flowers.

Bloom Season: All year

Habitat/Range: Rocky pine savannas of southern Florida and the Bahamas.

Comments: *Aletris* means "to grind," alluding to the cornmeal-like texture of the flowers. Aletris was a legendary Greek slave who ground corn. The name *bracteata* means "having bracts." A decoction derived from the roots was thought to be a sedative and was given to soothe upset stomachs and relieve the abdominal pain associated with colic. This species is locally common in Everglades National Park but does not occur north of the park.

WHITE WATERLILY
Nymphaea odorata Ait.
Waterlily Family (Nymphaeaceae)

Description: The round, floating leaf blades reach 6"–10" wide with a narrow basal cleft. The solitary, highly perfumed, 3"–4" flowers open by midmorning and close by late afternoon. The white petals may be lightly blushed with pink and the flowers typically float on the water surface.

Bloom Season: February–November

Habitat/Range: Freshwater ponds, lakes, swamps, and canals across the eastern United States to Canada and the Bahamas.

Comments: *Nymphaea* is Greek for "water nymph." The name *odorata* refers to the fragrant blossoms and this species is regarded as the most fragrant of all waterlilies. Waterlilies held a prominent place in the art and mythology of Egyptian, Chinese, and Mayan cultures and the rhizomes of some species contain psychotropic alkaloids and were used as a hallucinogen. This species is commonly cultivated and is often used as a parent in fascinating hybrids for water garden enthusiasts. Bees and beetles are attracted to the abundant nectar in the flowers. After checking for alligators and cottonmouth water moccasins it is well worth wading out to savor the floral fragrance.

CARTER'S ORCHID
Basiphyllaea corallicola (Small) Ames
Orchid Family (Orchidaceae)

Description: The single leaf of this rare orchid is practically impossible to find because it is only about 2" long and ⅛" wide. The flower stem stands 3½"–6" tall and is topped by several flower buds that rarely open because they are cleistogamous (pollinated in bud).

Bloom Season: October–November

Habitat/Range: Pine rocklands and hammock margins of southern Florida (Miami-Dade and Monroe Counties) and the Bahamas.

Comments: *Basiphyllaea* refers to the basal leaf. The name *corallicola* means "growing on coral," alluding to the coralline rock on which it often grows. Joel Jackson Carter (1843–1912) first discovered it in Florida in 1903 while bouncing along on a horse-drawn wagon across Longview Prairie south of Miami with botanists Alvah Augustus Eaton (1865–1908) and John Kunkel Small (1869–1938). Eaton was upset because he had switched seats with Carter that day.

MOSS ORCHID
Cranichis muscosa Sw.
Orchid Family (Orchidaceae)

Description: There is a basal rosette of 4–8 broadly elliptic leaves that are 1"–3" long and ½"–1½" wide, usually growing among mosses. The raceme of flowers averages 3"–6" tall with each flower measuring about ⁷⁄₁₆" wide.

Bloom Season: December–March

Habitat/Range: On moss-covered tree bases, stumps, and logs from the Neotropics to Collier County, Florida.

Comments: *Cranichis* means "helmet," alluding to the helmetlike lip. The name *muscosa* means "mossy," alluding to its habit of growing among mosses. The first time this orchid was discovered in Florida was May 1903 in Lee County (probably the Fakahatchee Swamp) and then again the same year in Miami-Dade County. It was not seen in Florida again for 101 years when AmeriCorps volunteer Karen Relish (1963–) discovered a flowering population on a moss-covered log deep in the Fakahatchee Swamp in January 2004. It is a state-listed endangered species.

GHOST ORCHID

Dendrophylax lindenii (Lindl.) Benth. ex Rolfe
(Also *Polyradicion lindenii* [Lindl.] Garay; *Polyrrhiza lindenii* [Lindl.] Cogn.)
Orchid Family (Orchidaceae)

Description: The photosynthetic roots of this leaf-less epiphytic orchid are flecked with white and radiate outward like spokes on a wheel. The growing tips are green. The 3"–4" flowers are solitary or in pairs (rarely clustered).

Bloom Season: May–August

Habitat/Range: Hardwood swamps and sloughs of southwestern Florida and Cuba.

Comments: *Dendrophylax* means "tree guardian" and alludes to the epiphytic habit of this small genus of orchids. The name *lindenii* honors Belgian botanist Jean Jules Linden (1817–1898) who discovered this orchid in Cuba in 1844. Botanist Allan Hiram Curtiss (1845–1907) first discovered it in Florida in 1880. The largest population in Florida is in the Fakahatchee Swamp but it also occurs sparingly in the Big Cypress Swamp and Corkscrew Swamp. Naturalist Charles Torrey Simpson (1846–1932) discovered it in April 1885 growing on royal palms *(Roystonea regia)* along the Rodgers River in what is now Everglades National Park. The flowers of this endangered species perfume the night air to attract the giant sphinx moth as a pollinator. Ghost orchids often grow on the branches of pond-apple *(Annona glabra),* the larval host plant of the giant sphinx moth.

SPURRED NEOTTIA

Eltroplectris calcarata (Sw.) Garay & Sweet
Orchid Family (Orchidaceae)

Description: The silky, elliptic leaf blades range from 4"–6" long and 1½"–2½" wide. The 2" flowers are arranged at the top of an erect spike. The sepals and petals are linear-lanceolate and the frilly lip is recurved.

Bloom Season: December–March

Habitat/Range: Hardwood hammocks of Florida (Highlands and Miami-Dade Counties), West Indies, Colombia, and Brazil.

Comments: *Eltroplectris* and *calcarata* both allude to the flower's free-hanging nectar spur. This state-listed endangered species occurs in Everglades National Park but is sporadic and rare. Alvah Augustus Eaton (1865–1908) discovered it in Florida (Miami-Dade County) in 1905. Feral hogs have decimated the population in Highlands Hammock State Park (Highlands County) and by the late 1980s it disappeared from hammocks east of Everglades National Park, perhaps due to a lowered water table.

NIGHT-SCENTED ORCHID

Epidendrum nocturnum Jacq.
Orchid Family (Orchidaceae)

Description: The reedlike leafy stems of this epiphyte may reach 3' long with elliptic, leathery leaves that measure 3"–5" long and ½"–1" wide. The lip of the flower is 3-lobed, with 2 winglike lateral lobes and the central lobe tapering to a narrow point.

Bloom Season: July–December

Habitat/Range: Hardwood hammocks and wooded swamps of the lower Florida mainland and the Neotropics.

Comments: *Epidendrum* is Greek for "on tree," referring to the epiphytic habit. The name *nocturnum* means "nocturnal" and alludes to the captivating scent emitted by the flowers at night. The pungent scent attracts sphinx moths that hover like hummingbirds around the flowers at sunset. The pollinia stick to the head of the moth as it sips nectar and is then transferred to another flower. Botanist Abram Paschell Garber (1838–1881) first discovered this state-listed endangered species in Florida in 1877.

MICHAUX'S ORCHID
Habenaria quinqueseta (Michx.) Eaton
Orchid Family (Orchidaceae)

Description: The succulent leaves of this terrestrial orchid are alternately spaced up the stem at flowering. Flowering plants are 6"–14" tall with 2"–6" long and ¾"–1" wide lanceolate leaves. The ¾" flowers are spindly and the white lip is in 3 threadlike divisions.

Bloom Season: August–January

Habitat/Range: Marshes, prairies, and wet flatwoods from South Carolina to Texas south through mainland Florida.

Comments: *Habenaria* means "rein," alluding to the reinlike spurs on the lip. The name *quinqueseta* means "five bristles," for the narrow portions of the calyx and corolla. The common name is for botanist Francois André Michaux (1770–1855) who first discovered this species in South Carolina. It ranges south into Everglades National Park and is similar to the rare *Habenaria distans* of Collier County that has leaves in a basal rosette and tuberlike growths on the roots.

HATCHET ORCHID
Pelexia adnata (Sw.) Poit ex Rich.
Orchid Family (Orchidaceae)

Description: The elliptic leaves average 2½"–4½" long and 1¼"–2" wide. Flowers are about ¼" wide on a hairy, erect spike that is typically 6"–10" tall, often blotched with white.

Bloom Season: March–June

Habitat/Range: In humus or on mossy logs in hardwood swamps and hammocks of southern Florida (Collier and Miami-Dade Counties) and the Neotropics.

Comments: *Pelexia* means "helmet" and refers to the dorsal sepal that is united with 2 petals to form a hood. The name *adnata* refers to the lateral sepals that clasp the column foot. This species was first discovered in Florida by the author in 1978 while exploring a Miami-Dade County hammock. By 1985 it had disappeared but was rediscovered in the Fakahatchee Swamp (Collier County) in 2004 by Florida State Park biologist Mike Owen (1960–) and AmeriCorps volunteer Karen Relish (1963–). The Spanish common name is *hachuela,* or "hatchet."

SNOWY ORCHID

Platanthera nivea (Nutt.) Luer
Orchid Family (Orchidaceae)

Description: This terrestrial orchid has keeled, lanceolate leaves that measure 2"–8" long and ⅜"–¼" wide. The erect stalk produces 20–50 glistening flowers arranged cylindrically with individual flowers measuring about ¼" long and ⅛" wide. The narrow lip is bent backward at the center.

Bloom Season: May–June

Habitat/Range: Wet flatwoods and prairies of the southeastern United States south in Florida to the Big Cypress Swamp.

Comments: *Platanthera* means "broad anther." The name *nivea* means "snowy," in reference to the sparkling, snow-white flowers. Attempts have been made to place this species in the genus *Habenaria*. More plants flower if there has been fire in its habitat during the previous year but individual plants have a very short bloom period. It often blooms in standing water and may skip flowering in dry years. The floral scent is reminiscent of grape jelly.

JUG ORCHID

Platythelys querceticola (Lindl.) Garay
(Also *Erythrodes querceticola* [Lindl.] Ames; *Platythelys sagreana* [A. Rich.] Garay)
Orchid Family (Orchidaceae)

Description: The very frail, succulent stems average 3"–6" tall and are lined with alternating lanceolate leaves averaging ⅜"–1" long and ¼"–½" wide. Flowers are white to greenish and are only about ⁵⁄₁₆" wide.

Bloom Season: October–March

Habitat/Range: Terrestrial in humus of forests and wooded swamps of Florida, Louisiana, and the Neotropics.

Comments: *Platythelys* means "broad woman" and is a fanciful allusion to the broad, flat beak (rostellum) on the upper edge of the stigma. The name *querceticola* refers to its habit of growing near oaks *(Quercus)*. This species is extremely difficult to locate even when it is nearby. Scattered populations occur in the hammocks of Long Pine Key in Everglades National Park through the Big Cypress and Corkscrew Swamp region northward in Florida.

LACELIP LADIES'-TRESSES
Spiranthes laciniata (Small) Ames
Orchid Family (Orchidaceae)

Description: The copious hairs on the erect flowering stems are swollen at the apex (capitate). The leaves are linear lanceolate, mostly basal, averaging 4"–8" long and ¼"–⅜" wide. The flowers are about ¼" wide.

Bloom Season: May–July

Habitat/Range: Prairies, open cypress swamps, and roadsides along the coastal plain from New Jersey south through Texas and Florida.

Comments: *Spiranthes* translates to "coil flower," alluding to the spiraling flower arrangement of many species. The name *laciniata* refers to the fringed lip. This orchid can line roadsides by the thousands, especially in northeast Florida, and is often common along roadsides and in sunny prairies of the Everglades region as well. An important feature that distinguishes it from the spring ladies'-tresses *(Spiranthes vernalis)* is the swollen tip on the hairs but to see them will require a hand lens.

LONG-LIPPED LADIES'-TRESSES
Spiranthes longilabris Lindl.
Orchid Family (Orchidaceae)

Description: The flowers of this terrestrial orchid are in tight ranks up the stem, often in a spiraling arrangement. There are 3–5 linear-lanceolate leaves that measure 3"–6" long but may not be present at flowering. The pubescent flowers are ⁵⁄₁₆" wide with a long lip and spreading lateral sepals.

Bloom Season: November–December

Habitat/Range: Flatwoods and prairies from Virginia to Texas south in Florida to Collier County.

Comments: The name *longilabris* refers to the long lip (labellum) of the flower. This state-listed threatened species ranges south in Florida to the Big Cypress Swamp (Bear Island) and the Corkscrew Swamp region. It was historically present in Miami-Dade County. The late bloom season combined with the widely spreading lateral sepals help separate this species from other white-flowered *Spiranthes* that occur in the region.

FRAGRANT LADIES'-TRESSES
Spiranthes odorata (Nutt.) Lindl.
Orchid Family (Orchidaceae)

Description: This aquatic or semi-aquatic orchid is typically less than 12" tall when in flower but can be much taller. The leaves are narrowly lanceolate and range from 3"–6" long and ½"–¾" wide. The flower spike is lined with very fragrant, ¼" flowers.

Bloom Season: Mostly October–December

Habitat/Range: Freshwater wetlands from Virginia to Texas through mainland Florida.

Comments: The name *odorata* means "with an odor," referring to the tantalizing scent that fills the air around the flowers. It often blooms in standing water but may be found in wet soil of cypress domes and wooded swamps throughout the Everglades region. It is worth wading out to take in the perfume emanating from the blossoms if it is found growing in standing water. It was once regarded as a variety (var. *odorata*) of the very similar *Spiranthes cernua* found in the Apalachicola National Forest.

GREENVEIN LADIES'-TRESSES
Spiranthes praecox (Walter) S. Watson
Orchid Family (Orchidaceae)

Description: The linear to linear-lanceolate leaves of this terrestrial orchid are spreading and average 4"–8" long and ¼"–½" wide. The flowers may be loosely or tightly spiraled, usually with a series of thin green (or pale lemon-yellow) veins on the lip.

Bloom Season: February–June

Habitat/Range: Moist roadsides, flatwoods, and pine savannas from New Jersey to Texas south through mainland Florida.

Comments: The name *praecox* means "precocious" or "untimely," in reference to its early blooming season. Plants without the characteristic green veins on the lip are referred to as forma *albolabia* (white lip). Some plants in north-central Florida produce green flowers. This is one of the most common members of the genus in Florida but is not known from Everglades National Park. It sometimes hybridizes with the following species to form *Spiranthes x meridionalis*.

SPRING LADIES'-TRESSES
Spiranthes vernalis Engelm. & A. Gray
Orchid Family (Orchidaceae)

Description: This is one of the most common terrestrial orchids thoughout much of Florida. The linear leaves average 4"–6" long and up to ⅜" wide. The erect flower spike is covered with pointed hairs and is lined with ⁷⁄₁₆" flowers, often with some degree of spiraling but some plants hold the flowers in a single rank. It averages 6"–10" tall when in flower.

Bloom Season: February–May

Habitat/Range: Flatwoods, prairies, and roadsides from Massachusetts to Nebraska south to Texas and Florida.

Comments: The name *vernalis* relates to the vernal equinox, or "belonging to spring," in reference to its flowering season. It is common along mowed road swales and in open prairies. Its early flowering season helps separate it from other white-flowered species, especially the similar lacelip ladies'-tresses *(Spiranthes laciniata)* that typically blooms in summertime.

SOLDIER ORCHID

Zeuxine strateumatica (L.) Schltr.
Orchid Family (Orchidaceae)

Description: This annual terrestrial orchid is 1"–4" tall when in flower. Narrowly lanceolate, green or bronze leaves sheath the stem. A terminal spike bears small, yellow-lipped, white flowers crowded together. Each flower is only about ³⁄₁₆" wide.

Bloom Season: December–February

Habitat/Range: Principally in mulched areas, lawns, and roadsides of central and southern Florida. Native to Asia.

Comments: *Zeuxine* means "a yoking," in reference to the partial union of the lip and column. The name *strateumatica* means "company" or "army," a fanciful allusion to clusters of plants resembling soldiers standing at attention. It was first reported in Florida in 1936 and is thought to have arrived in grass seed imported from China. It is also called lawn orchid due to its habit of showing up in lawns. It can be especially common along roadsides throughout the Everglades region.

PALE PASSIONFLOWER

Passiflora pallens Poepp. ex Mast.
Passionflower Family (Passifloraceae)

Description: The evenly 3-lobed leaves make this native passionflower easy to identify. The leaves range from 1"–3" long and the lobes are rounded. The showy flowers are 2" wide and produce round, yellow, 2" fruits. It climbs by tendrils.

Bloom Season: All year

Habitat/Range: Hardwood hammocks and swamps of southern Florida and the West Indies.

Comments: *Passiflora* is Latin for "passion flower" and relates to the crucifixion of Jesus. When Spanish physician Nicolás Monardes (1493–1588) published his herbal in 1574 he called these plants *Flos passionis*, or "flower of passion." Ever since then the plants have become intertwined with mystical Christian beliefs that the flower parts depict the crucifixion of Christ. The name *pallens* refers to the pale flower color of this state-listed endangered species. Heliconian butterflies rarely use this species as larval food.

GOATSFOOT

Passiflora sexflora Juss.

Passionflower Family (Passifloraceae)

Description: The goat's-foot-shaped leaves of this vine vary from 2½"–5" wide and about half as long. The leaves are opposite tendrils used for climbing and the stems and leaf blades are covered with fine, soft hairs. The clustered flowers measure ⅜"–½" wide. The rounded, ⅜" fruits are pubescent and ripen purplish black.

Bloom Season: All year

Habitat/Range: Hardwood forests of Florida (Miami-Dade County) and the Neotropics.

Comments: The name *sexflora* refers to it sometimes producing clusters of 6 flowers. The leaves serve as larval food for zebra longwing, Julia, and gulf fritillary butterflies but extrafloral nectaries on the leaves are intended to offer protection for the plant by attracting ants that attack butterfly larvae. It is a state-listed endangered species that has a habit of disappearing from some areas but then reappearing months or even years later.

ROUGH HEDGEHYSSOP

Gratiola hispida (Benth. ex Lindl.) Pollard

Plantain Family (Plantaginaceae)

Description: The very narrow, needlelike, dark green leaves are coarsely hairy (hispid) and measure ¼"–½" long, crowded along the stems. The leaves are often curled under at the margins (revolute). The flowers measure about ½" wide and appear along the stems.

Bloom Season: May–November

Habitat/Range: Dry flatwoods and scrub of the southeastern United States south through mainland Florida.

Comments: *Gratiola* means "agreeableness" or "pleasantness," and is said to allude to the medicinal qualities bestowed on this group of plants. The name *hispida* refers to the coarse hairs on the leaves. This species can be found in the dry flatwoods of the CREW Marsh in Collier County, especially along the Cypress Dome Trail. The plant looks somewhat like wild pennyroyal *(Piloblephis rigida)* but the leaves are darker green and have no minty odor when crushed.

BRANCHED HEDGEHYSSOP
Gratiola ramosa Walter
Plantain Family (Plantaginaceae)

Description: The many-branched, pubescent stems of this species reach 4"–12" tall. The leaves are opposite, oblong to ovate, and average ⅜"–⅞" long and about ¼" wide. The leaves are widely clasping where they meet the stem with a few coarse teeth along the margins. The tubular flowers are about ½"–⅝" long with white lobes and a yellow tube with brown lines.

Bloom Season: All year

Habitat/Range: Flatwoods, pond margins, and open marshes from Maryland to Louisiana south through mainland Florida.

Comments: The name *ramosa* means "branched." Of the 8 native members of this genus in Florida this is the only species that occurs in Everglades National Park. Most species in this genus occur in the central and northern counties of Florida but this and the previous species range south into the Everglades region. Some species have a long history of medicinal uses in Europe and North America.

PENINSULA AXILFLOWER

Mecardonia acuminata (Walter) Small subsp.
peninsularis (Pennell) Rossow
Plantain Family (Plantaginaceae)

Description: This endemic subspecies has angled stems that branch near the base. The toothed leaves are typically ½"–⅝" long (never longer than 1" on this subspecies) and about ¼" wide. White, 5-lobed, tubular flowers are on long stalks with the posterior lobes of the flowers united about ⅔ of the length.

Bloom Season: April–November

Habitat/Range: Endemic to marshes and damp soils of central and southern Florida.

Comments: *Mecardonia* honors Antonio de Meca y Cardona, an 18th-century Spanish patron of the Barcelona Botanical Garden and Marquis of Ciutadilla. The name *acuminata* means "tapering to a long narrow point," referring to the leaf shape. The name *peninsularis* means "growing on a peninsula," in this case, Florida. It is also called pixie foxglove and is a worthy subject for wild gardens or container culture.

DOCTORBUSH

Plumbago zeylanica L.
(Also *Plumbago scandens* L.)
Leadwort Family (Plumbaginaceae)

Description: Doctorbush has vinelike branches to 3' long or more with alternate, elliptic-lanceolate leaves ranging from 1¼"–4" long and up to 2⅜" wide. The flower spikes reach 4"–5" long and bear white, tubular flowers to about ⅝" wide. The anthers are blue. The linear fruits are prism shaped and cling to hair and clothing.

Bloom Season: All year

Habitat/Range: Coastal strand and open disturbed sites of the southern United States, the Neotropics, Hawaii, and Southeast Asia.

Comments: *Plumbago* was used by Dioscorides (AD 40–80) for a metal and a plant, hence also the name leadwort. The name *zeylanica* means "of Ceylon" and refers to modern-day Sri Lanka. Leaves and roots applied to the skin cause reddening and blistering, giving rise to the Spanish name *malacara* (bad face) and *erva de diablo* (devil's herb). This is a larval host plant of the cassius blue butterfly.

BACHELOR'S BUTTON
Polygala balduinii Nutt.
Milkwort Family (Polygalaceae)

Description: The stems of this species reach 8"–24" tall and are often branched near the base. The lower leaves are spatulate and the upper leaves are lanceolate with pointed tips. Small flowers are on erect spikes with the elliptic wings measuring about ⅛" long.

Bloom Season: All year

Habitat/Range: Wet pinelands, prairies, and coastal swales from Florida and Georgia west along the Gulf Coastal Plain to Texas.

Comments: *Polygala* means "much milk," in the fanciful belief that milkworts could increase milk flow in cattle. Flemish physician Rembert Dodoens (1517–1585) wrote of milkworts in 1578 that they "engendreth plentie of milk; therefore it is good to be used of nurses that lack milk." The name *balduinii* honors American botanist William Baldwin (1779–1819) who made important contributions to Florida botany. It is common throughout the Everglades region.

BOYKIN'S MILKWORT
Polygala boykinii Nutt.
Milkwort Family (Polygalaceae)

Description: The erect stems average 5"–10" tall but sometimes reach 20". The stems can be sparsely or densely leafy. The lower leaves are elliptic to linear lanceolate with narrowly linear to narrowly lanceolate upper leaves, both produced in whorls. The flower spikes are cylindrical with small white or greenish-white flowers crowded along the top of the spike.

Bloom Season: All year

Habitat/Range: Wet pinelands and prairies from Florida and Georgia to Louisiana.

Comments: The name *boykinii* honors Georgia physician and botanist Samuel Boykin (1786–1846), for whom the genus *Boykinia* (Saxifragaceae) was also named. It is locally common in the Everglades region, especially in Everglades National Park. Members of this genus have been used medicinally for depression, insomnia, coughs, and even venomous snakebite. Others are used to make alcoholic beverages and fiber.

MILD WATER-PEPPER
Polygonum hydropiperoides Michx.
Buckwheat Family (Polygonaceae)

Description: This wetland species has tubelike sheaths along the stem above the leaf bases. The leaves are narrowly lanceolate and average 1½"–4" long and ¼"–½" wide. Small, white to pinkish flowers are on jointed stalks with 4–6 petal-like sepals. Individual flowers are about ⅛" wide.

Bloom Season: March–November

Habitat/Range: Freshwater wetlands from Ontario and New Brunswick south to Florida, Texas, and Mexico.

Comments: *Polygonum* means "many knees" and refers to the swollen nodes along the stems. The name *hydropiperoides* refers to the resemblance of this species to *Polygonum hydropiper*. Some species are called smartweeds because of the spicy bite of the leaves when chewed. The leaves of this species have a mild taste. The stems root easily and can form extensive, spreading colonies in wet areas. Some species are used medicinally to treat asthma.

SOUTHERN DEWBERRY
Rubus trivialis Michx.
Rose Family (Rosaceae)

Description: The twigs and flower stems of this species are armed with stout thorns along with coarse, glandular hairs. The compound leaves have 3–5 leaflets that are mostly elliptic to narrowly ovate with serrate margins. Flowers are white to pink, solitary, and measure about 1" wide.

Bloom Season: January–May

Habitat/Range: Sandy flatwoods from Pennsylvania to Colorado south to Texas and Florida.

Comments: *Rubus* is an ancient name of the well-known blackberry. The name *trivialis* means "ordinary" and relates to it being common throughout its natural range. The fruits can be eaten raw or used in jams and jellies. They are a favorite of Florida black bears and a variety of birds, including American robins and wild turkeys. The blackberry looper and the stinging caterpillars of the io moth feed on the leaves. It ranges south into the Big Cypress Swamp (Bear Island) and Corkscrew Swamp regions.

VIRGINIA BUTTONWEED
Diodia virginiana L.
Madder Family (Rubiaceae)

Description: The stems of Virginia buttonweed are reddish green and reach 8"–24" long. The pubescent leaves are lanceolate, opposite, and range from ¾"–2½" long and ⅜" wide, often with red margins. Solitary, hairy, 4-lobed, white flowers are produced from the leaf axils and average ⅜" wide. The red or green fruits are oblong.

Bloom Season: March–September

Habitat/Range: Freshwater wetlands from New Jersey to Missouri south through mainland Florida.

Comments: *Diodia* is Greek for "thoroughfare" and was so named because some members of this genus often grow along waysides. The name *virginiana* means "of Virginia." It is regarded as a turf-grass weed in poorly drained areas and is difficult to control, adding credence to the old saying, "One man's weed is another man's wildflower." This family includes some well-known cultivated species, namely gardenia, pentas, coffee, ixora, and jasmine.

FAIRY FOOTPRINTS
Houstonia procumbens (J. F. Gmel.) Standl.
(Also *Hedyotis procumbens* [J. F. Gmel.] Fosberg)
Madder Family (Rubiaceae)

Description: The elliptic to round leaves of this creeping, ground-hugging species average ¼"–⅜" wide and may be slightly longer. The white, 4-lobed flowers measure about ½" across and sometimes have blue markings. The flowers can be terminal or axillary and barely extend above the leaves.

Bloom Season: Mostly September–March

Habitat/Range: Sandhills, dunes, and flatwoods of the southeastern United States.

Comments: *Houstonia* honors Scottish botanist William Houston (1695–1733) who collected plants in the Neotropics but died from heat stroke in Jamaica. The name *procumbens* relates to the procumbent growth habit of this species. It is also called innocence and roundleaf bluet. In Florida it ranges south into Everglades National Park but is more common in the Big Cypress and Corkscrew Swamp regions.

EVERGLADES FALSE BUTTONWEED

Spermacoce terminalis (Small) Kartesz & Gandhi
Madder Family (Rubiaceae)

Description: The stems of this endemic species
reach about 12" tall with leaves that measure
⅜"–1" long and ¹⁄₁₆"–⅛" wide. There is a row
of straight hairs on the underside of the leaves
along the midrib. The flowers are in compact,
round, terminal clusters (sometimes in the axils
of the second pair of leaves down the stem) to
about ⅜" wide.

Bloom Season: All year

Habitat/Range: Endemic to pinelands and coastal
areas from central Florida south to the Florida Keys.

Comments: The name *terminalis* refers to the
terminal heads of flowers. The very similar shrubby
false buttonweed *(Spermacoce verticillata)* has
heads of smaller individual flowers that occur in
most of the leaf axils along the stem, not just the
top 1 or 2 leaf axils. It is an extraordinarily common weed in disturbed sites throughout the Florida
peninsula, naturalized from the Neotropics.

FLORIDA DIAMONDFLOWERS

Stenaria nigricans (Lam.) Terrell var. *floridana*
(Standl.) Terrell
(Also *Hedyotis nigricans* [Lam.] Fosberg var. *flori-
dana* [Standl.] Wunderlin)
Madder Family (Rubiaceae)

Description: The threadlike, prostrate or ascending stems have opposite, very narrowly linear
leaves widely spaced along the stems. The leaves
measure ⅜"–¾" long and ¹⁄₃₂"–¹⁄₁₆" wide. The
4-lobed (occasionally 5-lobed) snow-white flowers
are about ³⁄₁₆" wide. The mature capsules of this
variety are subglobose.

Bloom Season: All year

Habitat/Range: Pine rocklands and disturbed
sites of southern Florida (Miami-Dade and Monroe Counties).

Comments: The name *Stenaria* is from the Greek
stenos and refers to the narrow leaves. The name
nigricans means "blackish," alluding to the color
of dried specimens. The name *floridana* means "of
Florida." This variety was first collected in Coconut
Grove, Florida, in 1895 by botanist Allan Hiram
Curtiss (1845–1907).

WATER PIMPERNEL
Samolus ebracteatus Kunth.
Brookweed Family (Samolaceae)

Description: The spoon-shaped, grayish-green leaves with red veins make this plant easy to identify when not in flower. The leaves form a basal rosette and are mostly 1"–3" long with an erect flower spike that rises from the center of the plant. The spike is topped by a loose array of white or pinkish flowers. The flowers measure ⅜" wide.

Bloom Season: All year

Habitat/Range: Freshwater and brackish marshes, flatwoods, and ditches from Nevada and Texas to Florida, Mexico, and the West Indies.

Comments: *Samolus* is of Celtic origin and is the Latin name of a plant used by Druids to treat diseases of cows and pigs. The name *ebracteatus* means "without bracts." This species is common in the Everglades region and is often found growing along trails that bisect its habitat. Pineland pimpernel *(Samolus valerandi* subsp. *parviflorus)* is infrequent and has much smaller flowers.

BALLOON VINE
Cardiospermum corindum L.
Soapberry Family (Sapindaceae)

Description: Balloon vine climbs by tendrils and has compound leaves with incised or crenate, finely pubescent leaflets. The white flowers are about ¼" wide and ⅜" long. The ¾"–1¼" fruits are inflated, changing from green to red to brown as they age.

Bloom Season: All year

Habitat/Range: Hammock margins and canopy gaps of southern Florida (Miami-Dade and Monroe Counties). Pantropical.

Comments: *Cardiospermum* means "heart seed," alluding to the shape of the white hilum on the black, round seeds. The black "eye" of a black-eyed pea is a hilum. Carolus Linnaeus (1707–1778) used the name *corindum* for this or a similar plant. This is a larval host plant of the silver-banded hairstreak, gray hairstreak, and the critically imperiled Miami blue butterfly. It is also called faux persil (false parsley) and heartseed. Amazonian men believe bracelets made of the seeds will ward off snakes.

215

LIZARD'S TAIL
Saururus cernuus L.
Lizard's Tail Family (Saururaceae)

Description: This common wetland species has bronze-colored, succulent stems with heart-shaped, alternate leaves measuring 4"–6" long and 1½"–3" wide. The leaves smell like minty licorice when crushed. The spikes of fragrant flowers arch like a bent fishing pole and each flower is about ¼" long, consisting of 6–8 creamy white stamens.

Bloom Season: All year

Habitat/Range: Freshwater wetlands from Ontario across much of the eastern United States south through mainland Florida.

Comments: *Saururus* is Greek for "lizard tail," alluding to the shape of the flower spike. The name *cernuus* means "drooping" or "nodding," in reference to the lax tip of the flower spike. Butterflies visit the flowers but it is seldom cultivated because it requires permanently wet soil. It has been widely used medicinally across its native range as well as by Creeks as an herbal tea during the Green Corn Ceremony.

SOUTHERN FOGFRUIT
Lippia stoechadifolia (L.) Kunth
(Also *Phyla stoechadifolia* [L.] Small)
Verbena Family (Verbenaceae)

Description: Southern fogfruit has erect or arching stems to 2' tall with opposite, toothed, linear-lanceolate leaves that measure ¾"–2" long and ³⁄₁₆"–⅜" wide. Tiny white flowers turn pinkish violet with age and are arranged in a circle around a stalked, axillary head.

Bloom Season: All year

Habitat/Range: Freshwater wetlands of southern Florida to the West Indies and Mexico.

Comments: *Lippia* honors Italian botanist Augustus Lippi (1678–1701). The name *stoechadifolia* refers to the similarity of the leaves to *Lavandula stoechos* (Lamiaceae). This is a larval host plant of the white peacock and phaon crescent butterflies. The common name apparently relates to its habit of growing in low, wet areas where fog settles but the name is sometimes corrupted as "frogfruit." It is a state-listed endangered species but can be locally common.

CREEPING CHARLIE
Phyla nodiflora (L.) Greene
(Also *Lippia nodiflora* [L.] Michx.)
Verbena Family (Verbenaceae)

Description: This mat-forming species has coarsely toothed, opposite leaves to 1" long and ⅜" wide. Axillary flower stalks are about 1½"–2½" long and topped by a flower head that is round when young, but becoming cylindrical with age. The flowers are ⅟₁₆" wide, opening white then turning pinkish violet.

Bloom Season: All year

Habitat/Range: A variety of natural habitats and lawns of tropical and subtropical regions of the world.

Comments: *Phyla* is Greek for "clan" or "tribe," alluding to the tight head of flowers. The name *nodiflora* means "knotted," also alluding to the flower head. Although this plant is generally regarded as a lawn weed, the flowers are a butterfly nectar source, the leaves serve as larval food for the white peacock and phaon crescent butterflies, and it makes an excellent substitute for lawn grass.

BOG WHITE VIOLET
Viola lanceolata L.
Violet Family (Violaceae)

Description: The leaves of this species are linear lanceolate, narrowing toward winged petioles and varying from 1"–6" long and ⅛"–⅜" wide. Flower stalks surpass the leaves and are topped by a solitary, ⅜" flower with conspicuous purple veins on the lower petal.

Bloom Season: December–August

Habitat/Range: Nova Scotia to Minnesota south through Texas and Florida.

Comments: *Viola* is the classical name for the violet. The name *lanceolata* refers to the lance-shaped leaves. Violets have been cultivated for their beauty and fragrance for more than 2,000 years and were once highly regarded as medicinal plants to cure gout, insomnia, epilepsy, and pleurisy. The scent is called "flirty" because, when inhaled, compounds in the fragrance can temporarily keep it from being detected by the human nose until the nerves recover. It is common in the Corkscrew Swamp region and can form large colonies.

PRIMROSELEAF VIOLET
Viola primulifolia L.
Violet Family (Violaceae)

Description: The variable leaves of this species range from ovate to reniform (kidney-shaped) in outline, usually with distinct petioles, and average ¾"–1" wide. They also vary from glabrous to shaggy pubescent. The flower stalk usually surpasses the leaves and is topped by a single ⅜" flower.

Bloom Season: February–June

Habitat/Range: Flatwoods, bogs, and wet forests of the United States and New Brunswick.

Comments: The name *primulifolia* relates to the similarity of the leaves to those of a primrose *(Primulaceae)*. This is a rare species in the Corkscrew Swamp region, which is its southernmost range in Florida. Some botanists treat this species as a fertile hybrid between *Viola lanceolata* and *Viola macloskeyi* (as *Viola* x *primulifolia*). Most botanists, however, treat it as a distinct species. Although the flowers are similar to the previous species, the leaves are much different.

CAROLINA YELLOWEYED GRASS
Xyris caroliniana Walter
Yelloweyed Grass Family (Xyridaceae)

Description: The twisted, narrowly linear leaves are erect or ascending and measure 8"–20" long and ⅛"–¼" wide. The base of the sheath is chestnut brown. The flowering spikes of this species are exceeded in height by the leaves. The flowers measure ½"–⅝" across and emerge from an ellipsoid cone.

Bloom Season: May–November

Habitat/Range: Flatwoods, sandhills, and scrub from North Carolina to eastern Texas south through Florida and Cuba.

Comments: *Xyris* is Greek for "razor," in reference to the 2-edged leaves. The name *caroliniana* means "of Carolina." Plants of this species occurring along the lower Gulf Coastal Plain from Florida to Mississippi have flowers with white petals but they are yellow in the northern parts of its range. The petals of the yellow-flowered species treated in this guide unfold in the morning but the petals of this species unfold in the afternoon.

GLOSSARY

Achene—small, dry, one-seeded fruits.

Alternate—arranged one after another along a stem or axis, usually in succession on the opposite side than the previous; often referring to the arrangement of leaves along a stem.

Annual—completing its life cycle from seed to maturity and death in one year.

Anther—the fertile, pollen-bearing part of a stamen.

Appressed—pressed close to or lying against something.

Aril—an exterior, usually fleshy, covering that at least partially surrounds the seeds.

Ascending—arching upward.

Axil—the angle that is formed by a leaf or petiole and the stem.

Axillary—produced or arising from an axil.

Basal—relating to the base; generally used in relation to the leaves.

Biennial—growing from seed to maturity and death in two years.

Bipinnate—compound leaves divided into segments with each segment also divided into segments.

Bract—a reduced leaf or leaflike structure subtending a flower or inflorescence.

Calyx—the outer set of flower parts, usually green, composed of the sepals, which may be separate or joined together.

Capsule—a dry, indehiscent fruit that releases seeds through splits or holes.

Clasping—partly surrounding another organ at the base.

Column—the structure in the center of an orchid flower formed by the fusion of the stigma, style, and stamens.

Compound leaf—a leaf divided into two or more leaflets; these may have leaflets arranged like the rays of a feather or radiating from a common point like a star.

Corm—the enlarged, fleshy base of a stem; tuberlike.

Corolla—the colored petals of a flower that constitute the inner floral envelope.

Deltoid—shaped somewhat like an equilateral triangle.

Disk—the tubular flowers in the aster family, as distinct from the ray flowers.

Elliptic—broadest at the middle and gradually tapering to a point at both ends.

Endemic—a native species restricted to a given area or region.

Entire—the margins of a leaf that are without teeth, lobes, or divisions.

Epiphyte, epiphytic—growing on another plant as in many ferns, orchids, bromeliads, and mosses; not a parasite.

Fruits—seed-bearing organs.

Genus—a grouping of closely related species, such as the genus *Solidago*, encompassing many species of goldenrods; sometimes a genus can comprise only a single species if there are no other living relatives.

Herbaceous—producing fleshy stems.

Inflorescence—the flower cluster of a plant, or the disposition of the flowers on an axis.

Involucre—bracts at the base of a flower or flower cluster.

Keel—a longitudinal fold or ridge, referring particularly to the two fused petals forming the lower lip of a typical flower in the pea family (Fabaceae).

Lanceolate—shaped like the head of a lance or spear.

Leaflet—a distinct, leaflike segment of a compound leaf.

Lectotype—the specimen chosen as the type specimen when the type cannot be defined.

Linear—a very long and narrow leaf with sides that are parallel or nearly so.

Lip—a modified petal in a flower, especially orchids, and usually differing in size, color, and form from the other two petals.

Margin—the edge of a leaf or petal.

Midrib—central leaf vein, often raised.

Neotropics—the region encompassing the West Indies, Mexico, Central America, and tropical South America.

Node—point of origin of leaves on a stem.

Obovate—broader above the middle and rounded on both ends.

Opposite—paired directly across from one another along a stem or axis.

Palmate—spreading like fingers of a hand.

Panicle—a compound racemose inflorescence.

Parasite, parasitic—an organism that derives nourishment from another, the host.

Pendent—suspended or nodding.

Perennial—living three or more years.

Petal—one division of the corolla, often the most brightly colored parts of a flower.

Petiole—the stalk of a leaf.

Pinnate—divided or lobed along each side of a leaf stalk, resembling a feather.

Pistil—the female, or seed producing, part of a flower, consisting of the ovary, style (if present), and stigma; a flower may have one to several separate pistils.

Pod—a dry fruit that splits open along the sides.

Pollen—tiny, often powdery, male reproductive cells formed in the stamens and typically necessary for reproduction.

Pollinia—a sticky mass of pollen transported as a whole during pollination, especially in the Orchidaceae.

Pseudobulb—the thickened, above-ground stem of certain orchids.

Pubescent—with short, dense, soft hairs; a general term to indicate the presence of hairs.

Raceme—unbranched stem with stalked flowers, the newest flowers forming at the top.

Rachis—The primary axis of an inflorescence or a pinnately-compound leaf.

Ray flower—flower in the aster family (Asteraceae) with a single, strap-shaped corolla resembling one flower petal; ray flowers may surround the disk flowers in a flower head or, in some species such as dandelions, the flower heads may be composed entirely of ray flowers.

Rhizome—creeping, underground, horizontal stem.

Rosette—a cluster of leaves arranged in a circle at the base of a plant.

Scape—a leafless flower stalk arising near ground level.

Sepal—a leaf or segment of the calyx.

Serrate—possessing sharp teeth.

Sessile—without a stalk.

Simple leaf—a leaf that has a single blade, although this may be lobed or divided.

Spadix—a spike of flowers on a succulent axis enveloped by a spathe.

Spathe—a broad, sheathlike bract enveloping a spadix.

Spatulate—spoon shaped.

Spike—an elongated, unbranched cluster of stalkless or nearly stalkless flowers.

Stalk—as used here, the stem supporting the leaf or flower cluster.

Stamen—the male unit of a flower that produces the pollen, typically consisting of a long filament with a pollen-producing tip.

Standard—the usually erect, spreading upper petal in many flowers of the pea family (Fabaceae).

Stigma—the portion of the pistil receptive to pollination, usually the top of the style, and often appearing fuzzy or sticky.

Stipule—bract or leafy structure occurring in pairs at the base of the leaf stalk.

Style—the portion of the pistil between the ovary and the stigma; typically a slender stalk.

Succulent—fleshy and juicy, usually thickened.

Tendril—a slender, coiled, or twisted filament with which climbing plants attach to their support.

Terminal—projecting from the end or apex of a branch.

Toothed—bearing teeth.

Tuber—thick, creeping, underground stems; sometimes also used for thickened portions of the roots.

Tubular—narrow, cylindrical, and tubelike.

Type—the specimen used to describe a species or subspecies.

Umbel—a flat or convex cluster of flowers in which the pedicels arise from a common point, much like an umbrella.

Vein—vascular bundle of a leaf that carries water, minerals, and nutrients.

Venation—the vein pattern.

Whorl—an arrangement of three or more leaves at a node or other common point.

Winged—a thin band of leaflike tissue attached edgewise along the length, as in a winged petiole.

Wings—the two side petals flanking the keel in many flowers of the pea family (Fabaceae).

Woody—producing wood.

NATIVE PLANT DIRECTORY

To view native wildflowers in their natural habitats, the reader is encouraged to visit the parks and preserves listed below. To find out more about wildflowers and other plants native to southern Florida, the reader may wish to contact the local native plant societies and conservation organizations. The Florida Native Plant Society has chapters throughout the state and these are diverse groups of amateur and professional plant enthusiasts organized to share information about the study, conservation, and propagation of plants native in their regions. Conservation organizations and regional native plant societies hold plant sales and offer guided field trips. Rangers and naturalists also offer guided field trips in many parks and preserves.

NATIONAL PARKS AND PRESERVES

Website: www.nps.org

Big Cypress National Preserve
52105 Tamiami Trail East
Ochopee, FL 33141
(239) 695-1201

Everglades National Park
40001 State Road 9336
Homestead, FL 33034
(305) 242-7700

STATE PARKS AND PRESERVES

Website: www.floridastateparks.org

Bill Baggs Cape Florida State Park
1200 Crandon Blvd.
Key Biscayne, FL 33149
(305) 361-5811

Collier-Seminole State Park
20200 Tamiami Trail E
Naples, FL 34114
(239) 394-3397

Fakahatchee Strand Preserve State Park
137 Coastline Dr.
Copeland, FL 34137
(239) 695-4593

COUNTY PARKS AND PRESERVES

Broward County Parks and Recreation
Website: www.broward.org/parks

Collier County Parks and Recreation
Website: www.colliergov.net

Lee County Parks and Recreation
Website: www.leeparks.org

Miami-Dade County Parks, Recreation and Open Spaces
Website: www.miamidade.gov/parks

NATIONAL AUDUBON SOCIETY

Corkscrew Swamp Sanctuary
375 Sanctuary Rd. West
Naples, FL 34120
(239) 348-9151
Website: www.corkscrew.audubon.org

SOUTH FLORIDA WATER MANAGEMENT DISTRICT

Corkscrew Regional Ecosystem Watershed (CREW)

CREW Marsh

23998 Corkscrew Rd. (CR 850)

Estero, FL 33928

(239) 657-2253

Website: www.crewtrust.org

CONSERVATION ORGANIZATIONS

Fairchild Tropical Botanic Garden

10901 Old Cutler Rd.

Miami, FL 33156

(305) 667-1651

Website: www.fairchildgarden.org

Florida Native Plant Society

Website: www.fnps.org

(Organized into regional chapters throughout Florida)

Florida Trail Association

Website: www.floridatrail.org

(Organized into regional chapters throughout Florida)

Friends of Fakahatchee

Website: www.friendsoffakahatchee.org

The Nature Conservancy

Website: www.nature.org

North American Butterfly Association

Website: www.naba.org

(Organized into regional chapters throughout Florida)

Sierra Club
Website: www.sierraclub.org
(Organized into regional chapters throughout Florida)

Tropical Audubon Society
5530 Sunset Dr.
Miami, FL 33143
(305) 667-7337
Website: www.tropicalaudubon.org

SELECTED REFERENCES

Austin, Daniel F. *Florida Ethnobotany.* CRC Press, Boca Raton, FL, 2004.

Correll, D. S. & H. B. Correll. *Flora of the Bahama Archipelago.* A.R.G. Gantner Verlag K.-G., FL-9490 Vaduz, 1982.

Godfrey, Robert K., and Jean W. Wooten. *Aquatic and Wetland Plants of the Southeastern United States.* University of Georgia Press, Athens, GA, 1979.

Luer, Carlyle A. *The Native Orchids of Florida.* New York Botanical Garden, New York, NY, 1972.

McCormack, Jeffrey Holt, et al. *Bush Medicine of the Bahamas.* JHM Designs Publications, Charlottesville, VA, 2011.

Wunderlin, Richard P. and Bruce F. Hansen. *Guide to the Vascular Plants of Florida, Third Edition.* University Press of Florida, Gainesville, FL, 2011.

INDEX

ABOUT THE AUTHOR

Roger L. Hammer is a professional naturalist retired from Miami-Dade Parks & Recreation Department and a volunteer instructor at Fairchild Tropical Botanic Garden in Coral Gables, Florida. He received the first Marjory Stoneman Douglas Award presented by the Dade Chapter of the Florida Native Plant Society in 1982 for "outstanding, consistent, and constant service in the areas of education, research, promotion, and preservation of native plants." Tropical Audubon Society honored him with the prestigious Charles Brookfield Medal in 1996 for "outstanding service in the protection of our natural resources." In 2003 he received the Green Palmetto Award in Education from the Florida Native

Plant Society. In 2008 he was the keynote speaker at the Nineteenth World Orchid Conference and in 2013 he was a keynote speaker at the Florida Native Plant Society's annual state conference. In 2012 he received an honorary Doctor of Science degree from Florida International University and a lifetime achievement award from the Florida Native Plant Society, Tropical Audubon Society, and the North American Butterfly Association. He is an avid canoeist, kayak fisherman, wildflower photographer, gardener, and rum connoisseur. Roger is also the author of *Florida Keys Wildflowers* (Globe Pequot, 2004), *A FalconGuide® to Everglades National Park and the Surrounding Area* (Globe Pequot, 2005), and *Florida Icons: 50 Classic Views of the Sunshine State* (Globe Pequot, 2011). He lives in Homestead, Florida, with his wife, Michelle.

For more information on Roger, visit rogerlhammer.com

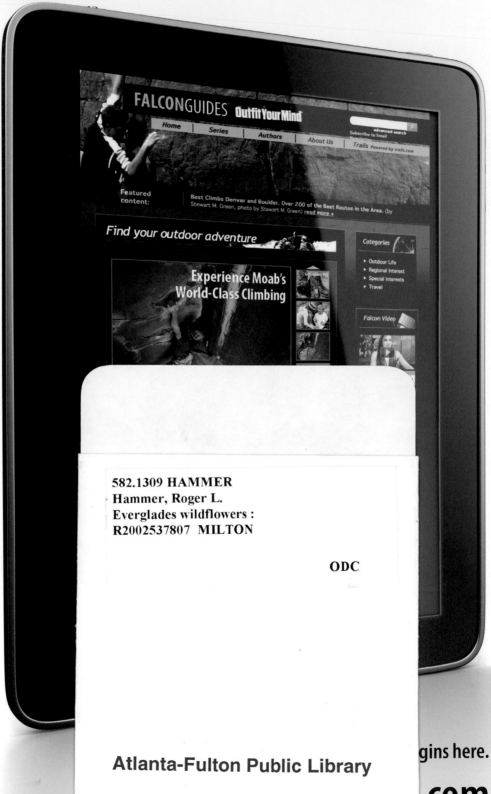